Contents

Foreword

[handwritten annotation: an alternative means / language of gaining "voices"]

Merengue dance music—soul, voice, mind and motion of the Dominican Republic—takes shape, in time perspective, within these pages. The author, Paul Austerlitz, not only researches but plays this music. He writes from the center of merengue happening. Here saxophones honk signature *cinquillo antillano* metric patterns in all directions, here song texts blossom into bittersweet social commentary and critique, here women carousel and carousel, moving together tightly with their dancing men, in a dance that has a handle on inciting and channeling the pleasures of love and commitment.

Read this book. Savor the creative energy of a Latino nation. Dominican voices, live voices, guide us to what we need to know. Straight through the text Austerlitz turns over the microphone to performers, historians, and other relevant sources in the Dominican Republic. Their insights, shared in interviews, become the bedrock of an important book.

It is important because half an island, the Dominican Republic, now provides dance music for virtually all the Americas, especially in New York and the black Caribbean. Once again, creative black culture eludes snares of prejudice and circumstance to teach the world a lesson by continuity and confidence.

Part of the lesson is this: Merengue provides an in-your-face exception to Wittgenstein's famous premise, namely, that the meaning of something is its use. For what about misuse, *compay?* The meaning of merengue transcends the propagandistic purposes to which it was put by the Dominican dictator Trujillo, who, like Huey P. Long, campaigning in Lousiana in the thirties with country musicians amiably attendant, wrapped himself in popular music. Trujillo also used the people's music as a way of sticking it to oligarchic snobs who looked down upon both the president and the dance as racially and socially inferior.

Austerlitz documents the impressions of Dominicans as to what it was like to live under one of the thoroughgoing despotisms of this century. Forbidding emigration, Trujillo converted his nation into one vast house of detention. But that didn't stop a few intrepid *merengueros,* one of whom became a hit of New York Puerto Rican dancehalls in the early fifties. Merengue took root, at the New York City Palladium and elsewhere. Around 1956 *Time* was publishing a diagram that purported to teach anyone, but anyone, how to move to the merengue beat. That was the first merengue impact on the United States. The second, far stronger, is taking place today. In 1996 there are merengue dance places up and down the Upper West Side of Manhattan, heavily frequented by Dominicans. Here *salsa,* as Willie Colón, the *salsero,* ruefully put it to me a few years ago, is played "only as a novelty."

In other words, cultural conquest and transnational happening richly defines major portions of this music. In fact, Austerlitz will be read for some time by those interested in the relationship of modern popular music to the pleasures and the predicaments of multicultural, transnational living. This place-mixing, time-confusing, class-baffling power helped break down merengue's boundaries of origin. The *tambora* beat of the merengue invaded Haiti in the fifties, and there combined with Haitian *mereng* and big-band *mambo* voicings, triggering a new dance music called *konpa.* In Brazil the beat of merengue caught the attention of certain musicians, during the eighties, in Belem and Porto Seguro. When they mixed it with *samba* there was a brief explosion, and the name of the explosion was *lambada.*

Meanwhile, back in the Dominican Republic, certain musicians worked the bass licks of disco in the seventies into the texture of merengue in order to compete with incursions of Saturday Night Fever from the north.

It is interesting that the Spanish roots of merengue were already "transnational"—bridging the musics of Muslim Spain and Christian Spain—before they ever got to the Caribbean. The musical impact of Moors and Berbers, starting with the invasion of Spain by the Berber general Tarik in 722 A.D. continued, even after the expulsion of the Muslims and the Jews in 1492. This gave, according to the brilliant argument of the late Richard Alan Waterman, Spanish America a "head start" in mixing Western music with African. The music of Spain, especially in Andulucía, a.k.a. Al-Andalus in Arabic, was indelibly affected by the percussive temper of Moroccan music, to say nothing of Islamic microtonality, melismas, acid timbres, and pinched nasal delivery.

As if that aspect of an originating heritage were not complicated enough, Dominican music has always been "transnational" in terms of its relation to the Black Republic. Haiti forms the western one-third of the island Hispaniola, of which Dominicans inhabit the eastern portion. The merengue tambora roll—[rest] tu-ku-tu-KUN—marched into Haiti from the Dominican Republic in the fifties and became, as we have seen, the enabling basis of the konpa beat and music. But there are other strands of connecting influence. The *cinquillo* (a five-stress pattern), in its *danzón* avatar in Cuba, RAM-pa-pam-pa-PAM, was present in the earlier Haitian mereng. It also is found, at melodic levels, in specific forms of Dominican merengue. The histories of Haitian mereng and Dominican merengue inevitably intertwine. As I write these words the presidents of the two republics have met and have agreed to start the dissolving of the "sugarcane curtain" that has separated them since the days of Dessalines. This, hopefully, will eventuate in a new range of island scolars willing to transcend race and nationalism to write the unified history of the black music of Hispaniola.

This book points the way toward that ideal zone of understanding. Austerlitz is a leading scholar of merengue. But he wears his erudition lightly. Through all the exposition he remains a *buen elemento,* able to pick up a sax and play merengue with his peers. His informants clearly consider him a colleague and share with him aesthetic judgments and considerations. You can't achieve this with a questionnaire. You can't let warlocks of the World Wide Web convince you that electronic windows are substitutes for live conversations with live musicians playing live music for live dancers in real—as opposed to virtual—reality. The message of merengue, like rap, mambo, samba, and dancehall, ultimately may boil down to this: Subvert the threat of a posthominid future with collective honesties of sweat and motion.

ROBERT FARRIS THOMPSON

Preface

As both performer and scholar, I have had a long-standing engagement with Dominican music. Born in Finland and raised in New York City, I was exposed to Latino culture at a young age, but had no contact with merengue until the early 1980s, when I returned to New York after four years at college. An aspiring jazz saxophonist in love with Afro-Caribbean music, I joined a Latin jazz group. Work was scarce for this band, and musician friends said I could find gigs playing merengue, a genre of popular music from the Dominican Republic that was fast becoming a favorite in New York's Latin clubs. Merengue saxophone riffs interacting with percussion rhythms produced the happiest sounds I had ever heard. With a shortage of merengue saxophonists in the city, bandleaders appreciated my willingness to spend extra rehearsal time learning the music, and I appreciated the warmth with which merengue musicians received me into their world. I performed mostly with semiprofessional groups but was lucky enough to do occasional gigs with first-rate musicians, including Joseíto Mateo, the "king of merengue." As I became more and more committed to Latin music, I moved to upper Manhattan's Dominican neighborhood, learned to speak Spanish, and adopted customs from my new friends.

ethno-musicologist

As a graduate student in ethnomusicology at Wesleyan University, where I had planned to concentrate on African music, I wrote my master's thesis on the role of the saxophone in merengue (Austerlitz 1986). Inspired by John Chernoff's book on African music (1979), in which Chernoff combines participant observation as a drummer in Ghana with an interpretive anthropological approach, I applied my experiences with Dominican music to my ethnomusicological research.[1] The contacts I had made with Dominicans in New York opened many doors when I conducted fieldwork there and in the Dominican Republic during the summer of 1985. The thesis written, I began course work for a Ph.D. and played with Connecticut-based Latin bands, made up mostly of Puerto Ricans. Merengue had begun to gain a foothold among non-Dominicans, and my band mates, relatively new to Dominican music, welcomed my experience. I played in these bands both for money and for fun—it was an enjoyable part-time job—but I also applied the ethnomusicology that I studied during the week at Wesleyan to my weekend Latin gigs and vice versa. This symbiosis continued in 1990 and 1991; when I conducted fieldwork in the Dominican Republic for my dissertation (Austerlitz 1992), I often played with Dominican musicians, sometimes to offset my living expenses, at other times to sit in as a guest merengue-jazz soloist with musicians I had interviewed.

I continued to perform Caribbean music in the United States, incorporating merengue and other influences into my own compositions, after I received a doctorate in 1993. That playing Latin music and working as an ethnomusicologist nourish each other prompts me to reconsider the concept of "the field." In a sense, I am constantly conducting field research, since playing Caribbean music has become integral to my life. When I perform in merengue nightclubs and self-consciously observe the situation, I am doing fieldwork. But when I lose myself in the experience of a Latin gig, I am not in the field; I am pursuing my creativity. My immersion in Latin music has provided my most valuable ethnomusicological insights.

A similar situation developed for Chernoff, who went to Ghana to conduct an ethnomusicological study; only when he became so enmeshed in the local culture that he had "lost [his] desire to write anything about what [he] was learning" was he "ready to begin the kind of education that [he] wanted to get in African music" (1979: 9). He notes that philosophy, literary criticism, and psychoanalysis use similar interpretive approaches; for example, literary critics speak of "putting oneself under the governing claims of the text" in order to gain entry into the "world of the text" (187). Paradoxically, the very subjectivity of this approach increased my awareness of the insider/outsider dialectic. Once I had adopted mannerisms, habits, and values from my Latino friends, I began to feel out of touch with my own background. After some introspection, I learned to value my status as an outsider to merengue as much as I enjoyed my closeness to it, finding that the questions I asked as a non-Dominican differed from those Dominicans asked.

According to Florence Kluckhohn in her seminal work on sociological participant observation, the participant observer, "forced to analyze his own roles, is, on the one hand, less misled by the myth of total objectivity in social research, and, on the other, more consciously aware of his own biases" (1940: 343). This strategy thus brought me into such intimate contact with the subject of my study that I sometimes felt like an authentic Caribbean music performer—a cultural insider, in some small way—yet my very closeness to merengue kept me acutely aware that I will always be an outsider to Dominican music, an insight that has colored my ethnomusicology of that music as well as my work as a performer and composer.[2]

What first drew me to merengue was its euphoric sound, but I soon found myself equally fascinated by its social meanings. Almost without exception, the Dominicans I met spoke with great pride of this music. For example, merengue star Joseíto Mateo told me that to him, the music's success on the global stage "is the success of the Dominican. It is the Dominican who has ascended, who has arrived in other countries" (all translations are mine unless otherwise noted). This intimate link between merengue—its stylistic and social history—and Dominican identity comprises the focus of this book.

Today perhaps the most requested form at Latin dances throughout the Americas, merengue fascinates not only music fans but cultural observers. Several Dominicans, along with anthropologist Deborah Pacini Hernandez, have explored the subject, but this book marks the first exhaustive study of merengue in English.[3]

Because, as ethnomusicologist Mark Slobin writes, "today music is at the heart of individual, group, and national identity, from the personal to the political" (1992: 1), thinkers from many academic disciplines pay attention to popular music. Conversely, while I come out of a performance background,

I draw on the perspectives of both anthropology and cultural studies as I investigate merengue in relation to nationalism, race, migration, social class, commodification, gender, and sexuality. My intent has been to infuse a humanistic perspective with attention to musical style; for musicologists, notated musical examples illustrate merengue melodies, rhythms, and harmonies. A companion CD, produced by Rounder Records, documents the historical and rural merengue styles, and contemporary commercial merengue recordings are available in record stores.

In my long acquaintanceship with merengue, I have grown intrigued with its interplay at the national, transnational, and regional levels.[4] One of the most provocative and influential recent ideas about nationalism is Benedict Anderson's suggestion that nations are socially constructed "imagined communities" (1983, 1991). Noting that "nationalism is a cultural artifact," Anderson argues that nations are imagined because "the members of even the smallest nation will never know most of their fellow-members, . . . yet in the minds of each lives the image of their communion" (1991: 4, 6). Like Eric Hobsbawm and Terence Ranger's (1983) idea of "invented traditions," Anderson's proposition underscores the social construction of human reality. As symbolic constructs, however, traditions are constantly reinvented by definition; the *ways* that traditions are created are as meaningful as is the notion that they are invented (see Handler and Linnekin 1984, Balibar 1991: 93). Christopher Waterman notes that "for the student of expressive culture the most intriguing part of Anderson's thesis is the notion that imagined communities are to be distinguished not by their falsity or genuineness, but by 'the style in which they are imagined'" (1990b: 376). That Joseíto Mateo sees merengue's global popularity as marking a triumph of the Dominican people suggests to me that this music lies at the heart of the Dominican national imagination. The primary goal of my work is to unravel the nature of this musico-national nexus.

To look at merengue as a global phenomenon, I link field and written data from the Dominican Republic, New York City, and Puerto Rico (and to a lesser extent, Haiti and Cuba) to transnational economic and political currents, enlisting "multi-locale system ethnography" that treats "multiple, blindly interdependent locales" in relation to larger systems (Marcus 1986: 171).[5] Dominican culture and politics have long been marked by sharp divisions between several regions of the country, and in spite of the advent of a Dominican diaspora, much of the population continues to live in rural areas and perform local musics. Regionalism is thus of central importance to merengue's past as well as its present. In considering merengue's national and transnational dimensions as they relate to its past and present operation as a regional and rural music, I draw on field data I collected in several regions of the Dominican Republic.

Because I believe, with ethnomusicologist Kay Shelemay, that exploring one time period in depth can "illuminat[e] the historical continuum from which it emerged" (1980: 233), here I examine the history of Dominican merengue from the mid-nineteenth century to today but focus on the late twentieth century, when the music spread around the world. The two perspectives overlap: I gathered many historical data in the field through interviews, and in spite of the late-twentieth-century focus, I have hung some of that material on a historical framework.[6]

In the Introduction, I lay out my theoretical approach to merengue and national identity, suggesting that the music derives its efficacy as a Dominican symbol by simultaneously encoding several often contradictory aspects of Dominican life. The body of the book consists of two parts: Part I (Chapters 2 to 4) considers merengue from the mid-nineteenth to the mid-twentieth centuries, while Part II (Chapters 5 to 8) looks at merengue from 1961 to 1995. In Chapter 2, on merengue's early history, I look at the contradictions of race and class in the Dominican Republic and other Caribbean countries during the nineteenth century. Focusing on the Cibao region of the Dominican Republic in Chapter 3, I discuss the role that Cibao-style merengue played in a cultural nationalist movement that developed in resistance to the 1916–1922 U.S. occupation of the country. In Chapter 4 I explore the dictator Rafael Trujillo's use of merengue as propaganda and as a symbol of the state from 1930 to 1961. Treating the late twentieth century in Chapter 5, I look at the connections between stylistic continuity and change and merengue's commodification and transnationalization. In Chapter 6 I consider innovative trends in merengue and other Dominican popular musics in relation to race, class, and sexual politics. Merengue among Dominicans in the United States and Puerto Rico, and the music's growing relevance to non-Dominicans, are the subjects of Chapter 7. In Chapter 8 I consider the meaning that rural and regional culture continue to have for contemporary Dominican life, exploring the impact of local variants of merengue on transnational forms of the music. In the book's final chapter I draw conclusions about the music's position on Dominican society by comparing and critically examining the various stages of its history.

My involvement with merengue has brought treasured acquaintances into my life. I am perhaps most indebted to the many Dominican musicians, scholars, merengue fans, and music industry personnel with whom I conferred in the Dominican Republic, New York City, and Puerto Rico. I will never forget the warm receptions that I received from these people; the depth of Dominican hospitality has truly enriched my life. Folklorist Fradique Lizardo was consistently generous with his knowledge and time, as was singer and music historian Arístides Incháustegui. Great thanks are due to Joel Cabrera Torres, who accompanied me on field trips to rural areas of the Dominican Republic in 1990 and 1991, providing counsel and camaraderie. The merengue musicians who helped with this study are too numerous to list, so I will name only those whom I met more than once, or who took special interest in my work. I will always cherish the memories of my meetings with the late merengue and jazz master saxophonist Tavito Vásquez, and prize the relationship that I developed with his relatives Raymundo Vásquez and Noelia de Vásquez in the city of Santiago. Verbal and musical dialogue with Tony Vicioso and other members of the group Asa-Difé were both personally enriching and seminal to my education in Dominican music. Maestro Julito Figueroa taught me much about merengue, speaking as eloquently on his drums as he did with words. Rafaelito Román and Félix del Rosario were helpful and hospitable, and I especially treasure my experiences performing with them. Cheché Abreu taught me as much about human kindness as he did about merengue. Joseíto Mateo, Luis Pérez, Crispín Fernández, Agapito Pascual, Juan Luis Guerra, Andrés de Jesús, Julio Alberto Hernández, Millie and Jocelyn Quezada, Johnny Ventura, Victor Waill, and all of the other musicians whom I interviewed were friendly and generous with their expertise.

The Wenner-Gren Foundation for Anthropological Research has consistently supported my research. In 1990 and 1991, it funded a ten-month field trip to the Dominican Republic for the early research upon which this book is based, and in 1995 it again supported fieldwork (this time in the Dominican Republic, Puerto Rico, and New York City) and the writing of this book. It is a pleasure to thank my long-term advisor at Wesleyan University, Mark Slobin, who has steadfastly guided me since my early days as a graduate student. Gage Averill started teaching at Wesleyan University just in time to become my dissertation advisor, and he continues to guide my thinking about music and politics. I am extremely fortunate to have partaken of his ethno-musicological acumen. Thanks are also due to the third member of my dissertation committee, Elizabeth Traube, whose sharp mind excited me about anthropology and cultural studies. I am greatly indebted to Deborah Pacini Hernandez, who recommended my work to Temple University Press and read the final draft of this book, providing many valuable suggestions. The founder of Dominicanist ethnomusicology in the United States, Martha Ellen Davis, has been forthcoming with encouragement and advice since I first met her in the mid-1980s. I also express heartfelt thanks to Jeffrey Magee for his expert editing and keen insights into American musics, which were shared over many enjoyable cups of coffee. Doris Braendel of Temple University Press has consistently supported this project, copy editor Bobbe Needham offered invaluable input, and Darrin Kiessling guided me through the production process. Victor Camilo was more than generous with his excellent photos, and Marty Cuevas provided invaluable assistance with obtaining rights to merengue lyrics.

I also wish to thank my family. I consider it a privilege to be the son of the late Robert Austerlitz, whose scholarly excellence inspired me, and whose comradeship delighted me. My sister Monica's *joie de vivre* and love of music have always been inspiring. Lastly, I thank my best friend and beautiful wife, Karoll, for her help with Spanish translations, for her biting insights into Latino and Anglo cultures, and, most importantly, for her great love.

P.A.

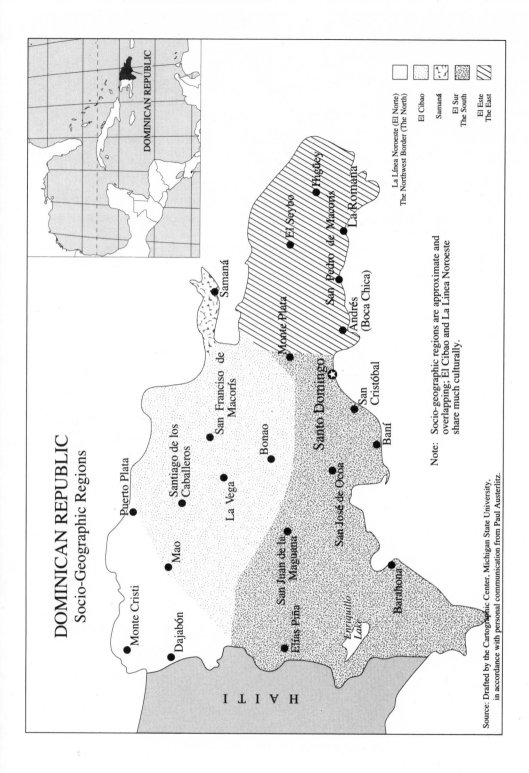

DOMINICAN REPUBLIC
Socio-Geographic Regions

DOMINICAN REPUBLIC

HAITI

Monte Cristi
Dajabón
Puerto Plata
Mao
Santiago de los Caballeros
La Vega
San Franciso de Macorís
Bonao
Samaná
San Juan de la Maguana
Elías Piña
Enriquillo Lake
San José de Ocoa
Barahona
Monte Plata
Santo Domingo
San Cristóbal
Baní
Andrés (Boca Chica)
San Pedro de Macorís
El Seybo
Higüey
La Romana

La Línea Noroeste (El Norte)
The Northwest Border (The North)

El Cibao

Samaná

El Sur
The South

El Este
The East

Note: Socio-geographic regions are approximate and
        overlapping; El Cibao and La Línea Noroeste
        share much culturally.

Source: Drafted by the Cartographic Center, Michigan State University,
        in accordance with personal communication from Paul Austerlitz.

Chapter 1

Introduction

According to an often quoted anecdote, merengue originated in 1844, the year that the Dominican Republic was founded, to satirize a Dominican soldier named Tomás Torres who had abandoned his station during the Battle of Talanquera in the War of Independence. The Dominicans won the battle, and while celebrating the victory at night, soldiers mocked the cowardly Torres in the first merengue:

Toma' juyó con la bandera	Thomas fled with the flag,
Toma' juyó de la Talanquera:	Thomas fled from Talanquera;
Si juera yo, yo no juyera,	If it had been I, I wouldn't have fled:
Toma' juyó con la bandera.	Thomas fled with the flag.[1]

Related by journalist Rafael Vidal to composer and folklorist Julio Alberto Hernández (1927: 6), this account first appeared in print in 1927, when merengue was beginning to gain currency as a national symbol. A melody and similar words appeared in the same year in another publication, Julio Arzeño's *Del folklore musical dominicano*. Arzeño, however, did not consider the song a merengue, classifying it as a "patriotic song" instead (1927: 127).[2] The Battle of Talanquera story is clearly dubious history, but it is a powerful myth that solidly links music and national identity in a bond that has endured through most of merengue's history.

We will probably never know with certainty the true origin of this music, but theories about it express deep-rooted feelings about Dominican identity. One theory links merengue to the Haitian mereng. Although they differ in important ways, the Dominican Republic and Haiti share many cultural characteristics. Like merengue in the Dominican Republic, mereng (in Haitian Creole; *méringue* in French) is a national symbol in Haiti. According to Jean Fouchard, mereng evolved from the fusion of slave musics such as the *chica* and *calenda* with ballroom forms related to the French *contredanse* (1988: 5–9). Mereng's name, he says, derives from the *mouringue* music of the Bara, a Bantu people of Madagascar (1973: 110, 1988: 77–82). That few Malagasies came to the Americas renders this etymology dubious, but it is significant because it foregrounds what Fouchard, and most Haitians, consider the essentially African-derived nature of their music and national identity.[3] Dominican merengue, Jean Fouchard suggests, developed directly from Haitian mereng (1988: 66).

Dominicans are often disinclined to admit African and Haitian influences on their culture. As ethnomusicologist Martha Davis points out, many Dominican scholars "have, at the least, ignored African influence in Santo Domingo. At the worst, they have bent over backwards to convince themselves and their readers of the one hundred percent Hispanic content of their culture. This is not an uncommon Latin American reaction to the inferiority complex produced by centuries of Spanish colonial domination" (1976: 9). According to merengue innovator Luis Alberti, for example, merengue "has nothing to do with black or African rhythms" (1975: 71). The Dominican proclivity to deny connections with Africa is related to anti-Haitian sentiment, and relationships between the national musics of Haiti and the Dominican Republic have often been ignored or downplayed in Dominican merengue scholarship. In several standard Dominican sources that mention merengue in Puerto Rico and other countries, competent scholars neglect to acknowledge even the existence of Haitian mereng (del Castillo and García Arévalo 1989: 17; Lizardo 1978a, b; Nolasco 1956: 321–41). In fact, for Esteban Peña Morel, one of the few Dominicans to admit a connection between merengue and mereng, this link renders merengue inappropriate as a Dominican symbol; he suggests another genre, the *mangulina*, as more representative of national culture (1929, sec.3:1, 3).[4]

In the 1970s, some Dominican intellectuals and artists began to challenge this Eurocentrism by celebrating the African contributions to Dominican culture and looking at connections to Haiti. The musicologist Bernarda Jorge, for instance, noted that "anti-Haitian sentiment and the tendency to hide and/or minimize the African roots of our [Dominican] culture on the part of the bourgeois intelligentsia have obstructed understanding and study not only of merengue, but of numerous forms of Dominican culture through the years" (1982b: 33).

Such views met with considerable criticism. When Dominican folklorist Fradique Lizardo discussed the African influence on Dominican culture (1979) and asserted that "merengue's origin is in Africa," the respected dance music composer Luis Senior described himself as "horrified" by Lizardo's assertion and claimed that it was "unpatriotic" to call merengue African (Ysálguez 1975a: 50, 1976c: 50). Lizardo's theory of merengue's origin resembles Fouchard's, for he writes that the Bara of Madagascar perform a dance called "merengue," adding that they play a drum similar to the *tambora* prominent in Dominican merengue. Lizardo suggests that Bara and other African musics were combined with a Cuban form called the *danza* to produce Caribbean merengue (1978a; also see 1978b: 11–13).[5] However, knowing that few Malagasies came to the Americas, that drums similar to the tambora are distributed widely in Africa (and Asia), and that several styles of merengue (both in and out of the Dominican Republic) do not use the tambora weighs against Lizardo's theory that merengue derives specifically from the Bara.

Whatever their differences, almost all of the origin theories point to connections between merengue and European-derived ballroom dance musics such as the danza (Fouchard 1988: 15–21; Hernández 1969: 65; Lizardo 1978a; Nolasco 1939: 60, 1948: 164–65, 1956: 322; Rueda 1990b). Flérida de Nolasco believes that merengue's association with these forms indicates that its origins are in Europe (1948:164–65). Although Manuel Rueda acknowledges the possibility of some African influence on merengue, he also believes that its European influences demonstrate merengue's Euro-American nature, and he discredits the idea that merengue is Afro-Caribbean (1990b). Julio Hernández, however, points out that European-derived musics came under African influence in the Americas, arguing that while merengue developed from European forms, it is a syncretic, Afro-Hispanic genre (1969: 53). Singer Joseíto Mateo, the "king of merengue," concurs; he pointed out to me in an interview that racial amalgamation naturally produces syncretic music: "Dominican whites and blacks [originally] had their own musics, just as in the United States the blacks have their own music. But gradually, what is called a fusion of the two races came about, the blacks and the whites. And so, a *música mestiza* was formed; that is, a mixed music. The white contributes his part, and the black contributes his drums."

For most Dominicans, then, to discuss merengue's origin is to discuss Dominican national and racial identity. Eurocentric thinkers emphasize merengue's European elements, Afrocentric scholars emphasize its African elements, and those who celebrate racial amalgamation point to its syncretic nature. Yet while they may disagree on the nature of Dominicanness, all come together on one point: Merengue expresses Dominican identity.

A Mixed-Race Community

With a population estimated at 80 percent mixed African and European, 15 percent black, and 5 percent white, the Dominican Republic has aptly been termed a "*comunidad mulata*," or mixed-race community (Pérez-Cabral 1967: 75).[6] The African-derived element in this mix is considerable: According to Martha Davis, among others, the country, "without doubt, should be considered an Afro-American nation—that is, a New World nation in which the African cultural influence figures prominently, if not predominantly" (1976: 2). The European element in Dominican culture is far from negligible; however; the upper classes, as well as the *campesinos*—the country people, or peasants—in certain regions, are of predominantly Spanish origin. Still, the racial line is fuzzy, for Spaniards and Africans were not strangers when they met in the Americas; Spain had come into a great deal of contact with Africa during the seven hundred years Moors had occupied the Iberian peninsula. As Fernando Ortiz reminds us, the forces occupying Spain came from as far away as Timbuktu (1952–55, 3: 64), and, as Philip Curtin notes, many Spanish entrants to the Caribbean were "free settlers of partial African descent" (1969: 31). The line between Spaniard and African was further blurred because, as Juan Bosch suggests, economic conditions in colonial Santo Domingo may have produced the *"de facto*, if not *de jure*, liberation of the slaves, to the extent that they might already have behaved as free men in 1659, although they were not free legally" (1988: 121). By the end of the eighteenth century, black and mixed-race freedmen outnumbered both whites and slaves in Spanish Santo Domingo.

Poised between Old World civilizations, Dominicans brewed a unique culture steeped in both African and Spanish traditions. Its myriad musics include a wealth of African-derived styles such as *palos, congos*, and *sarandunga* drumming, which are performed by Afro-Dominican religious brotherhoods; European-influenced forms such as *chuines*, which draws on Canary Islands music; and many styles, such as merengue and mangulina, that fuse African and European elements (see Davis 1976, 1981; Lizardo 1975).

Mountainous terrain and poor roads have kept the five primary areas of the Dominican Republic relatively isolated from each other; regionalism has been central to both music and politics in the country (see the map).[7] *El Sur* (The South), the largely arid southwestern portion of the country, contains large cattle ranches and Santo Domingo, the capital of the Republic, while sugar cultivation as well as ranching dominate *El Este* (The East). The lush northeastern Samaná peninsula was settled by black entrants from Haiti, the English-speaking Caribbean, and the United States. The fertile, rolling mountains of the country's most densely populated central region, *El Cibao*, have been used mainly for small-scale fruit, vegetable, tobacco, and coffee cultivation. The region shares many cultural characteristics with *La Línea Noroeste* (northwest border).

Variants of merengue developed in several regions of the country, but only the Cibao version gained national prominence, perhaps because of the region's high status. The country's oligarchy was long concentrated in the Cibao's largest city, Santiago de los Caballeros (literally, "Santiago of the Gentlemen"). And while Dominicans of both African and European descent live in all areas of the Republic, the Cibao's people claim the highest proportion of European ancestry (although parts of the South also have populations of largely European descent). Racially speaking, in general "the South and East of the country became true centers of *mulatos* . . . [while] several areas of the Cibao maintained a preponderance of white population more or less devoid of African physical characteristics" (Pérez-Cabral 1967: 132–33).[8] This high concentration of European blood, of oligarchs, and of the population in general precipitated what H. Hoetink terms a "*hierarchy of regions*, in which the Cibao had always been dominant" (1982: 50).

Syncretism and Articulation

A Dominican friend told me on several occasions that she would like to view some of my videotapes of rural Dominican festivals, but only tapes that "do not involve the saints or the dead"; the worship of saints and religious homage to ancestors in the Dominican Republic are associated with African-derived beliefs that my friend considered taboo. Because most Dominican rural festivals are, in fact, held in honor of saints or deceased community members, it was difficult for me to find tapes that she could view.

The gap between the Dominican Republic's dominant, Hispanocentric ideology and its cultural reality causes mixed feelings similar to the "socialized ambivalence" that Melville Herskovits noted in Haiti. Melville Herskovits wrote that this predicament manifests itself in a Haitian's "possession by the gods of his [African] ancestors . . . despite his strict Catholic upbringing," and that his "desire to understand and worship the gods of his ancestors" is followed by "utter remorse after having done this" (1937: 295–96).

Many Dominicans reveal similar mixed feelings about local music and national identity. Like my friend, many in the urban middle and upper classes who find the rural arts intriguing symbolic expressions of national character eschew them in practice because most Dominican musics are associated with African-derived religious practices. Most Dominicans thus prefer to think of the Cibao variant of merengue as representative of their traditional culture. Davis, who has conducted extensive research on Afro-Dominican drumming, relates that when she says she studies "folk music, Dominicans on the whole say, 'Oh, you mean the [Cibao-style] *merengue*.' Long drum and other strongly African influenced types of music are not perceived as 'folklore'" (1976: 10). At least, they are not perceived as *presentable* folklore. Ironically, merengue is often performed as a recreational component of the very African-influenced rituals that Eurocentric Dominicans eschew.

Erika Bourguignon noted a relationship between mixed feelings and syncretism, arguing that while the latter "helps to present a complete picture of the universe, . . . ambivalence is essentially disruptive not only to a harmonious world-view, but even to successful self-identification" (1951: 173; also see 1969). But judgments that rest on rigid compartmentalizations don't do justice to life's complexity; as Renato Rosaldo writes, many cultural phenomena "escape analysis because they fail to conform with standard expectations" (1988: 79). Explicating his influential notion of "double-consciousness" in 1903, W.E.B. Du Bois noted that mixed feelings cut both ways, sometimes widening rather than limiting people's horizons: Although the African-American "ever feels . . . two warring ideals in one dark body," which may "seem like the absence of power, . . . it is not weakness,—it is the contradiction of double aims" ([1903] 1989: 3). Far from being a flaw, the predicament that Herskovits describes in Haiti is a natural outgrowth of the colonial encounter, a result of the inculcation of hegemonic values.[9] The reality would seem to be that, as Frantz Fanon writes, ambivalence is "inherent [in] the colonial situation" (1983: 67; also see Ferrán 1985; Smith 1983: 93–95; Wilcken 1992). Out of such complex feelings springs a rich and multifaceted creativity; through the years, Dominican musicians have adapted with remarkable finesse to changing realities by incorporating non-Dominican elements into merengue. Particularly in changing times, this wealth of signification has lent the music special aesthetic relevance.

One-sided theoretical frameworks for considering merengue are thus inadequate. Theodor Adorno believes that popular culture promotes the interests of the ruling class (1976), while commentators such as John Fiske argue that it belongs to "subordinated and disempowered" elements of society (1989: 4). Calling attention to the deficiencies of both views, Jim McGuigan calls for a "critical populism" to replace the sometimes naively celebratory tone of "cultural populist" scholarship on one hand and Adorno's position on the other (1992: 5). As Stuart Hall explains, "Popular culture is neither, in a 'pure' sense, the popular traditions of resistance . . . nor is it the forms that are superimposed on and over them. It is the ground on which the transformations are worked" (1981: 228, quoted in Middleton 1990: 7). He thus proposes that we look at popular culture in terms *of articulation*, because this term "carries the sense of languageing, of expressing," but more importantly, because "in England . . . we also speak of an articulated lorry (truck), a lorry where the front (cab) and back (trailer) can, but need not necessarily, be connected to one another. . . . So the so-called 'unity' of a discourse is really the articulation of different, distinct elements which can be rearticulated in different ways because they have no necessary 'belongingness'" (Grossberg and Hall 1986: 53).

Thus, syncretic, multivalent, and fluid, merengue has endured as a symbol of Dominican identity for its very success in articulating the contradictory forces at play in Dominican life.

Prologue to the Dominican Nation, 1493–1844

The Dominican Republic shares with Haiti a West Indian island situated between Cuba and Puerto Rico; it was called Quisqueya by its native inhabitants, a name Dominicans still use (see the map). Christening it *La Española* (Hispaniola in English), Columbus claimed it for the Spanish crown and founded the first permanent European settlement in the Americas, Santo Domingo de Guzmán, on its southern coast in 1493. Santo Domingo eventually became the capital of the Dominican Republic.[10] Only a century after Columbus's arrival, virtually all the native Tainos and Caribs had perished, and enslaved Africans comprised the majority of the island's inhabitants. As Spain colonized more lucrative areas of the Americas, such as gold-rich Mexico and Peru, Hispaniola became a neglected part of the empire. Frenchmen, many of them buccaneers, took advantage of Spain's disinterest and in the seventeenth century began to settle the western part of the island, an area ceded to France under the Peace of Ryswick in 1697. The Spanish colony remained Santo Domingo, and the French settlement became Saint-Domingue. While the French possession was soon home to a large population, mostly enslaved Africans, inhabitants of the sparsely settled Spanish area were for the most part a rich racial mix.

Over the half-century from 1795 to 1845, the island saw one war after another. Slave revolts shook Saint-Domingue in the late eighteenth century; Spain and England supported the slaves, hoping to destabilize France's most important colony. In a bid for the favor of Saint-Domingue's masses, revolutionary France abolished slavery, and the black leader Toussaint L'Ouverture defeated the Spanish and English in the name of France in 1795. As a result, Spanish Santo Domingo was ceded to France under the Treaty of Basil. Occupied with its own revolution, France did not take possession until 1801, when L'Ouverture entered the territory, abolishing slavery as his first official act. Meanwhile, Napoleon Bonaparte had decided to reinstitute slavery on Hispaniola and use the island as headquarters for a new French empire in the Americas. His forces wrested control of Hispaniola in 1802, capturing L'Ouverture and sending him to France. While France secured the Spanish side of the island, former slaves on the Saint-Domingue side, now led by Jean Jacques Dessalines, refused to submit to their former French masters and expelled Napoleon's forces. In 1804 these free people founded the Republic of Haiti, the world's first black republic and the second independent state in the Americas.[11]

Hoping to banish slavery and European domination from the entire island once and for all, Haitian president Dessalines invaded Spanish-speaking Santo Domingo in 1805 but could not oust the French. Although many Dominicans of color had sided with him, the Haitian leader felt betrayed and committed abuses while retreating; according to Frank Moya Pons, he killed over four hundred people in the towns of Moca and Santiago (1986: 130). Stressed in Dominican historiography, this massacre played a tractable role in the formation of a Dominican national identity that has often been defined by its opposition to Haiti.

The French enacted policies that put them out of favor with the Spanish-speaking Dominican elite. With help from Spain and England, the Dominicans expelled the French in 1809, and their territory was returned to the Spanish Crown. Many Dominicans had mixed feelings about living under colonial rule when much of Latin America was seeking independence, and this period came to be known as the era of *España boba* (foolish Spain). After little more than a decade, a group of Dominicans led by José Nuñez de Cáceres overthrew the Spanish colonial government, establishing El Estado Independiente del Haití Español (The Independent State of Spanish Haiti) in 1821 in alliance with Simón Bolívar's Colombia Federation. Haitian president Jean Pierre Boyer was haunted by the possibility that the French would return and reinstitute slavery. Boyer's forces met little resistance when they entered Santo Domingo in 1822, and the island was unified under the Haitian flag. Haiti emancipated the slaves, although they were tied to the land they worked, and according to Davis, a "cultural renaissance" followed, as islanders could practice African-derived customs without fear of persecution by the colonial authorities (1976: 17).

Economic problems fomented discontent on both the French and Spanish sides of the island, and both launched plots to depose the Haitian president. On the Dominican side, liberal intellectuals founded a secret society, La Trinitaria (The Trinity), headed by Juan Pablo Duarte, which strove to establish a new sovereign state independent from Haiti. The overthrow of Boyer in Haiti in 1843 created conditions favorable to La Trinitaria's plan, and after a short war of independence, the Dominican Republic was founded on 27 February 1844.

Race, Nation, and Music

Behind merengue's link to Dominican national identity lies a century and a half of racial, class, and ethnic discomfort. The white Dominician elite, for example, found itself unallied with both black Dominicans and Europeans. Many Dominicans of color, did not consider Haitian president Boyer an outside aggressor when he took control of Spanish Santo Domingo in 1822. As Frank Moya Pons affirms, the Haitian leader offered the Dominican masses more than the Euro-Dominican ruling class did: "[T]he majority of the population was mulatto, and many were favorably disposed to the unification with Haiti. To them, the Haitian government promised land, the abolition of taxes, and the liberation of the few remaining slaves" (1995: 123).

The white Dominican elite found being subsumed into a black republic unacceptable. Because Spain was less than forthcoming with support for this constituency, many privileged Dominicans believed that the best way to preserve their social position was to break away from Europe (see Royce 1982: 89–90). Benedict Anderson shows that many Latin American independence movements arose in response to threats of black or indigenous uprisings; Simón Bolívar himself once said that a slave revolt was "a thousand times worse than a Spanish invasion" (in Anderson 1991: 49). These were the sentiments of the Dominican ruling class, which gained independence from Haiti rather than from colonial Spain.

The demographics of the Dominican state founded in 1844 were clearly at odds with the Eurocentric worldview of its leaders. At about this same time, the idea that nations or ethnicities are linked to sovereign states and bounded territories became prevalent in western Europe and the Americas—the term *nation* originally applied to any group of people with a shared history, what today we call an ethnic group (Hobsbawm 1990: 14–17).[12] As Linda Basch, Nina Glick Schiller, and Cristina Szanton Blanc write, the development of national identity is a "hegemonic process" that invokes—or invents—a shared historical past that advances the interests of a country's dominant classes (1994: 36). While the resulting sense of national identity may be flavored by preexisting ethnic feelings,[13] it is essentially a social construct—to borrow Etienne Balibar's term, a "fictive ethnicity" (1991: 96). This term is particularly apt for the Hispanic sense of self that developed in the Dominican Republic, whose culture owes so much to Africa.

In terms of music, then, what is more natural than for the urbane, Eurocentric Dominican cultural nationalists to be attracted to the syncretic merengue rather than to Afro-Dominican drumming? As propagated by Johann Gottfried Herder, Central European romantic nationalism, taught that nations express their essences and highest manifestations in language and artistic expression (see Wilson 1973). Although the New World patriots espoused Enlightenment ideas rather than romantic nationalism, the latter influenced the arts in the Americas during the late nineteenth and early twentieth centuries (see Béhague 1979: 96). Upper-class and bourgeois composers may have enlisted local rural musics as national symbols, but they embraced only those forms consonant with the dominant worldview. Singling out merengue for canonization allowed a *"selective tradition"* to be "passed off as *the* tradition" (Williams 1991: 414).

While its rise to prominence was originally linked to the agenda of the ruling class, Dominicans of all social classes eventually came to consider merengue an authentic expression of nationhood. The music remained central not only to national identity as outside influences inundated the Republic in the late twentieth century, but also to the transnational identity that developed as many Dominicans sought work abroad. Like other migrants of this era, they have adapted differently than earlier migrants. While developing allegiances to their new countries, these "transmigrants" also remain loyal to their homelands, forging multiple identities that subtly resist political and economic domination (Basch, Glick Schiller, and Szanton Blanc 1994: 7). Dominicans have created social, economic, political, and artistic networks to extend their home culture into transnational spaces, and merengue has had a high profile in this "transnational nation-state" (Basch, Glick Schiller, and Szanton Blanc 1994). The music's visibility outside of the Republic gained it new, non-Dominican audiences, and today Dominican merengue is integral to the soundscape of Latinos in all of the Americas.

PART I

The History
of Merengue,
1854–1961

Chapter 2

Nineteenth-Century
Caribbean Merengue

While best known as a Dominican music, merengue was a pan-Caribbean genre already in the nineteenth century. Haiti, Venezuela, Colombia, and Puerto Rico each developed local forms of the music; with the exception of the Puerto Rican version, all are still played today. Like another pan-Caribbean form, the *danza*, the Caribbean merengues fused the European *contredanse* with local, African-derived elements; they are thus aptly called *Afro-Caribbean contredanse transformations*.[1] In their duality, the contredanse transformations reflected the contradictions of nineteenth-century Spanish Caribbean society, which was divided along intertwined lines of race and class. While the light-skinned urbane gentry sustained close ties to Europe, much of the rural population maintained African-derived practices. Still, interracial marriage was not unusual, and communication across class lines took place.

    The contredanse originated in England, where country dances became popular among the nobility during the mid-seventeenth century.[2] This *English country dance* was introduced to the court of the French king Louis XIV, an avid amateur dancer. Performed in groups with set figures, it acquired a genteel nature in the French court, and there came to be called the con-

[handwritten marginal note: contredanse Form]

tredanse (Sachs [1937] 1963: 397, 414–24; Yih 1989).[3] When the dance caught on in colonial Saint-Domingue, its musical accompaniment was impregnated by African influences. Jean Fouchard writes that Haitian mereng developed in the mid-nineteenth century from a local contredanse derivative, the *carabinier* (1988: 96–97, 111). As a dance, mereng's novelty lay in its performance by individual couples instead of groups. (I will hereafter refer to such forms as *independent couple dances*.) As a musical type, mereng was first played on wind instruments but later developed into a rural and bourgeois song form and a nationalist art music. (The well-known mereng "Choucounne," popular at the turn of the century, is the source of the Harry Belafonte hit "Yellow Bird" [Averill 1989a: 63]). The several kinds of mereng feature a rhythm typical of much Caribbean music, which I call the *Caribbean cinquillo* (the Caribbean quintuplet); see musical example 1 (on Haitian mereng see Averill 1989a: 61; 1994; Dumervé 1968: 207–12; Larghey 1994; Saint-Cyr 1981–82; Vincent 1910: 271–82).[4]

Musical Example 1
The Caribbean Cinquillo

Fleeing the black-led Haitian revolution, many Saint-Domingue French colonists and their African slaves moved to the Spanish Caribbean in the early nineteenth century, bringing their expressive forms with them. According to Alejo Carpentier, the Saint-Domingue, or "French," influence on the Cuban *contradanza*, which was also called the *danza*, bore the distinct mark of African, and specifically Afro-Haitian, music (1961: 71–78).[5] Impregnated with local Afro-Cuban elements, the danza was of course censured by Eurocentric Cubans. Cultural nationalists, however, embraced it for the same reasons it was denounced, and like mereng, the Cuban danza became a nationalist art music. Utilizing sectional form and a dance figure called the *paseo* (Orovio 1981: 294), it had a formative influence on another Cuban genre called the *danzón*, which, like mereng, was an independent couple dance and used the Caribbean cinquillo rhythm.[6]

In 1842 and 1843, Cuban regimental bands brought a danza variant, the *upa*, to Puerto Rico. An independent couple dance, the upa was sometimes known as a *baile a dos* (dance for two), sometimes as merengue. Like the danza in Cuba, merengue's popularity in Puerto Rican ballrooms was undercut by criticism of its novel couples dance style, considered lascivious, and its African-influenced elements. Calling it a "corrupting influence," Puerto Rican governor Pezuela prohibited merengue in 1849, imposing a fine of fifty pesos on those who tolerated it in their homes and a sentence of ten days in prison on those who danced it (Nolasco 1956: 338; Rodríguez Demorizi 1971: 129). The governor's campaign may have contributed to merengue's decline in Puerto Rico; it was no longer performed there after the 1870s (Díaz Díaz 1990: 12).

Merengue nevertheless affected the development of a Puerto Rican form of the danza. Like the Cuban danza, it employed a multipart form: The paseo section was danced in a group, while the merengue section was danced by independent couples (Díaz Díaz 1990: 10–11). Puerto Rican danza music was often performed by brass bands and featured the baritone horn (*bombardino*) outlining the Caribbean cinquillo rhythm. Like Haitian mereng, the Puerto Rican danza also developed into a rural music sung to the accompaniment of plucked string instruments. Also like its relatives in Haiti and Cuba, it became a romantic nationalist concert music, usually composed for piano. The danza maintained its status as a national symbol of Puerto Rico into the twentieth century (Cadilla de Martínez 1950; Díaz Díaz 1990; Manuel 1994: 251–56; Quintero Rivera 1986; Rosado 1977).

Venezuelan merengue emerged in Caracas salons during the late nineteenth century and reached the height of its popularity in the 1930s. According to Venezuelan ethnomusicologist Luis Ramón y Rivera, it developed from the *danza* to become a "notable national piece" (1976: 85). Like its counterpart in Puerto Rico, Venezuelan merengue was criticized for its lascivious hip motion (Soto 1993: 42, 43). A local form of merengue also developed in the Caribbean coastal region of Colombia, but its early history lies in obscurity.[7]

This comparative perspective clearly reveals merengue's Afro-Spanish basis, even if it doesn't resolve the question of the music's origin. On the one hand, Carpentier's argument that the Cuban danza, so closely related to merengue, had been influenced by Saint-Domingue colonists fleeing the Haitian revolution tempts speculation about a Haitian source (1961: 71–78), a possibility that gains some support from the etymology of the Spanish word *merengue*, which derives from its French cognate, *méringue* (Corominas 1954: 351).[8] On the other hand, according to Haitian scholar Sténio Vincent, the similarities between mereng and the danza traveled from the Spanish Caribbean to Haiti rather than the other way around (1910: 273). In the final analysis, no hard evidence links merengue's early history to any particular nation.

The Campaign against Merengue in the Ballrooms

As in Puerto Rico and Venezuela, merengue played to mixed reviews in the Dominican Republic. The frequency with which contemporary writings refer to merengue indicate its popularity in the Republic, but most of these writings condemn it. The appalled authors were prominent young intellectuals who published in *El Oasis*, a literary journal of the capital. The earliest extant document, from 1854, reflects the horror with which urbane intellectuals reacted to the licentious commotion provoked by the new music:

> And when the merengue begins, dear God! One man grabs the woman sitting opposite him. Another fellow runs around, not knowing what to do, and then tugs on a young lady's arm, asking her to *merengue*. A third man elbows himself across the room. Even those who have the appearance of sophistication participate in all kinds of mischief, which they later blame on their partners. This labyrinth of confusion lasts until the end of the piece. (Rodríguez Demorizi 1971: 111–12)

The best writers in the country used their literary gifts in reproach of the new fad. Manuel Jesús de Galván's eleven-stanza poem "Complaint of the Tumba against the Merengue" decries the "lewd and contemptible" merengue's displacing the stately *tumba*, a contredanse-derived group dance, in the ballrooms:

La tumba, que hoy vive desterrada	The tumba, exiled today
por el torpe merengue aborrecible;	By the lewd and contemptible merengue,
que en vil oscuridad yace olvidada,	Lies in odious obscurity, forgotten.
llorando su destino atroz, horrible;	Wailing in horrible and insufferable exile,
ya por fin, penetrada de furor	Finally penetrated by fury,
expresa de este modo su dolor.	She expresses her pain thus:

Progenie impura del impuro averno,	Impure progeny of impure Hell,
hijo digno del diablo y una furia,	Child of the Devil and a Fury,
merengue, que aun siendo niño tierno	Merengue, when but a tender babe,
te merengueó en sus brazos la lujuria,	Miscreant and insulator of chastity,
tú, villano, que insultas al pudor,	You were rocked in lecherous arms.
dame mi cetro, infame usurpador.	Give me my staff, ignoble usurper.

(Rodríguez Demorizi 1971: 114)

A look at both the body of Galván's work and the historical context in which he wrote suggests a link between his animosity for merengue and the anti-African, pro-European sentiment that prevailed within his social class. In the period following the establishment of Dominican independence in 1844, power passed from idealistic bourgeois nationalists to conservative *caudillos* (literally, men on horseback; leaders or strongmen), who drew their power from "a well established system of rural chieftainship by means of which the rural population was organized. Each region had its *caudillo* who maintained order within his territory at the same time that he defied the efforts of the central government to control him or his dependencies" (González 1972: 44).

Competing caudillos Pedro Santana of the East, with whom Galván became associated, and Buenaventura Báez of the South rose to national prominence in midcentury; each held the presidency more than once. Haiti's repeated attempts to retake the country during this period were repelled by Santana and others. (As noted, many rural Afro-Dominicans supported unification with Haiti; the anti-Haitian sense of Dominican identity had not yet taken hold among the masses [Moya Pons 1995: 123, 1988: 236]). The caudillos' anti-Haitianism was based more in Eurocentrism and expectations of personal advance than in patriotism; Santana and Báez repeatedly tried to annex the Dominican Republic to France and other European powers in return for military and financial support. "Santana's envoys knocked on the door of practically every European monarch, making similar offers to Great Britain, Spain, and even the tiny kingdom of Sardinia" (Martínez-Fernández 1991: 574). Santana finally succeeded in annexing the Dominican Republic to Spain in 1861, a move that met widespread disapproval. La Restauración de la República (The Restoration of the Republic) was proclaimed in 1863, and sovereignty was restored in 1865 after an arduous War of Restoration with

Spain that was significant in promoting Dominican identity among the masses (Moya Pons 1986: 243).

Galván, possibly the best-known writer of Dominican fiction, was involved with the annexationist camp: He had served as Santana's secretary and played an instrumental role in negotiating the Spanish annexation of 1861 (Somer 1991: 250). Like other Latin American writers of the period, he participated in an *indigenista* (indigenist) literary movement that celebrated Native American culture. Galván's best-known work, the novel *Enriquillo* ([1882] 1989), is based on a true story about a *cacique*, a Native American leader who rebelled against Spanish domination.[9] Although *indigenismo* may have represented a genuine anticolonial posture in countries whose populations consisted largely of Native Americans and *mestizos* (persons of mixed indigenous and Spanish ancestry),[10] in the Dominican Republic it served largely as a strategy for rejecting African heritage (see Alcántara Almánizar 1987: 164). *Enriquillo* contributed to a trend in which Dominicans of mixed African and Spanish descent identified themselves as *indios* (Indians) rather than with their African heritage.[11] "From the time Galván published *Enriquillo*, almost immediately institutionalized as required reading in Dominican schools, Dominicans are Indians or mestizos, descendants of Enriquillo's valiant tribesmen and the Spaniards to whom they were bound by love and respect, whereas blacks are considered foreigners, Haitians" (Somer 1991: 252).

The novel helped propagate the dominant anti-Haitian sense of Dominican identity by diluting pro-Haitian tendencies among the middle classes of mixed ancestry during this period, which was marked by the growth of a lucrative sugar industry that attracted black immigrants from the English-speaking Caribbean and Haiti (see Fennema and Loewenthal 1987: 28). As Frank Moya Pons notes, "one of the great paradoxes of Dominican national formation is that as the Hispanic population became darker, the Dominican mentality became whiter" (1988: 238). This whiter mentality was integral to urbane Dominicans' attitudes about dance and music.

The waltz had been denounced as lascivious in Europe; an observer in nineteenth-century Erlangen, Bavaria, described couples waltzing "as close together as possible, and thus the turning went on in the most indecent positions. . . . It is the custom of the country, and not as bad as it looks, they say: but I can now quite understand why they have forbidden the *waltz* in certain parts of Swabia and Switzerland" (Sachs [1937]1963: 430).

While Euro-Caribbeans viewed the waltz as complementary to the formality of group dances, they rejected the local independent couple dance, the merengue. Thus in 1849 a Puerto Rican observer called the waltz "the inseparable companion of the contradanza, and it is considered a necessary consequence; the young lady who agrees to dance a contradanza knows that she must also dance a waltz with the same partner" (Díaz Díaz 1990: 13). Yet of the déclassé merengue, Ulises Francisco Espaillat, a well-known Dominican intellectual who once served as president of the Republic, wrote the following 1875 reproach in the form of a dialogue, under the pen name María:

> "Why has María declared herself an enemy of merengue? Is she crazy?"
> "It is accepted in all the civilized countries!"
> "You are wrong . . . not in all. It is not known in Europe or in any of the South American Republics."
> "But it is danced in Havana."
> "In Philadelphia, you say?"
> "No, in Havana."
> "Ah . . . !" (Rodríguez Demorizi 1971: 136–37)

The Puerto Rican and Dominican elites denounced merengue not only because it was an independent couple dance, but also because it was associated with Cuban and other Afro-Caribbean cultures.

Galván was greatly troubled by the swinging hips of merengue dancers. In the eighth stanza of the "Complaint of the Tumba against the Merengue," he expresses outrage that Euro-Dominican sisters and daughters should act so lewdly:

¿Decid, merengueadores,	Speak, merengue dancers;
no os enfada	doesn't it trouble you,
cuando dáis con parejas	When you go with a *sandungera*
sandungueras,	[dance] partner,
pensar que alguna hermana o	To think of a beloved sister or
hija amada	daughter
a otro prueba que es ágil de caderas?	Demonstrating the agility of her hips?
¡No tenéis corazón, no tenéis alma	You must have neither heart nor soul
para sufrir ese aguijón en calma!	To endure this injury in peace!
(Rodríguez Demorizi 1971: 115)	

Hip motion characterizes much African-influenced dance. For example, the *yuka*, a fertility dance associated with the Congolese-Cuban *mayombe* religion, and its descendant the *rumba guaguancó* employ a pelvic thrust that mimics the sex act. Euro-Americans have often misinterpreted African-influenced choreographic expressions of fecundity as lewdness; African American dance provoked censure in the United States during the Harlem renaissance and during the rock 'n' roll vogue. Such movements have also struck some Euro-Americans as excessively agitated. A New York State preacher's 1922 opinion that "jazz may be analyzed as a combination of nervousness . . . and savage animalism" (Merriam 1964: 242) resembles Espaillat's suggestion that merengue damages the nervous system: "'When do you plan to start dancing merengue again?' . . . 'When the medical profession learns to cure attacks of the nerves'" (Rodríguez Demorizi 1971: 136).

Even had Espaillat failed to note that he had made local ladies angry by "condemning the *favored merengue* without appeal" (italics added) (Rodríguez Demorizi 1971: 136), all of these impassioned writings against merengue indicate that the music had followers in the ballrooms. The same Africanisms that offended some Euro-Dominicans apparently appealed to others, a conflict inherent in the futile project of forging a Eurocentric identity in an African American country.

Stylistic Characteristics of Salon Merengue

We are probably safe in concluding that nineteenth-century salon merengue in the Dominican Republic resembled its cognate forms elsewhere in the Caribbean, although a paucity of historical evidence precludes definitive statements. Like Puerto Ricans, Dominicans seem to have used the terms *merengue* and *danza* interchangeably; a 1909 Dominican writing asserts that "merengue was called danza in this country for a period of time" (Espaillat 1909: 61), and another early source describes what is "called *Merengue* in Santo Domingo . . . [as] the primitive, melancholy, tender, [and] expressive original of the elegant genre that certain Antillian composers have elevated to artistic eminence [that is, the danza] (Deschamps n.d.: 275).

As elsewhere, Dominican merengue dance used hip motion and was performed by independent couples. In midcentury, the musical ensemble that played merengue in ballrooms consisted of combinations of flute; string instruments such as violin, guitar, mandolin, *tiple*, and *cuatro*; the *timbal*, tambora, or *pandereta* drums; and a scraper called the *güiro*.[12] Marching-band instruments arrived in the Dominican Republic during the 1863–65 War of Restoration, and salon *orquestas* began using the clarinet and baritone horn. These instruments were also important to the Puerto Rican and Cuban danza and the Haitian mereng (López Morillo 1982: 80–81; Rodríguez Demorizi 1971: 152–53). Additionally, an 1874 newspaper article mentions that merengue was sometimes performed on the piano (Rodríguez Demorizi 1971: 124).

Juan Bautista Alfonseca (1810–65) is the earliest known Dominican composer of merengue. Although his obituary does not mention merengue by name, it speaks of the composer's adaptation of the danza to a peculiarly local sensibility: "A musical innovator, Señor Alfonseca understood the people's nature and modified the [Latin] American danza, giving it an entirely new, rhythmic, merry, and sensual air" (Rodríguez Demorizi 1971: 125). Most merengue researchers agree that this adaptation was merengue (Hernández 1969: 63; Nolasco 1939: 59–60, 1948: 164–65, 1956: 341; Rodríguez Demorizi 1971: 124) Although Alfonseca was a member of the cosmopolitan gentry, titles of his pieces such as "The Sancocho" (a typically Dominican soup) and "Oh Coconut!" indicate that his music was associated with local culture (Rodríguez Demorizi 1971: 125). None of Alfonseca's manuscripts survive, but Flérida de Nolasco provides a merengue attributed to him entitled "Juana Quilina" (see musical example 2).[13] Only the first two lines of the "Juana Quilina" text survive:[14]

Musical Example 2
Juana Quilina
Attributed to Juan Bautista Alfonseca
(from Nolasco 1956: 341)

Juana Quilina va llorando	Juana Quilina is crying
Porque la llevan merengueando.	Because they are taking her merengue-ing.
(Nolasco 1939: 60, 1948: 164;	
Rodríguez Demorizi 1971: 125)	

Rodríguez Demorizi suggests that this song refers to an incident reported in an 1855 police record, in which an unruly guest broke a string instrument, a cuatro, over a musician's head at a party at the home of one Juan Aquilino (1971: 123).

Alfonseca performed merengue and other local forms such as the mangulina at ballroom dances, and his obituary mentions that his music was characterized by a "national style" (Henríquez y Carvajal in Jorge 1982a: 31; Rodríguez Demorizi 1971: 125). Having participated in the 1844 independence movement, Alfonseca believed that local music was a fitting symbol for the young nation, but when he composed the country's first national anthem, he made it a mangulina, not a merengue (Nolasco 1956: 321). In fact, there is little evidence to suggest that merengue, a pan-Caribbean form, was considered typically Dominican during this period.

Merengue in the Rural Regions

While merengue was expelled from the elite ballrooms, it flourished in the countryside. With the Eurocentric Dominican identity confined to "a minority that controlled the educational and communications systems" in the period following the establishment of independence, the population was estimated as 97 percent rural in 1880 (Moya Pons 1988: 236, 213)—and the culture of the rural majority was steeped in African traditions. Africans arrived regularly at least until the end of the eighteenth century (Hoetink 1982: 181), the Haitian occupation of 1822–44 promoted settlement by Haitians and others of African descent, and black immigration continued in the later part of the nineteenth century. The extent and nature of religious expression in the 1800s reveal the strong African-derived element of rural society. Dominican life was characterized by "an extraordinary religiosity," according to Moya Pons (1988: 215), which manifested itself in frequent Afro-Catholic religious festivals, usually held in honor of saints or deceased community members.

Catholic saints were often syncretized with African deities, and documents attest to the occasional use of African languages in ritual contexts as late as 1784 (Hoetink 1982: 183). Music and dance were integral to Afro-Dominican religion, and social dance was also popular; a mid-nineteenth-century account reports that campesinos "dance during all the fiesta days" (López Morillo 1983: 80).

Rural merengue likely developed from its urban cousin in the same way that the rural *danza* evolved from its urban counterpart in Puerto Rico. In this case, each region of the Dominican Republic would have adapted the music to local instruments and aesthetics to create the variants performed today (see Chapter Eight). Supporting this view is the fact that while the regional variants use widely differing instruments, rhythms, and melodies, all are independent couple dances performed in the ballroom dance position.

Although merengue was performed throughout the Dominican Republic during the nineteenth century according to Nolasco (1956: 324–35), we have most of our information from the country's most populous region, the Cibao. Midcentury *merengue cibaeño*, or Cibao merengue, was performed on plucked string instruments such as the cuatro, the tambora drum, and a scraped calabash, the güiro (Rodríguez Demorizi 1971: 153). Rural groups also sometimes added wind instruments in imitation of salon orquestas (Hoetink 1982: 206). Still used throughout the Dominican Republic in many musical types, the tambora is a double-headed drum made from a hollowed log or from boards arranged to form a barrel-shaped cylinder. Goatskin membranes, attached to each end of the drum with hoops, are tied together with rope arranged in Y-shaped configurations and used to tune the instrument.[15] Nineteenth-century tambora players held the drum sideways in their laps, playing it with a stick in each hand (Lizardo 1988: 29). Made from a dried, hollowed calabash with horizontal serrations cut around its front and holes bored in its back, the güiro is scraped with a *gancho* or *púa* (literally, hook or spike) made from a piece of wood into which bits of hard wire are inserted.

String instruments in merengue cibaeño gave way to the accordion, which began arriving in the region during the 1870s. Germany was an important trading partner for Cibao tobacco growers, and according to oral tradition, Germans bartered their one-row button accordions for tobacco (Hernández interview); shopkeepers Joaquín Beltrán and Bernabé Morales were famous for selling the best accordions as well as the best rum (Rodríguez Demorizi 1971: 157).[16] The new instrument came under attack soon after it was integrated into merengue. Many Dominicans considered string instruments more sophisticated than the loud and harmonically limited one-row accordion, which could play only tonic and dominant chords in one major key.[17] The popular poet Juan Antonio Alix addressed this issue in two poems using the *décima* form.[18] In one, "El cuatro y el acordeón," the cuatro tells the accordion that string instruments have been in the Republic longer than the newfangled German import, that fads come and go, and that the accordion will likely also be replaced someday:

. . . *Soy en mi Nación*	. . . In my country
Ei primero que soné.	I was the first to be heard.
Y si hoy me dan con el pié	And if they kick me out now,
Será poique me combiene,	It'll be because I want it that way,
Y ei que a ti amoi te tiene	And he who loves you,
Aunque tú lo vea así,	As you see it,
Te jará peoi que a mí,	Will treat you worse than me
Si otra cosa mejoi viene.	If something better comes along.
(Alix 1961: 73)	

The cuatro goes on to insult the accordion for being an inferior instrument that can only play in one key:

Encoideón yo te haré bei	Accordion, I'll show you
Que aunque me tienen en poco,	That even though they don't value me,
En todo tono yo toco	I can play in all keys,
Lo que tú no pue jasei.	Which is something that you cannot do.
(Alix 1961: 74)	

    In 1887, the municipal government of Santiago de los Caballeros went so far as to propose that the national Congress impose a tariff on accordions to discourage their importation. A Santiago lawyer expressed the municipality's position thus: "Accordions are not necessary articles, and only serve to bring vagabonds together. They do not contribute to the edification of the country, as does the cuatro, which is more sonorous, more harmonious, more perfect, and thus, more useful" (Jorge 1982a: 32). Given the tenor of the times, the accordion may also have been rejected because it accentuated the music's African and percussive elements at the expense of the Hispanic and harmonic elements (Pacini Hernandez 1989a: 251).[19] Still, despite the instrument's hostile reception, accordion-based merengue flourished in the Cibao under the influence of artists such as accordionist Juan María Rosa (Pichardo n.d.a).

We have clues to the musical style of rural nineteenth-century Dominican merengue, drawn by Dominican composer Julio Alberto Hernández from the memories of elderly musicians in interviews early in the twentieth century. According to them, most rural merengues dating from the late nineteenth century consisted of four-measure melodies, repeated many times with improvised variations (Hernández 1969: 63): "These beautiful melodies were from the era of Lilís [the dictator Ulises Heureaux, who ruled from 1886 to 1899] and earlier. . . . Most of the examples were no longer than four measures, performed with lively variations" (Hernandez in Incháustegui 1988: 9).

Because the early accordions could not execute minor keys, accordion-based merengue was necessarily in the major mode. Merengues predating the adoption of the accordion, however, occur in both major and minor. For this reason, the minor-mode merengue theme collected by Juan Francisco García (musical example 3) likely dates to the mid–nineteenth century.[20] Marked by the Caribbean cinquillo rhythm, the song's lyrics speak about the girls of a Cibao town:

Musical Example 3
A Nineteenth-Century Merengue Melody Collected by Juan Francisco García;
"Juangomero" Theme
(from Hernández 1969: 64)

·*La muchacha de Juan Gome [un pueblo]*	The girls of Juan Gómez [a town]
son bonita y bailan bien,	Are pretty and dance well.
pero tienen un defecto	But they have one defect:
Que se rien de to ey que ven.	They laugh at all who come their way.
(Hernández 1969: 54)	

Songs of this era often commented on local and world events, and many focused on the respected regional caudillo. The following merengue seems to endorse Lilís (Ulises Heureaux) and disparage Benito Monción and Casimiro N. de Moya, although its exact meaning is cryptic:

Generai Benito,	General Benito,
yo se lo decía,	As I told him,
qu'en ei Aguacate	Cuco left
ei Cuco salía.	The Aguacate.[21]
¡Cayó Moya,	Moya lost,
ganó Lilí;	And Lilís won.
yo . . . poi mí!	Me . . . for myself!
(Nolasco 1956: 333).	

Early Merengue and Articulation

Considering Dominican merengue's early history and tracing the development of related forms in Haiti, Cuba, Puerto Rico, and Venezuela tells us a good deal about both the Dominican social order and the music's social meanings. The contredanse transformations typify recreational dance musics, which, according to Carlos Vega (1966), often spread from colonizing powers to urban subcenters; from there they are further disseminated to, and reinterpreted by, rural populations according to local aesthetics. The resulting musical types occupy a middle ground that straddles class, urban/rural, vernacular/art, and national boundaries.

The contredanse transformations share the attributes listed in Table 2.1. As dances, they developed from European ballroom forms, were performed by independent couples, and often used an African-influenced motion of the hips. As musical types, they were marked by Afro-Caribbean elements, especially the cinquillo rhythm. Although they seem to have first emerged in elite salons, these forms were adopted and adapted by rural musicians. Associated with both European-derived cosmopolitanism and local African-influenced elements, they connected, or articulated, the social forces at play in Caribbean life (Grossberg and Hall 1986: 53). As a result, the contredanse transformations were attractive to cultural nationalists in Haiti, Cuba, and

Table 2.1 The Afro-Caribbean Contredanse Transformations

	Dominican Republic: Merengue	Haiti: Mereng	Cuba: Danza, danzón	Puerto Rico: Merengue, danza	Venezuela: Merengue	Colombia: Merengue
Salon dance music	*yes*	*yes*	*yes*	*yes*	*yes*	*no*
Ambivalent reception in salons	*yes*	*yes*	*yes*	*yes*	*19th century: no; 20th century: yes*	*not applicable*
Nationalist art music	*19th century: no; 20th century: yes*	*yes*	*yes*	*yes*	*no*	*no*
Rural interpretations	*yes*	*yes*	*no*	*yes*	*yes*	*yes*
Caribbean cinquillo	*yes*	*yes*	*danza: no; danzón: yes*	*yes*	*no*	*no*

Puerto Rico. Eurocentric Caribbeans, however, repudiated them because of their novel independent-couple dance choreography and links to Afro-Caribbean culture. Banished from elite contexts in the Dominican Republic, merengue flourished in rural areas of the country, and the Cibao variant, which was later to gain national and global fame, developed its characteristic instrumentation of accordion, tambora, and güira.

Chapter 3

Merengue Cibaeño,
Cultural Nationalism,
and Resistance

The U.S. marines landed in the Dominican Republic in 1916. Their arrival marked the beginning of a eight-year military occupation that Dominicans countered with both armed struggle and a cultural movement that celebrated all things Dominican, including merengue cibaeño.

General Ulises "Lilís" Heureaux had risen to the Dominican presidency in 1886, establishing a thirteen-year dictatorship that was politically stable but brutal and financially mismanaged. Its legacy of economic problems left the Republic in fiscal ruin after the dictator's death in 1899, and some of the country's European creditors sent battleships to collect debts in 1900 and 1903. President Theodore Roosevelt of the United States interpreted these actions as threats to the Panama Canal's security. In 1905 he negotiated an arrangement with the Dominican government under which the country's customs offices would be run by U.S. officials, who would equitably distribute revenue among foreign and domestic creditors. Although this scheme pulled the Republic out of debt, many Dominicans resented Yankee meddling in their internal affairs. The resulting tension, combined with the close ties several powerful Dominicans maintained with Germany, was too much for the North Americans, and in 1916 President Woodrow Wilson sent in the U.S.

marines, establishing the military occupation that lasted until 1924 (Moya Pons 1995: 279–320).[1] As Howard Wiarda writes, all political power rested in the hands of the occupying forces, who "assumed arbitrary power and at times abused their authority. Patriotic Dominicans of all shades of political opinion disapproved of the occupation" (1969: 31).

Uneasy interaction with the marines permeated all facets of social life, including musical activity, and the development of merengue during the occupation was intimately tied to the reaction to North American domination. Resistance to the occupation was waged on military, diplomatic, and cultural fronts in several regions of the country. In the East, *gavilleros* (insurgents, or bandits) led by local caudillos engaged the marines in guerrilla warfare from 1917 to 1922. Meanwhile, a program of diplomacy and propaganda, aimed at swaying international opinion against the occupation, was waged by upper-class Dominicans in the Cibao region. According to Bruce Calder, the program of protest eventually forced the United States "to abandon the occupation" (1984: 241, 249–59). This campaign worked hand in hand with a cultural movement that celebrated Dominicanness and embraced the Cibao variant of merengue, merengue cibaeño, as a national symbol.

Merengue Típico Cibaeño

Although merengue had once been performed in elite ballrooms, by the beginning of the twentieth century it was entrenched as a *típico* (typical, authentic, or folk) form played only by campesinos and those who dwelled in barrios. Rural expression was far removed from the lifeways of middle- and upper-class ubanites; as Manuel Andrade noted in 1930, campesino customs "seem as strange to the average Dominican of the city as they would to a European" (1930: 404). The lives of barrio dwellers, however, paralleled those of rural Dominicans. Contact across class lines, which continued to be important to merengue's development, was common in urban areas. The Cibao's largest city, Santiago de los Caballeros, became a focal point for the development of *merengue típico cibaeño,* or Cibao folk merengue.[2]

As we have seen, this music was sung—often with a tight, nasal technique—to the accompaniment of the button accordion, tambora, güira, and sometimes the baritone horn or alto saxophone. Accordionists led groups, composed, and sang; Santiago natives Francisco "Ñico" Lora and Antonio "Toño" Abreu were the best-known accordionist/bandleaders of the period and the architects of the merengue style that later gained national and transnational prominence.[3] While one-row accordions were used in the early part of the century, two-row models, capable of executing several major and minor keys, became more and more prevalent. *Tamboreros*, or tambora players, still held the drum sideways in their lap but now played it with a stick in the right hand and the palm of the left hand, rather than with two sticks as they had done in the nineteenth century.[4] The calabash güiro, which fell into disuse at the beginning of the twentieth century (possibly due to a scarcity of gourds of the proper shape), was replaced by a metal version. Dominicans generally call the metal version *güira* and the calabash version *güiro* (see Lizardo 1988: 243–57). (Tambora and güira rhythms are illustrated in musical examples 4 and 5.)[5]

As in the late nineteenth century, rural and barrio merengueros occasionally used the baritone horn in emulation of salon orquestas. As composer Julio Alberto Hernández explained to me, in elite ballrooms "the baritone played a special role [in danza performance]. It performed a rhythmic accompaniment. . . . They improvised típico rhythms, tropical rhythms, which had a certain character. . . . There were some excellent baritone players, with special embouchures. Often, people listened to the baritone rather than dance." Barrio groups sometimes substituted an alto saxophonist when a baritone player was not available, and the early merengue saxophone style, based on the baritone's capacity, soon gave way to an approach more consonant with the saxophone's disposition. Saxophonist Antonio Lora, who often performed with his father, Ñico, told me that musicians came to prefer the bright and flexible alto saxophone to the subdued and slow-speaking baritone horn; it blended better with the flashy and nimble accordion. This is not surprising, since the saxophone and accordion are both reed instruments and have similar ranges. And as Hernández explained to me, "Since saxophones are more flexible than baritones . . . , well, they played lots of variations and pirouettes, up and down."

Avelino Vásquez and Pedro "Cacú" Lora were the first saxophonists to play merengue regularly and were the best of their day. Under their influence, use of this instrument became increasingly common in merengue after about

1910; Vásquez and Lora were thus the architects of the original merengue saxophone style (Hernández 1969: 61; Lora, Pichardo, and T. Vásquez interviews; Pichardo n.d.b: 5). While the saxophone was seen as a típico, or authentic, merengue instrument (Alberti 1975: 87), it was not present in all groups and was rarely used in rural areas, being unavailable there. The *urban* nature of merengue típico cibaeño belies the conventional notion that "folk" music is rural. All the contredanse transformations borrowed stylistic elements across class lines, a process stimulated by urban life and central to their appeal.

Contexts and Dance

But whether in the city or in the country, cibaeños danced the merengue—at informal fiestas, *galleras* (cock-fighting rings), and brothels. Rebutting romantic images of peasants cavorting in rags, Agustín Pichardo writes that "campesinos went to fiestas in their best clothes . . . and never barefoot" (n.d.a: 2). As in the nineteenth century, dances often ended as brawls (Incháustegui 1988b:11). Perhaps trying to downplay this unsavory fact, Pichardo explains that "the campesino did not customarily dance with a machete at his waist, since anyone who entered with a knife, revolver, or machete was disarmed at the door" (n.d.a: 2). Country folk often danced in an open-sided, thatch-roofed structure, an *enramada* (or *enramá*); several days of packing with lime, water, and earth made its dance floor shiny and perfectly level (Alberti 1975: 69). Pichardo recalled for me "places in the country where dances were held every Saturday and Sunday. And people danced on the ground, which was specially prepared to look nice." Musicians usually received food and drink in lieu of cash for their services and performed almost nonstop, pausing only periodically to consume food and rum (Hernández 1969: 64; Lora interview). As Hernández told me, "Playing dances in the country was hard work; playing and playing, drinking and drinking, hardly ever taking a break." (Even today, rural festivals in the Dominican Republic feature continuous live music.) Young ladies were accompanied by female chaperones who spent the night gossiping and sampling various treats; the culinary highlight was often a *sancocho* soup served at midnight (Alberti 1975: 70).

On Sunday afternoons, dances called *pasadías* were often held in the outlying areas of Santiago. These were public events for which dancers paid an admission price. According to Lora in our interview, all social classes attended "When a group of good típico musicians with saxophone and accordion went to the country to play, everyone went to the dance; the rich and the poor. Society didn't exist; there wasn't this thing of a 'club.' Rich and poor danced together and spent their money together. The people were very united." Lora's recollection of such unity may be more rosy than the reality, since class lines have always been tightly drawn in Santo Domingo. As Deborah Pacini Hernández notes, Lora's comment in this interview likely refers to members of leading rural families rather than to the Santiago elite (1989a: 74–75).

Merengue cibaeño is danced in the classic ballroom dance position.[6] The man's left hand clasps the woman's right, the man's right arm circles the woman's waist, and the woman's left hand rests on the man's shoulder. The man slides his left foot to his left and follows it with his right to bring his feet together, while the woman mirrors him. Continuing in this way, the couple moves sideways across the dance floor. In spite of references to hip motion in nineteenth-century merengue, evidence suggests that dancing merengue cibaeño involved little or no such motion in the early twentieth century (Lizardo p.c.; Pichardo interview). According to Pichardo, who often danced to the music of Lora, early merengue cibaeño was performed rather slowly. He also remembered in our interview that the man performed improvised figures around the woman and that merengue stimulated courtship: "In those days, the woman carried the rhythm, while the man danced in another way, performing figures. . . . The country man won the love of a woman using his feet, by dancing, . . . just as you have seen the rooster courting the hen." Informal dancing competitions often took place, according to a prominent Cibao musician, Luis Alberti: "The best merengue dancers of the area showed off. It was a marvelous spectacle, just like any other competition, but this time, of dance. Each couple showed off their best steps, hoping to receive the greatest amount of applause from the people that were watching" (1975: 69).

Not only the music but the lyrics of merengue cibaeño appealed to dancers and listeners. In a witty, light-hearted tone, songs commented on everyday life and serious political issues. Often made up on the spot, they could speak to the immediate context. Pichardo described to me Lora's skill as an improviser: "I often danced where he played, and he had a certain thing—he was an inspired man. You could go up to him and say, 'Ñico, I'm in love with that girl; make up a merengue for me.' And he sings a merengue named for the girl and named for you: 'This guy is good for you! Marry him!' Oh yes, yes, yes; I saw that happen many times!" Most merengues, however, were composed before they were performed, and Lora is credited with creating more than five-hundred songs (Pichardo and Lora interviews). Many of Ñico Lora and Toño Abreu's pieces are still played today.

As one might predict, a form often performed in bordellos had a bawdy side, as in this man's confession of his weakness for harlots:

Todos los cueros	All the whores
Son de Santiago,	Are from Santiago,
Y en Santiago	And in Santiago
Ellas viven bien.	They live well.
Y poi culpa de esa maldita	And because of this damnation,
De Santiago soy también.	I'm from Santiago too.
(Ysalguez 1975a: 51;	
Incháustegui 1988b: 11)	

Most such merengues refer to sex obliquely, using double entendre. The following song offers an extended metaphor about a woman who is not a virgin:

EL JARRO PICHAO
(The punctured bucket)

Que yo me iba pa' la Vega	I went to La Vega [a Cibao town],
Y pase por Bonao	And passed through Bonao [another town].
A mi me dieron agua	I was given some water
En un jarro pichao	In a punctured bucket.
Pichao, pichao	Punctured, punctured,
Mamá el jarro está pichao.	*Mamá,* the bucket is punctured.

Pichardo told me that, like newspaper articles, Ñico Lora's merengues addressed the issues of the day: "If someone was killed, [Lora] came out with a merengue about it, or if someone became powerful politically. . . . He was like a journalist, because he commented on everything with his accordion." Lora composed "La libertad de Cuba" in 1899, "El aeroplano" in 1903, and "La guerra mundial" ("The world war") in 1914 (Pichardo n.d.a). Just as nineteenth-century merengueros had commented on the caudillos of their day, twentieth-century singers praised or denounced current leaders. Julio Alberto Hernández told me that merengue was integral to political campaigns: "There were political leaders who said that politics is nothing more than merengue and rum, because they used to give peasants lots of rum so that they would vote for certain candidates. For example, Desiderio Arias was a leader whom many merengueros and other country people ·were crazy about."

Desiderio Arias was the dominant political and military figure of the North in the early twentieth century. U.S. diplomatic correspondence in 1914–16 refers more often to him than to the president of the Dominican Republic, according to Nancie González, who concludes that the U.S. military considered him "the single most important stumbling block" to the imposition of U.S. rule during the period leading up to the occupation (1972: 43). As it turned out, when the U.S. marines invaded in 1916; Arias retreated, an act that failed to diminish the caudillo's popularity. A merengue composed in his honor, still popular today, proclaims that his refusal to take up arms strengthened, rather than undermined, his honor and patriotism:[7]

DESIDERIO ARIAS

Primera Parte	Part One
Dice Desiderio Arias	Desiderio Arias asks
Que lo dejen trabajar.	That we let him till the soil,
Porque si él coje el machete,	Because if he takes up the machete,
Ni Dios sabe lo que habrá.	God only knows what he will do.
Las armas que hoy él maneja	The weapons which he now prefers
Son las armas de sembrar.	Are the weapons of planting.
Y él es en agricultura,	Our foremost general
Nuestro primer general.	Has become a farmer.

Segunda Parte	Part Two
Ay que general, con tanto valor [repite];	Oh, what a general, how brave he is [repeat];
A nadie hizo mal, a nadie mató [repite].	He did no one harm; he killed no one [repeat].
Ay que general, con tanto valor [repite];	Oh, what a general, how brave he is [repeat];
Le gusta la paz, pero con honor [repite].	He wanted peace, but with honor [repeat].

As González writes, Arias was reputed to be a proud, patriotic, generous, humble, and intelligent (although self-educated) man. Unlike most caudillos, he inspired respect through his moral character rather than through fear (1972: 42).

Merengue sometimes served as a forum for discussing taboo topics; perhaps its light-hearted tone undercut the usual restrictions. Ñico Lora's song "La protesta," recited for me by accordionist Bartólo "El Ciego de Nagua" Alvorado, celebrates two manifestations of Dominican resistance to the U.S. occupation: the guerrilla war of the east and the Cibao-based diplomatic program of protest led by statesman Francisco Henríquez y Carvajal:

LA PROTESTA
(The protest)

Primera Parte	Part One
En el año diez y seis	The Americans came
Llegan los americanos,	In 1916,
Pisoteando con sus botas,	Trampling Dominican soil
El suelo dominicano.	With their boots.
Francisco Henríquez Carvajal,	Defending the flag,
Defendiendo la bandera,	Francisco Henríquez y Carvajal
Dijo,"¡No pueden mandar	Proclaimed that "Yankees
Los yanquis en nuestra tierra!"	Cannot rule our land!"
Segunda Parte	Part Two
El americano, como se	We'll attack them with machetes, we'll make
entromete [repite];	them leave [repeat];
Los haremos ir, dandole	The Americans, the intruders [repeat].
machetes [repite].	
Los haremos ir, con fuerza y	With power and courage, we'll make them
valor [repite];	leave [repeat];
El americano, por abusador [repite].	The Americans, the abusers [repeat].
En tierra de Duarte, no pueden	Carvajal said that Americans
mandar [repite];	[repeat]
Los americanos, dijo Carvajal	Cannot rule the land of Duarte
[repite].	[repeat].

Alvarado, who performs this merengue today, told me that "it was hard in those days; hardly anyone said things like that. But Ñico did it."[8] Rafael "Fello" Almonte, an accordionist active during the occupation, reports that whenever "La protesta" was played "we bought all the rum in the store, so everybody could drink." Although "La protesta" was not generally performed in the presence of North Americans, Almonte tells of a time when, having had a couple of drinks, he decided to sing it in front of some marines: "Although they understood parts of it, they laughed and danced. You should have seen those . . . Americans dancing merengue!" (Brito Ureña 1987: 59–60).

Sectional Merengue Cibaeño and the Pambiche, or Yankee Merengue

Two merengue cibaeño forms that were played during the early twentieth century are still performed today: *sectional merengue cibaeño* and the *pambiche*. The sectional type consists of a short introduction (paseo) and two longer sections, the merengue (or part one) and the *jaleo* (or part two). (As we have seen, sectional form and paseo sections also characterize the Cuban and Puerto Rican danzas.) Each section is marked by characteristic percussion rhythms and melodic types (see musical example 4).[9] The paseo is an eight-measure marchlike instrumental introduction that serves as a signal for couples to take the dance floor. It is followed by the merengue section, which features an eight-measure European-influenced melody sung and played instrumentally several times to the accompaniment of major-mode harmonies. The final and longest section, the jaleo, consists of a two-measure repeating pattern based on dominant and tonic harmonies.[10] With interlocking rhythms performed on tambora, güira, accordion, and saxophone (if present), the jaleo exhibits a highly African-influenced aesthetic. As John Storm Roberts puts it, the merengue/jaleo form is "similar to Afro-Cuban numbers, such as the *guanguancó*, which has a 'melodic' first part in the European sense, and a second part . . . during which the percussion goes to town" (1972: 104). Vocals in the jaleo consist of two rhyming couplets, with each line repeated once (see "Desiderio Arias" and "La invasión del '16" earlier in this chapter). In addition to referring to the final part of a merengue, the term *ja-*

leo can denote the repeating figures played on accordion and saxophone during the jaleo section. Merengue performances thus include several accordion and saxophone jaleos, or patterns, many of which are improvised; merengue accordion and saxophone playing consists largely of *inventando* (inventing) jaleos.

Musical Example 4
Three-Part Merengue Cibaeño: Con el alma
(from oral tradition) Composer: Toño Abreu

Musical Example 5
Pambiche: Pambiche es mejor que el dril
(from Alberti 1975: 71)

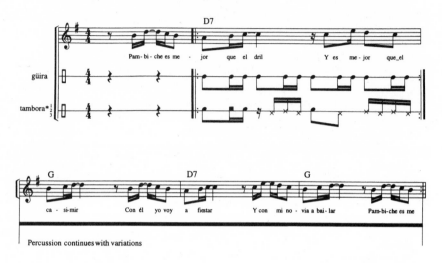

Percussion continues with variations

Merengue cibaeño pieces almost always end with one of several variants of the coda seen at the end of musical example 4. Played on the accordion (or sax-ophone, if present), the beginning of the coda cues the last two notes of the piece, which are executed by all the musicians together. Inserted at any time during the jaleo, the coda can unexpectedly signal the end of the piece. Early twentieth-century musicians, who sometimes played for donations from the public, used this effect to economic advantage: "The novel manner of ending merengues may have come from the custom of 'tossing' the music to someone who has been put in the spotlight. Merengue musicians in the countryside walked around the couples. Suddenly, addressing one man in particular, they exclaimed, 'You owe [for this merengue], my friend!' or, 'You pay for this one, my friend!' And so, that man had to pay for the merengue" (Fondeur n.d.: 2).

The other type of merengue típico cibaeño still played today, the pam-biche, features cinquillo-related tambora rhythms, major tonic and domi-nant harmonies, and a melody repeated many times with improvised vari-ations (see musical example 5). Although an often told story places the pambiche's origin during the U.S. occupation, Julío César Paulino and

Dálmaso Mercado affirm that the form existed before the occupation but received its *name* during that period (1983: 144; 1992).[11] Like the notion that merengue originated at the Battle of Talaquera, however, theories about pambiche's origin serve us best as indicators of merengue's symbolic significance.

As the story goes, the occupying marines who sometimes attended local fiestas danced badly, combining the one-step and fox-trot with merengue. Imitating the North Americans, Dominicans in the northern town of Puerto Plata created a dance called *merengue estilo yanqui* (Yankee-style merengue). A song about a fabric called Palm-Beach was associated with the dance:[12]

Palm-Beach es mejor que el dril,	Palm-Beach is better than drill,
Y es mejor que el casimir.	And it is better than cashmere;
Con él yo voy a fiestar,	I will celebrate with it,
Y con mi novia a bailar.	And dance with my girlfriend.
(Alberti 1971: 79)	

The cinquillo-based tambora rhythm in musical example 5 accompanied this song and the estilo yanqui choreography, and the style came to be called *pambiche*, a Dominicanization of the Americanism *Palm Beach*.[13] The story goes that merengue estilo yanqui was named *pambiche* because, just as the Palm Beach fabric is neither cashmere nor drill, pambiche is neither merengue nor fox-trot.

Ramón Emilio Jiménez, who lived in the Republic during the occupation, tells this version of the story: "Since the Americans could not dance to the lithe and delicate merengue rhythms, dancing with jumps instead, as an old musician put it, a type of merengue more suited to their rhythmic sense was created. This new style is nothing other than a slow and elongated jaleo with a syncopated rhythm that was easier for the foreigner, who does not have the sensibility of the native, to dance" (del Castillo and Arévalo 1988: 27). The anecdote stands occupation-era power relations on their head: Dominican creativity not only spawned "lithe and delicate merengue rhythms" that the clumsy U.S. occupiers could not contend with, but generated a new expressive form from the marines' incompetence. Perhaps this story continues to be told because its message remains relevant in the late twentieth century, a period marked by continuing neocolonial domination of the Dominican Republic by the United States.[14]

Merengue as Nationalist Art Music

A similar spirit of resistance found expression in a nationalist movement spearheaded by Cibao art music composers. Social worlds away from rural and barrio life, these young middle- and upper-class composers nevertheless were inspired by típico music, as one of them, Julio Alberto Hernández, remembered in our interview: "I lived in Santiago, in the center of the city. Every night, every night, I heard merengues being played in the barrios that surround the city—the tambora and the güira, especially the tambora. I gradually became interested in composing this [music]."

According to Hernández, the earliest merengue composed for concert performance marked "the beginning of the propagation of Dominicanism" (interview). Juan Francisco "Pancho" García's rondo "Ecos del Cibao" (Echoes of the Cibao) was published in 1918 and premiered at Santiago's Teatro Colón in the following year (Incháustegui 1973a). In hopes of precluding an unfavorable reaction from the many elite Dominicans who continued to look down on local music, García identified the work as a collection of danzas típicas instead of as merengue (Hernández interview). The composer suspected that cosmopolitan Dominicans might enjoy merengue in spite of themselves; he once said that he had used it in his music to prevent people from getting bored at concerts (Incháustegui 1974a). García himself later wrote about the rise of nationalism in Dominican music in relation to European romanticism:

> In the early twentieth century, Dominican musical nationalism developed. This music utilized folk songs and dances that had hitherto been relegated to the humble milieu of the lower social classes.
>
> For many years, the interesting phenomenon of romanticism, which developed in Europe and some parts of the Americas during the nineteenth century, had made folk art radiate with splendor. Poems and legends were collected and regional folk melodies and

rhythms were transcribed, thus contributing not only to their own exaltation, but also to their international diffusion. (1972: 23)

Other composers, including Esteban Peña Morel, Emilio Arté, and
Hernández, a García protégé, also began to write concert music based on local themes. Later called the national school of Dominican music (Coopersmith 1949: 22), this movement developed in tandem with folklore research.
Many composers were folk-music collectors, and scholars encouraged composers to use local material; in 1927, folklorist Julio Arzeño wrote that "we
must abandon exotic rhythms and be Dominican musicians," and that "when
true love of country increases . . . the stability of the Republic grows, and the
Fatherland thrives" (1927: 7, 135).[15] This musical movement was part of a
strategy of noncooperation with the United States. By encouraging the open
display of patriotism, cultural nationalism made it difficult for those few Dominicans who would have liked to cooperate with the United States to do so
openly, thus depriving the U.S.-controlled military government of Dominican collaborators.

García based "Ecos del Cibao" on merengue melodies he had collected.[16] Hernández explained in an interview that this piece, like all of García's merengue compositions, omitted the paseo and jaleo, consisting instead
of several central-section merengue melodies strung together and arranged
for chamber ensemble: "Pancho García composed a kind of potpourri . . . using folk merengues. But he only used the part that we call the verse, the central part, the melodic part. Also, he didn't call them *merengues*, calling them
danzas típicas instead. He arranged them for chamber ensemble, with violins
. . . and piano. He didn't use percussion instruments. . . . They were played
at society clubs as concert music, not for dancing."

Other composers took different approaches to adapting merengue to the
concert setting. Emilio Arté was the first to use the paseo, and others followed
suit (Hernández 1927; Hernández in Brito Ureña 1987: 55). Hernández's solo
piano merengue, "Santiago," has parts labeled paseo, merengue, and jaleo,
but the sections do not follow the order of three-part merengue típico cibaeño.
Instead, "Santiago" begins with a paseo, and continues with a jaleo, a
merengue, a reprise of the jaleo, and a "trio" (see musical example 6).[17] Composers also sometimes used the paseo/merengue/jaleo form. Some of the resulting pieces were original creations, others were transformations of típico

tunes, while yet others were simply transcriptions of existing three-part merengues for which the formally educated composers claimed credit.

Musical Example 6
Excerpt from Santiago
(from Hernández 1927)
Composer: Julio Alberto Hernández

Musical Example 7
A Merengue Melody Collected by Juan Francisco García
(from Hernández 1969: 63)

Certain melodies became favorites of classical and popular music composers. For example, García used the melody in musical example 7 in "Ecos del Cibao," String Quartet no. 2, and Symphony no. 1 (*La Quisqueyana*), while Hernández employed it in the song "Querer, querer, querer" (To love, love, love), composed in 1928 to text written by Emilio Morel.[18] In musical example 8, Luis Alberti's song "Compadre Pedro Juan" (Buddy Peter John) features a transformation of the melody into cinquillo-related rhythms.[19]

Juan Francisco García's best-known piece, "Juangomero," has two sections (see musical example 9).[20] The first part consists of the nineteenth-century minor-mode cinquillo-infused melody discussed in Chapter Two and illustrated in musical example 3. Conforming to neither three-part nor pambiche form, the structure of "Juangomero" is García's own. The composer learned the first theme from a blind singer named Sinó Agustín, who

Musical Example 8
Compadre Pedro Juan
(from oral tradition)
Composer: Luis Alberti

Musical Example 9
Juangomero
(from oral tradition)
Composer: Juan Francisco García

accompanied himself on the cuatro (Incháustegui 1974a). The second theme, which employs harmonies unusual to merengue (a secondary dominant leading to the subdominant), was García's creation (Incháustegui interview). García and most of his colleagues worked primarily in the realm of art music, but "Juangomero" became a staple of a merengue vogue that swept Cibao ballrooms.

Merengue and North American Popular Music in the Ballrooms

Shunned at high-society dances before the U.S. invasion, native music became popular in ballrooms as the nationalist cultural movement took shape. As Hernández recalls, Cibao socialists favored the danza, the waltz, and other cosmopolitan genres at the outset of the occupation: "High-society people did not customarily listen to [merengue], nor were they interested in it. Balls always began with a waltz. Polkas, mazurkas, and danzas were also played, especially danzas, tropical danzas more or less in the style of Puerto Rican danzas. . . . But merengue, no. They never played merengue at the balls, never" (interview). According to folklorist René Carrasco, when "Juan-gomero" was performed at the Cibao high-society Club Comercio in 1911, the hostess "immediately protested, saying that it was an insult to her social position, since that piece was inadmissible at such an occasion. Immediately, people were flashing revolvers, and the ball ended with a chastisement of the bandleader for introducing merengue at a society ball" (Ysalguez 1976c: 53). In 1912, when García played a merengue theme at a high-society ball, he dared not identify it as típico music, disguising it as the final section of a Cuban danzón (Incháustegui 1973a, 1974a).

Perhaps inspired by García's innovations, clarinetist and composer Juan Bautista Espínola Reyes, who led the most popular Santiago salon band in the late 1910s, took an interest in local music. Formed in 1917, Espínola's group specialized in the danzón and was comprised of two clarinets, one saxophone, two baritone horns, tuba, string bass, *timbaletas* (a small version of the timpanilike timbal, or timbales), and other percussion (Incháustegui 1974b; Tolentino interview). Like García's concert merengues, Espínola's ballroom merengues omitted the tambora and accordion and thus resembled the elegant danza more than rustic merengue típico cibaeño. In 1922, performances of Espínola's merengues "Terapéutica" (Therapy) and "Mi entusiasmo" (My enthusiasm) at the Casino Central in the Cibao town of La Vega met an enthusiastic reception; the public asked for them to be repeated many times (Hernández 1969: 65–66). Merengue soon found a permanent, though limited, place in the repertoires of Cibao dance bands; a practice of ending every ball with a merengue, usually "Juangomero," developed (Alberti 1975: 29, Tolentino interview). High society's about-face regarding merengue, from violent scorn before the invasion to enthusiastic acceptance during the occupation, illustrates the link between neocolonial domination and the rise of cultural nationalism.

The mood of resistance, however, did not entirely dim the allure of North American popular culture. As the story about the pambiche's origin suggests, Dominicans were intrigued by the dances that the marines brought to the island. Similarly, U.S. inventions such as the gramophone and radio piqued peoples' interest and spread North American music, for most of the existing recordings came from the United States. At the same time, however, these new mass media created opportunities for Dominicans to disseminate their own art.

In the early 1920s, the Victor Talking Machine Company made the earliest recordings of Dominican music, five danzones and three danzalike merengues composed by Juan Espínola and performed in New York City by the Orquesta Internacional. Julio Alberto Hernández's "Santiago" was also recorded in New York during this period. The first recordings made within the Dominican Republic itself appeared in 1928, when Victor recorded six selections at radio station HIX, including a salon version of Ñico Lora's merengue "La rigola." Because of the poor quality of the facilities in the Dominican Republic and the adverse effect of tropical heat on the wax cylinders, however, Victor decided not to record in the Republic anymore, but to record a group of Dominican artists in New York City instead. Whether any merengues were included in the latter session has not been reported, but one source believes that commercial constraints impeded this group's artistic quality (Incháustegui 1988a: 15–18).

Recorded music from North America began to make inroads on Dominican taste in the 1920s, when jazz-tinged dance music became popular. In 1921, Juan Pablo "Pavín" Tolentino founded Orquesta Bohemia, which soon displaced Espínola's group as Santiago's top dance band. What began as a danzón group with two clarinets, cornet, baritone horn, string bass, and percussion by the end of the decade had become a jazz band consisting of three saxophones (or clarinets), cornet, violin, baritone horn, tuba, banjo, trap drums, and other percussion (Tolentino interview). In the face of anti-U.S. sentiment, the jazz vogue did not meet with a wholly favorable reaction, and musicians boycotted North American music at the outset of the occupation (Alberti 1975: 33). Nevertheless, jazz-tinged popular music continued to gain favor; socialites liked its cosmopolitan image, while musicians found it a creative musical option.

In 1928, a new group, Jazz Band–Alberti, appeared in Cibao salons.[21] Its leader, Luis Alberti, was a great-grandson of J. B. Alfonseca, the nineteenth-century merengue innovator. As the two top bandleaders of the area, Tolentino and Alberti competed: When Orquesta Bohemia added a banjo to facilitate its jazz performance, Alberti had to get one; when Alberti learned several merengues on the piano accordion in 1933 and created arrangements that fused merengue with jazz, the following weekend Orquesta Bohemia brought in reinforcements—Manuel Lora's trio, one of the best típico merengue groups of the Cibao (Incháustegui 1973c). This was a significant innovation; as we have noted, earlier forms of salon merengue were stylistically removed from merengue típico cibaeño. The tambora, güira, and piano accordion, permanently incorporated into Alberti and Tolentino's bands, gained secure places in Dominican ballrooms.

Some of típico saxophone pioneer Avelino Vásquez's younger relatives, once members of Orquesta Bohemia, started their own group in 1932. Orquesta los Hermanos Vásquez (The Vásquez Brothers) became the number-one dance band of the region and remained popular into the late 1940s. The street where many of the Vásquezes lived and where the band rehearsed came to be known as La Calle Alegría (Happy Street), because the band's rehearsals were so enjoyable that people gathered to listen and dance (R. Vásquez p.c.; Morel p.c.). Orquesta los Hermanos Vásquez included several innovative saxophonists, who applied merengue accordion jaleos to the saxophone section of a jazz-style big band. According to Hernández, "The role of the saxophone in merengue acquired its traditional characteristics thanks to the contributions of celebrated popular musicians of Santiago, such as Pedro 'Cacú' and the Vásquez family, who converted the alley known as 'Happy Street' into a quarry of saxophonistic gyrations which served as the model for the modern orchestration of our típico dance" (1969: 61). By now the salient character of popular merengue as it was soon to be nationally and transnationally disseminated had been established.

Resistance and Contradiction

Based in several regions of the country, the manifestations of Dominican resistance to the occupation eventually met success, even if they formed an uneasy coalition. While it did not attain a military victory, the guerrilla action of the East successfully sapped marine morale. Meanwhile, the Cibao-based nationalist movement and international program of protest challenged the occupation on cultural and diplomatic fronts. The Cibao elites, however, looked down on the peasant armies of the East, and there was a cleavage between the military and cultural operations. But insurrection and resistance via expressive culture are analogous; Umberto Eco calls the latter "semiotic

guerrilla warfare" (1986: 135–44; see also Fiske 1989: 19). One cannot en-
gage a superior force in open combat. Instead, one undermines the enemy
and bolsters one's own psychological position through terrorism, sabotage,
and propaganda. Like the guerrilla action of the East, the virulent cultural
nationalism of the Cibao elites was a thorn in the side of the military government that demonstrated the falsity of U.S. officials' claim that Dominicans favored the occupation. Because the occupying forces could find few
collaborators, they were unable to create the semblance of a democratic
regime—according to Bruce Calder, a factor that made the occupation relatively short compared with U.S. occupations elsewhere in the Caribbean
(1984: 246–247).

Nationalist musical expression gained much of its efficacy by simultaneously encoding both resistance and North American cultural hegemony. By
domesticating the one-step and fox-trot, the anecdote about the pambiche's
origin is analogous to a guerrilla ploy that uses weapons manufactured by,
and captured from, the enemy.[22] At the same time, the origin story expresses
the allure of U.S. culture; típico musicians were *inspired* by the one-step and
fox-trot. Musicians and audiences in the ballrooms betrayed similar contradictory attitudes: while North American music was popular, it was also boycotted to protest the occupation. Tolentino, Alberti, and the Vásquez Brothers' innovative fusions of típico merengue and jazz were poignant
juxtapositions of stylistic elements derived from native and occupying powers. Such contradiction, according to John Fiske, lies at the heart of oppositional popular culture: "Popular culture is deeply contradictory in societies
where power is unequally distributed. . . . Contradiction can entail the expression of both domination and subordination, of both power and resistance. . . . [It] devolves to them [the subordinated groups] the power to situ-
ate themselves within this play of forces at a point that meets their particular
cultural interests" (1989: 4–5).

As in Europe, where musical nationalism most often developed as part of independence movements in smaller countries that were not sovereign nations,
Caribbean musical nationalism took shape primarily in nonsovereign countries.
Cubans' and Puerto Ricans' embrace of the danza as a national music was associated with independence movements, and the Haitian elite's interest in
Vodou music developed in opposition to Euro-American hegemony during the
1914–34 U.S. occupation of their country. Significantly, Dominican cultural

nationalism took shape only in the Cibao, the traditional home of many upper-class Dominicans, who rejected merengue until their country was stripped of sovereignty, when they embraced it as a national symbol. While not yet viewed that way by the rest of the country, merengue at the end of the 1920s was poised to play an influential role in national politics.

Chapter 4

Music and the State:
Merengue during the Era
of Trujillo, 1930–1961

Rafael Leonidas Trujillo Molina, who from 1930 to 1961 headed in the Dominican Republic one of the strongest and most absolute dictatorships ever established in Latin America, played a special role in the development of merengue. Like the European totalitarian leaders, the Dominican dictator understood that rural expressive forms can serve as effective symbols of national identity. In 1930, he took Ñico Lora and Toño Abreu along with him on speaking tours to sing merengues extolling his virtues and criticizing his opponents; as Luis Alberti remembers, when Trujillo campaigned for the presidency in 1930, he "based his . . . campaign on merengue. A típico quartet accompanied him to every town and championed him by singing about his promises and future glory" (1975: 74–75).

The merengue "Horacio salió" (Horace is gone) composed in 1930 correctly divined the nature of Trujillo's regime and celebrated the departure of President Horatio Vásquez:[1]

HORACIO SALIÓ
(Horace is gone)

Horacio salió	Horacio is gone,
y ahora entra Trujillo.	And now Trujillo is in.
Tenemos esperanza	We have faith
en nuestro caudillo.	In our caudillo.

Todo cambiará,	All will change,
en marcha caliente.	With fiery motion,
Pues ahora Trujillo	Because now Trujillo
es el Presidente.	Is the President.
Se acabó la bulla, se acabó.	No more noise, it's over.
Se acaban los guapos, se acabó.	No more bullies, it's over.
Ni "colú" ni "bolo," se acabó.	No *colú*, no *bolo*, it's over.
Eso de partidos, se acabó.	No more political parties, it's over.
(del Castillo and García Arévalo	
1989: 33)	

Trujillo was born into a lower-middle-class family in the small southern town of San Cristóbal in 1891. His father owned a small business and his maternal grandmother, a Dominican-born woman of Haitian parentage, was well known and influential in town. As a young man, Rafael Trujillo worked as a telegraph operator and a sugar plantation administrator. He also became involved in small-scale criminal activities (Crassweiler 1966: 25–32). Trujillo later joined the constabulary created by the occupying U.S. marines. Because most Dominicans were unwilling to cooperate with the occupation forces, opportunities for advancement were available, and Trujillo rose rapidly through the ranks. As a young officer, he was stationed in several parts of the country, serving as military commander of the Cibao and fighting insurgents in the East, and he stayed in the military after the U.S. forces left the Republic.[2] In 1928, Trujillo was promoted to chief of staff of the National Army, as it was then known, and he soon became the most powerful man in the country, having converted the army into an instrument of personal power. Using deception, ballot fixing, and violence, he became president of the Dominican Republic in 1930. Civil liberties were suspended and state-sponsored violence subdued elements that posed threats to the regime. All Dominicans were required to pay homage to *el benefactor*, as Trujillo was known.

Under Trujillo, the "provinces and local governments became almost paper entities in a system controlled from the capital" (Crassweiler 1966: 93–94), for centralized political power was integral to his program, a drastic change from the regionalism characteristic of Dominican politics. This centralization was made possible largely thanks to the U.S. occupation: The marines had built a network of roads that united the Republic geographically as never before. Additionally, Trujillo's rise through the national constabulary made him the first Dominican president with a truly national, rather than regional, base of support. He subjugated or destroyed the local leaders who had traditionally held power in their respective regions, among them the northern caudillo Desiderio Arias, who had once supported him. As Robert D. Crassweiler puts it, however, Arias was "incapable of genuine adherence to any other man's cause, and Trujillo was incapable of tolerating anything but total adherence" (1966: 94); when Arias fled the capital in 1931, Trujillo's forces followed, caught, and executed him. Because of Arias's popularity, several anecdotes about the execution circulated. The most colorful of these held that Arias's fate was similar to that of John the Baptist, maintaining that the caudillo's head was presented to Trujillo on a platter, surrounded by flowers. To preclude competition from beyond the grave, Trujillo forbade any open display of devotion to his rival, including performance of the merengue "Desiderio Arias" (González 1972: 44).

A National Merengue

Trujillo, who was not from the Cibao, adopted a music from this region as a national symbol; his status as a national rather than a regional caudillo allowed him to transcend established Dominican patterns not only of regional politics but of expressive culture.

In 1936, the dictator brought Luis Alberti's group to the capital to work as his personal dance band. Renamed Orquesta Presidente Trujillo, the band was required to specialize in merengue.[3] Merengue cibaeño had never been performed in elite ballrooms outside of the Cibao, and upper-class *capitaleños* (residents of the capital) were shocked to hear it at their functions (Mateo and Incháustegui interviews). But no one dared openly question the dictator's taste, and the socialites eventually accepted merengue, if they never adored it. The regime required all of the country's dance bands to feature merengue in their repertoires, and accordion-based merengue cibaeño groups performed throughout the country. Artists and intellectuals were expected to pay homage to the dictator, and often were intimidated into doing so. The composer García later wrote that "General Rafael Leonidas Trujillo Molina, who is today appropriately known as the Benefactor of the Fatherland and Father of the New Dominion, since the beginning of his judicious administration not only appreciated the true value of folk music as a genuine expression of nationhood, but also, with laudable patronage, secured our creoleism merengue as a popular symbol of authentic Dominican culture" (Rivera González 1960, 1: 10). Trujillo's iron will thus transformed a regional music, merengue cibaeño, into a state symbol recognized throughout the country.

A novel fusion of rustic and sophisticated stylistic elements characterized the merengue performed in the elite salons. Singer Joseíto Mateo described to me the impression that Luis Alberti's orquesta made on young musicians when it debuted in the capital in 1936:

> Luis Alberti went straight to high society, because it was an elite band, sponsored by Trujillo. Trujillo had them play in the salons, and when we first saw them, they looked fine. And also, he was a great musician. This was another class of merengue; the musicians played better. That is, they respected what is called the etiquette of music, with all its signs, markings such as crescendo, mordento, moderato, like [classical] music. They did that, so it sounded truly beautiful.

Alberti's band featured jazz-influenced interpretations of the traditional merengue cibaeño repertoire, augmenting big-band instrumentation with tambora, güira, and piano accordion. The latter instrument sounded similar to a button accordion, but its capacity to execute complex harmonies better suited Alberti's sophisticated style.[4]

Although Alberti's group remained popular, Super Orquesta San José, sponsored by one of the dictator's brothers, José "Petán" Trujillo, soon became the country's top dance band. Led by Papa Molina (Ramón Antonio Molina y Pacheco), this group featured the vocals of Joseíto Mateo, who became known as "the king of merengue." According to Mateo, Orquesta San José played a faster and livelier style of merengue than did Alberti (interview). Its innovations included omitting the piano accordion, adding the Cuban conga drums, and using syncopated Afro-Cuban rhythms in the bass.[5] As time went on, more and more band arrangements omitted the paseo section of three-part merengues. Alberti's group performed regularly at the Patio Español of the Jaragua Hotel from 1944 to 1954, while Orquesta San José specialized in radio broadcasts and played in the Night Club of the radio station La Voz Dominicana. The third most important dance band of the day and the only top band not sponsored directly by the Trujillo family was Antonio Morel y su Orquesta, a polished ensemble that had more freedom to perform and record as they wished, playing at society clubs and private parties (del Castillo and García Arévalo 1989: 37).

Several members of Santiago's Orquesta los Hermanos Vásquez moved to the capital to play with Orquesta San José. As mentioned in Chapter Three, the Vásquez Brothers had made important innovations in applying merengue accordion patterns to the saxophone section of a jazz band. The fusion of the essence of merengue cibaeño—jaleos—with jazz was the heart of the national music's link with both típico and cosmopolitan culture. It also gave the music its spicy danceability. Tenor saxophonist Rafael "Chachi" Vásquez's composition "Los saxofones" celebrates the merengue saxophone:

LOS SAXOFONES

Primera Parte (Merengue)	Part One (Merengue)
Oigan bien al saxofón,	Listen to the saxophone,
Con su sonar que domina;	With its commanding sound.
Al compas del acordeón,	To the beat of the accordion,
La tambora y de la güira.	The tambora and the güira.

Segunda Parte (Jaleo)	Part Two (Jaleo)
Toca tu saxofón, que yo quiero bailar [repite].	Play your saxophone, I want to dance [repeat].
Con su sondido así, me quiero enamorar [repite].	With its sound like that, I want to fall in love [repeat].

In a typically African-inspired aesthetic, the rhythms of merengue saxophone jaleos dovetail with the rhythms of the tambora and güira and the movement of dancers' feet, an almost irresistable combination.[6] Musical example 10 is a transcription and musical analysis of the jaleos in Antonio Morel's recording of "Los saxofones."

Musical Example 10
The Big-Bank Merengue Cibaeño Jaleo
(from Antonio Morel y su Orquesta's recording of "Los saxofones,"
MCA Coral DL8274)
Composer: Chachi Vásquez

*Tambora Key:

1 { ● right hand (stick) open tone
  { ■ left hand open tone
2   × right hand (stick) rim hit
3   × left hand bass slap

Analysis of Musical Example 10

The big-band merengue cibaneño jaleo, as performed on Antonio Morel y su Orquesta's recording of "Los saxofones" by Chachi Vásquez (see musical example above), is a typical jaleo and thus provides a good illustration of merengue cibaeño jaleo rhythm. A complete cycle of the rhythmic pattern has four pulses. The beginning of the cycle, most often defined by harmonic phrasing, may come at one of two places: after the roll in the tambora (shown as filled-in sixteenth notes here), or two beats before the roll. The former, more common, version is illustrated in musical example 10. Melodic rhythms in the two beats following the tambora roll leads usually feature Caribbean cinquillo-related rhythms, while the two beats preceding the roll generally articulate downbeats. Thus, the trumpet part here uses cinquillo-related syncopation at beats one and two, and eight-note values at beats three and four. The general pattern of emphasizing cinquillo-related rhythms for two beats and downbeats for two beats is basic to Cuban music as well as to much merengue cibaeño. In Cuban music this pattern is referred to as the *clave* (key).

The most prominent sound in merengue cibaeño percussion is the tambora roll, shown here as filled-in circular and square notes. Notice that this figure consists of four strokes, although it can give the impression of having five (the eighth-note bass slap that precedes the roll is easily misheard as part of the roll). Leading into the downbeat at the beginning of the four-beat cycle, the tambora roll gives dancers a lift before the downbeat grounds them at the beginning of the cycle. This downbeat is strong, since it is it is often played by the güira and bass (or marimba) as well as the tambora. The saxophone (or the accordion, or both), however, often omits it, coming in on the following sixteenth note instead. Typical saxophone jaleos, such as the one shown here, tend to echo the tambora roll with a similar sixteenth-note rhythm beginning immediately after the downbeat. The dancers thus receive a lift from the saxophones after being grounded by the downbeat in the güira, bass, and tambora. While saxophone jaleos usually omit the first downbeat, they generally articulate the third beat of the cycle, which, conversely, is not prominent in the tambora. These call-and-response rhythms in the tambora, güira, saxophone, and dance lend merengue its characteristic drive.

Steeped in merengue típico cibaeño and well versed in jazz, Tavito Vásquez, merengue saxophone pioneer Avelino Vásquez's nephew, became Orquesta San José's lead alto saxophonist and occasionally led his own dance band and típico group, Conjunto Alma Criolla (Creole Soul Band). One of the best musicians in the Republic, Vásquez was in a unique position to take the fusion of Dominican and North American musics to new heights of creativity. His revolutionary application of bebop improvisation to merengue renders him an important innovator of Dominican music, and his emotive tone, sophisticated harmonic sense, and uncanny melodic conception make him a jazz master by any standards.[7] Arranger Bienvenido Bustamante also played an important role in diffusing knowledge about, and enthusiasm for, jazz among Dominican musicians in the 1950s. Alto saxophonist Choco de León recorded small-group interpretations of the traditional merengue cibaeño repertoire whose extended jazz-influenced solos continue to serve as models of Dominican jazz today.

Although shared African-derived characteristics such as a metronomic pulse and interlocking rhythms made jazz and merengue a likely musical partnership, jazz's social meanings in the Dominican Republic differed from its meanings in the United States. In North America, where it was created by an oppressed minority group, jazz represented an alternative to dominant Euro-American culture. In the Dominican Republic, however, jazz became associated with elite, cosmopolitan culture and was often associated with the hegemonic and imperialist United States. While Dominican musicians looked to jazz for its creative musical options, their audiences were often attracted to it as a marker of social status.

Dance-band merengue showed a remarkable capacity to incorporate elements of other musics. For example, when Mexican *rancheras* and Brazilian *sambas* became popular, Dominican bands recorded merengue versions of the foreign hits.[8] Joseíto Mateo told me that this strategy, designed to help merengue compete with foreign musics, proved an aesthetically successful move as well: "Mexican music was very popular here [in the Republic]; Dominicans were crazy about Mexican music. Merengue wasn't selling. So I took rancheras [a type of Mexican song], and recorded them with merengue rhythm. . . . And so, that was my best LP." New hybrid genres included Luis Senior's *bolemengue*, a fusion of the Cuban *bolero* and merengue, in which the güira and tambora play slowly. Capitalizing on the importance of the saxophone in the Cuban *mambo* as well as in merengue, Pedro Pérez invented the *jalemengue*, which consisted of a mambo-inspired saxophone introduction followed by a jaleo (Incháustegui interview). A merengue arrangement of "Skokiaan," an internationally popular South African song, made a big hit in the late 1950s.[9] Recorded by Antonio Morel y su Orquesta and arranged by Félix del Rosario, the Dominican "Skokiaan" fused elements of South African *tsaba*, big-band jazz, and merengue cibaeño. While the Dominican, North American, and South African elements each retain their own aesthetic integrity, the arrangement's three black Atlantic sources share so many stylistic characteristics that they coalesce to a remarkable extent. That the original "Skokiaan" was a tsaba, a "syncretic style of [South] African urban music blending African melody and rhythm, American swing, and Latin American" music (Coplan 1985: 270), further underlines the breadth of pan-African musical cross-fertilization that was taking place.

Native forms other than merengue, especially the *salve*, became fodder for dance-band arrangements. Rural salve melodies are often in the minor mode, and their rhythmic accompaniment varies greatly from region to region. Big-band salve arrangements combined merengue cibaeño percussion rhythms with salve melodies and newly composed texts to produce a merengue/salve fusion marked by minor-mode melodies and melancholy tone. Bands also sometimes played arrangements of the mangulina.[10]

Trujillo's regime encouraged a cult of *personalismo*, and adulation of the tyrant approached deification. Parks and streets were named after the dictator and his family; the highest mountain in the country was renamed Pico Trujillo (Mount Trujillo); in 1936, the capital city of the Dominican Republic was renamed Ciudad Trujillo; and merengue composers were expected to write songs praising the dictator, often for cash incentives. In other cases they wrote Trujilloist merengues because they realized that it was expected of them, or because they had been subjected to "encouragement," government-backed threats of violence. As Jesús de Galíndez noted in the mid-1950s, examples of "sycophancy" were everywhere. "It is sufficient to walk through the streets of Ciudad Trujillo or of the smallest village, or to listen to the lyrics of many songs. Trujillo—Trujillo—Trujillo!" (n.d.: 201).

A four-volume collection published in 1960, *Antología musical de la era de Trujillo,* includes three hundred merengues and eighty-eight other songs dedicated to the dictator; highly regarded and talented composers contributed articles on merengue and Trujillo's role in promoting Dominican culture and nationalism (Rivera González 1960). Sample titles of merengues in the *Antología* illustrate the extent to which the dictator was exalted: "Fé en Trujillo" (Faith in Trujillo) and "Trujillo es grande e inmortal" (Trujillo is great and immortal). Other song names championed Trujillo's policies and political cohorts: "La alfabetación" (Literacy), "Trujillo el gran arquitecto" (Trujillo, the great architect), "Trujillo y Balaguer" (Trujillo and Balaguer) (Rivera González 1960: 214–15).

"San Cristóbal," a merengue named after Trujillo's hometown, enjoyed great popularity, largely because of its spicy saxophone jaleo (Pérez interview); it was included in the repertoires of every dance band (Incháustegui interview).[11] Its text gives equal play to adulation for the dictator and to his well-known relationships with many women:[12]

SAN CRISTÓBAL

¡Salve San Cristóbal,	Hail San Cristóbal,
Cuna de Trujillo!	The birthplace of Trujillo!
Ese gran caudilo,	This great caudillo,
Jefe de nación.	The leader of the nation.
Sus mujeres son	His women are
Las más lindas flores;	The prettiest flowers;
Ellas son primores	They are beauties
De gracia y encanto.	Of grace and charm.

Because much of the dance-band repertoire consisted of traditional merengue cibaeño, lyrics often referred to rural life in the Cibao. When performed at elite balls in the capital city, however, the lyrics connoted not the immediate environment but an idealized rural culture that symbolized nationhood.

Newly composed merengues could treat subjects not local to the Cibao. While "El Negrito del Batey," for example, remains true to Cibao musical style, it speaks of *bateyes*, sugar-cane workers' towns located mainly in the East and South of the country. Similarly, the merengue hit "Caña brava" celebrates sugar-cane cultivation, practiced mainly in the East and South. Such a marriage of Cibao music to texts that referred to the country's major industry, sugar cultivation of the East and South, embodied Trujillo's strategy of centralization and the integration of his propaganda, cultural, and economic programs.

Trujillo's cultural policy proved a double-edged sword: While it put creativity under strict control, it also created musical opportunities. The dictator supported municipal bands, which provided townspeople with free entertainment, and he also founded music schools. Moreover, Dominicans responded to the musical quality of Trujilloist music. Citizens of the era could acknowledge the music's role as propaganda while at the same time finding it aesthetically appealing: "In any party you might have, you'd almost always have to have a [pro-Trujillo] record, even if you didn't play it. Or even if you played it only once. Because if you didn't play it, it was as if you didn't identify [with the regime]. Now if a number was good . . . it was played because people liked it" (Francisco Amaro, quoted and translated in Pacini Hernandez 1989: 100). Even the dictator's most ardent critics would probably not contradict arranger Luis Pérez's opinion that the Trujilloist merengue "San Cristóbal" was "popular, maybe because of the way that it used the saxophones" (interview). But the importance that Dominicans gave Trujilloist merengue's aesthetics relative to its politics remains a complex question. A person I spoke with who had expressed deference to Trujillo offered a synthesis of the aesthetic and political reactions to the music: "People do not hear the merengue 'San Cristóbal' as a Trujilloist merengue. Rather, they think of its beauty."

Regional Musics and Racial Politics

While dance-band merengue spread throughout the country, regional musics remained popular in rural areas, where most Dominicans still lived; of the 1935 population, estimated at 1.5 million, 82 percent was rural (Duarte 1980: 191). Art that addressed the needs of this large constituency adhered to regionally based aesthetics.

Merengue became more popular than ever in the Cibao, where it was performed in contexts similar to those described in Chapter Three. Merengue típico cibaeño's status as a national symbol gave it primacy over other regional musics; several Cibao accordionists moved to the capital and became well-known figures whose music was disseminated nationally and internationally through the mass media. The best-known merengue cibaeño group of the Trujillo era, El Trio Reynoso, consisted of Pedro Reynoso on accordion and vocals, Domingo Reynoso on güira and vocals, and Francisco "Pancholo" Esquea on tambora. To evoke rural culture, Pedro Reynoso always performed barefoot (Incháustegui interview). The group's omission of the saxophone was also likely intended to project a rustic image, since high-profile groups in Santiago had long used this instrument (Roman interview). El Trio Reynoso added a bass instrument, the marimba, to the traditional instrumentation of accordion, tambora, and güira.[13] This innovation was employed by other merengue cibaeño groups, the most important of which were led by accordionists Luis Kalaff, Dionisio "Guandulito" Mejía, Isidro Flores, and Tatico Henríquez.[14]

In the 1930s, accordion-based merengue came to be called *perico ripiao* (literally, ripped parrot), a label that lends itself to rich etymological speculation. One man I spoke with who remembers the thirties era explained that this appellation came from a brothel in Santiago:

> Perico ripiao came into being around 1935 or '36, when merengue, merengue típico, entered the society. In a patio in front of the meat house here [in Santiago], on Independence Street, a "salon" called "El Perico Ripiao" was opened, . . . [and] all the women who went there were "free women" [that is, prostitutes]. You see, it has a double meaning; *perico ripiao* refers to [the male genitals]. It became very famous; people came from the capital, and people came from other towns. . . . They thought that the group that played there was called Perico Ripiao, but actually, Perico Ripiao was the salon itself. That's how the ensemble came to be called Perico Ripiao.

While the term *perico ripiao* may indeed derive from the name of the Santiago brothel, most Dominicans are not aware of this etymology, although Joseíto Mateo suggested to me that upper-class men learned to enjoy dancing the merengue cibaeño in houses of prostitution: "Upper-class men went to poor neighborhoods, which is where the prostitutes were. And they spent time there, and danced merengue. So they learned that it [merengue] was good."

On an entirely different note, saxophonist Andrés de Jesus detailed the following folk etymology: "To me, the term *perico ripiao* is slang for a simple type of music, like accordion music, since [early] accordions . . . played in only one key all the time. So, being a simple type of music, you see, I feel that it is fitting to call it 'ripped parrot.' A parrot is a small animal; if you tried to eat one, you'd hardly find any meat at all" (interview). Indeed, the term seems more aptly to connote the humble nature of accordion-based merengue than to hint at sexuality.

However labeled, merengue cibaeño, like "Hispanicism, whiteness, and Catholicism" was an ingredient in Trujillo's version of the national essence"; "merengue played an important role in the dictator's cult of nationalism and the exaltation of Hispanic values" (Jorge 1982a: 84, 93–94). Unlike the national music, much rural music was associated with African-influenced religious practices rejected by official dogma and by Trujilloist folklorist Flérida de Nolasco, who wrote that "Dominican folk music cannot be but a derivation of Spanish music, adjusted to the environment, corrupted when it has fallen into inexpert hands, and sometimes contaminated with black music, of savage stupidity" (in Davis 1976: 22).

Among the plethora of rural Dominican musics with close links to Africa are the local variants of merengue from regions other than the Cibao.[15] Joseíto Mateo, who grew up in the South, talked to me about the southern variant, merengue palo echao (or pri-prí), as it compares to merengue cibaeño: "There is merengue cibaeño, which is the merengue of the North. The merengue of this area [the South], of the capital and nearby towns such as San Cristóbal, . . . a different kind of merengue was danced: . . . merengue palo echao." Mateo made a racial distinction between the two variants. "You know that here [in the South] people practice a lot of this . . . African culture. . . . [But] merengue cibaeño is from the northern part of the country, where there are more white people." Trujillo's attraction to merengue cibaeño in spite of its African-derived elements was likely influenced by the Cibao's whiter ethnic make-up and link with the oligarchy, which had long placed it at the top of the Dominican regional hierarchy.

Trujilloism thus fostered the traditional Hispanophilic and anti-Haitian sense of Dominican national identity, excluding the explicitly African-influenced culture that typified the lives of the masses (and often of the elite) from state-sanctioned "national" culture. The extremity of Trujillo's anti-Haitianism and its association with his sense of Dominican identity is epitomized by the 1937 massacre of Haitians residing in the Dominican Republic, which his regime officially termed the "Dominicanization of the border." Haiti had twice the population of the Dominican Republic on half the amount of land, largely deforested. Because the Dominican-Haitian border was unregulated and poorly defined, many Haitians lived on Dominican territory. On 2–4 October 1937, Dominican soldiers decapitated, drowned, and used other means to kill Haitian men, women, and children residing in the Dominican Republic. Soldiers used a language test—pronunciation of the Spanish word *perejil* (parsley)—to distinguish black Dominicans from Haitians, since Haitians generally mispronounced the Spanish *r* as *l*. As a result, many dark-skinned Dominicans with speech impediments were killed.[16]

Not even Haitian house servants, who were often regarded as members of Dominican families, were spared. The only exceptions were Haitians working on U.S.-owned sugar plantations (Crassweiler 1966: 150–155), whose protection reflected the flip side of Trujillo's anti-Haitian racism: pro-U.S. blancophilia. Estimates of the number of victims range from 12,000 to 40,000; Trujillo's own unofficial estimate was 18,000 (Moya Pons 1986: 139).

To forestall the adverse public reaction Trujillo feared, especially in the United States, he convinced (perhaps bribed) Haitian president Sténio Vincent to send a formal letter to the Dominican government expressing the Haitian president's doubts that Trujillo had been associated with the massacre. Both leaders later signed a diplomatic communiqué stating that friendly relations between the countries had "not been impaired" by border incidents "in which several civilians were reported injured" (Crassweiler 1966: 156).

Trujillo considered the "Dominicanization of the border" a significant event in the development of Dominican national identity; he referred to it obliquely in a 1955 speech: "I received in 1930 . . . a people with a weak sense of identity, with their territory still undefined, and today I offer to my fellow-citizens a country the demarcation of whose frontiers has been completed" (quoted and translated in Crassweiler 1966: 295). His anti-Haitianism built upon well-established Dominican attitudes. Dominican primary schools had long taught that the bloodshed wrought by Haitian leader Jean Jacques Dessalines during his 1805 retreat from Santo Domingo was significant in the development of the Dominican nation; Dominican historiography of the Haitian occupations thus nurtured the anti-Haitian sense of Dominican identity.[17] According to Frank Moya Pons, Trujillo committed the 1937 holocaust in order to become an "anti-Dessalines" (1986: 140).

This dictator who persecuted Haitians was himself of partial Haitian descent, one among several contradictions in Trujillo's attitudes about Hatian and African influences in the Republic. For example, while the Dominican constitution's guarantee of "freedom of conscience and of worship" was respected in the case of the small Protestant and Jewish populations, "a law of September, 1943, established punishment for those practicing *voudou* or *lua*" (Galíndez n.d.: 124)—yet Trujillo himself was known to be involved with African-influenced magico-religious practices. Giving credence to "the beliefs of old Africa," Trujillo "frequently consulted those whom he believed to hold the power of divination. He used spells on occasion. Was there any danger hanging over the regime? Was this or that development in the country proceeding well? It is difficult to know these things thoroughly, and it would be wise to consult the spirits. A medicine man would be summoned and would report his findings" (Crassweiler 1966: 84, 85).[18]

Trujillo's mixed feelings about race and national identity hardly set him apart; he has been described as an archetypal blancophilic mixed-race Dominican (Perez-Cabral 1967: 185). In sum, while Trujillo massacred Haitians and propagated an anti-Haitian Dominican identity, he was of partial Haitian descent himself; while he proscribed blatantly African-influenced magico-religious customs, he practiced them himself; and while he chose a national music associated with what is arguably the country's most European region, merengue cibaeño itself has many African-derived characteristics. The music was an effective national symbol because it successfully articulated the contradictions of Dominican culture as well as of Trujillo's personality.

The pambiche "Pacone", performed by El Trio Reynoso on a 1952 radio broadcast, expresses both the denial and the ubiquity of African- and Haitian-influenced religion in the Dominican Republic. The song inquires into the whereabouts of spirits named Candelino, Buquí, and Belié Belkan. At first, the answer is *"pacone"*—"I don't know," in Haitian Creole. But the spirits soon indicate their arrival by saying *"bonswa"* (*bonsoir*, good evening):

PACONE
(I don't know)

Payu payu pacone	*Payu payu pacone*
Payu payu pacone,	*Payu payu pacone,*
Yo que te quiero de verdad,	I truly love you,
Yo que te quiero a tí, y na' ma'.	I love you, and that is all.
¿Donde está Candelino?	Where is Candelino?
Pacone, mamá.	I don't know, *mamá.*
¿Donde está Buquí el gamberro?	Where is that hooligan, Buquí?
Pacone, mamá.	I don't know, *mamá.*
¿Donde está que no lo veo?	Where is he? I can't see him.
Pacone, mamá.	I don't know, *mamá.*
¿Donde está Belié Belkan?	Where is Belié Belkan?
Pacone, mamá.	I don't know, *mamá.*
¡Bonswa, bonswa!	Good evening, good evening!

Dominican historian and singer Arístides Incháustegui, who lived through the Trujillo era, told me that this song refers to the fact that African-influenced magic and religion pervaded Dominican life in spite of the denial of their existence.[19] That the song was openly performed on radio demonstrates a laxness, or perhaps a selective enforcement, of Trujillo's ban on these practices.

Social Class and National Unity

Trujillo's use of merengue as propaganda was related to his populism, and his personal vendetta against high society likely influenced his decision to introduce merengue cibaeño to the salons (Incháustegui and Hernández interviews; Miniño 1983: 17). A native of the South rather than of the Cibao, Trujillo probably had no contact with merengue cibaeño as a child. Coming from a relatively humble background, however, he was surely exposed to southern dances such as mangulina, palos, and merengue palo echao in his early years. Trujillo likely became acquainted with merengue cibaeño when he served as military administrator of the Cibao during the U.S. occupation; Incháustegui told me that "Trujillo was in the military, and military men danced a lot of merengue in the countryside and in the towns." The dictator was not from the lowest Dominican class, but a chasm separated the social position of families such as Trujillo's and that of the leading families of the capital or the Cibao. Before his rise to power, Trujillo had made several unsuccessful attempts to join elite social clubs. It might not have been out of the question for a lower-middle-class man of partial Haitian descent to enter high society, but Trujillo's involvement in criminal affairs and his pursuit of women precluded such an exception. The fact that Trujillo was an army man also worked against him, since military officers were generally neither highly educated nor loved by the elite. Trujillo's rejection by high society was so complete that he had difficulty recruiting members of the oligarchy for important posts in the government (Crassweiler 1966: 82–83, 91–92; Incháustegui interview). Many high-born Dominicans

disliked him personally in varying degrees of intensity. . . . This is a painful conclusion for any man to accept, but in Trujillo's case it was made even more hurtful by reason of inordinate ambition, sensitive

pride, and awareness of his own abilities and resourses of will. The result was a grudge against the world. . . . Pulling down the high-born
and highly-regarded, and putting them at his feet; dominating every
facet of a hostile society . . . —these had become the purposes of his
existence (Crassweiler 1966: 83).

According to Crassweiler, Trujillo's sense of rejection was "one of the most
formative of all the influences playing upon him" (47).

His talent as a merengue dancer perhaps brought some small solace,
Arístides Incháustegui believes: "Trujillo had a problem with high society.
Since society originally did not accept merengue, he imposed it in these
places [the salons] in order to harass the upper class. And he danced better
than any of them, since he knew how to dance this. So people talked a lot
about how well Trujillo danced" (interview). Yet the upper class so disliked
Trujillo personally that his preference for merengue only exacerbated their
negative feelings about the music. As Luis Alberti writes, "merengue was his
favorite dance, and he always requested it. Since high society had rejected
merengue, this gave them even more reason, political reason, to resist it. As
soon as Trujillo turned his back, they forgot about merengue" (1975: 75).

In spite of the antipathy felt toward him by members of every social class,
Trujillo received genuine support from many constituencies, in part for the
advantages they received, in part for his dramatic flair. Beneficiaries of the
regime such as government officials, members of Trujillo's family, his business associates, and the Catholic Church supported the dictatorship. While
many oligarchs looked down on Trujillo, they benefited from the political
and economic stability that he provided. Many members of the less privileged
classes were attracted to the dictator's highly publicized material advances,
his social programs, and, as Crassweiler puts it, "the color and drama and
spectacle of Trujillo and the regime, or by a sense of nationalism stimulated
or satisfied" (1966: 358), for the dictator had "a sure grasp of those sensitive
areas of the national psychology" (78) and knew how to communicate with
the Dominican people. He wore full-dress military uniforms, often complete
with ornate ostrich-plumed bicorn hats, at formal occasions. An accordion-
based merengue group, a dance band, and a symphony orchestra sometimes
played simultaneously at outdoor concerts and political rallies. While the
Dominican art-music singer Incháustegui describes the result as "cacopho-

nic," such pomp was impressive not only to campesinos and barrio dwellers, but also to many middle-class Dominicans.

While it did not ingratiate him with the upper class, Trujillo's use of merengue bolstered his image among the masses. Although the regime maintained power by instilling fear and inflicting violence, the country's poor likely responded favorably to the dictator's dancing, and his compelling the elites to dance, to native, rural music. Identifying an enjoyable pastime such as merengue dancing with the state was an inexpensive and efficient means of propaganda. Dominican citizens, always in danger of being denounced by the authorities, could express support for the dictatorship by listening and dancing to merengue, safeguarding what few freedoms they had. What is more, they could give the impression of supporting the regime even when they did not, since dancing had always been popular among Dominicans.

With the growth of salon merengue, the music split into accordion-based groups for the poor and dance bands for the privileged. The merengue styles of Trujillo's era thus reflected the country's social structure, as they had in the past. As a result of merengue's status as a national symbol and its access to the mass media, however, the entire populace heard both types of merengue at outdoor public concerts and on radio and television. Through the use of merengue as propaganda, Trujillo thus succeeded in forging contact, and perhaps an illusion of fellowship, across class lines. Proclaiming that the national music is performed at both high-society balls and rural fiestas, the merengue "A bailar" celebrates the social unity that Quisqueyan, or national, merengue purportedly embodied:[20]

A BAILAR
(To dance)

Primera Parte (Merengue)	Part One (Merengue)
Vengan todos a bailar	Come, everyone, to dance
Este ritmo sabrosón.	To this tasty rhythm.
El merengue quisqueyano	Quisqueyan merengue
Es una revelación.	Is a revelation.
Lo baila en la enramá,	It is danced in the enramá[21]
Lo mismo que en un salon.	Just as it is danced in the salon.
El merengue es el mejor	Merengue is the best
Que se baila en sociedad.	That is danced in society.

Segunda Parte (Jaleo)	Part Two (Jaleo)
Vengan a bailar este merenguón (repite)	Come and dance this great merengue [repeat].
Es todo el sabor del cañaveral (repite)	It has all of the flavor of the sugar cane fields [repeat].
Ritmo del batey, y de la, enramá	Rhythm of sugar-cane towns and of the enramá;
Vengan a bailar, pa'lante y pa'tra'.	Come and dance, forward and back.

Petán the Merenguero and the Trujilloist Music Industry

A music lover, Trujillo's brother José "Petán" Arismendy shaped the development of the Dominican music industry while Trujillo was in power. Petán lived in the Cibao town of Bonao, which he treated as a personal fief. Unlike his brother, Petán was uninterested in political power and economic advancement, dedicating himself to more hedonistic pursuits. Miguelina Rodríguez Vidal, who lived in Bonao as a child and was a playmate of Petán's daughter, told me that Petán

> loved music, he liked art, he liked merengue. . . . He was something of a bohemian, the bohemian of the Trujillo family. . . . He was a nice, pleasant man; that is, the part that I knew as a little girl. . . . But others say he was a violent man who had many people killed. . . . Trujillo was interested in international connections for the benefit of his businesses or of his government, but not for their cultural benefit. Petán, on the other hand, was interested in this. He loved music, he loved merengue. . . . He had fiestas all the time.

She adds that the country club where most of the Bonao balls were held was located near Petán's home and that the dictator's brother walked there. Petán required that his guests arrive first at his home, wait for him outside, and then, to demonstrate respect, follow him on foot to the country club.

Rodríguez Vidal told me that at the club, the first dance of the night was reserved for Petán and his wife to dance alone: "No one was allowed to dance the first piece. That is, what happened was that everyone had to wait for Petán to get up to dance. He would get up and dance with his wife, and the band would follow behind him," playing on the dance floor nearby. Similarly, pianist Rafael Solano remembers that Rafael Trujillo often required band members to play in a circle around him on the dance floor, adding that the dictator "enjoyed these serenades, as much as I hated them" (1992: 91).

In 1942 Petán founded radio station La Voz del Yuna (The Voice of the Yuna), named after the Yuna River, which runs through Bonao. Although Trujillo's government sponsored its own official radio station, La Voz del Partido Dominicano (The Voice of the Dominican Party), La Voz del Yuna soon became the most important mass medium of Trujilloist propaganda. In 1945 the station moved to the capital and was renamed La Voz Dominicana (The Dominican Voice) (Crassweiler 1966: 212), and in 1952 it began to broadcast on television as well as on radio (Incháustegui interview).

La Voz Dominicana, Petán's pet project, served as an outlet for his love of music. He ran the station with an iron hand; employees had to adhere to his stringent standards of cleanliness and subservience on pain of dismissal, or even of death (Lora Medrano 1984: 125; Solano 1992: 42–45). Catering to Petán's taste for live music performance, La Voz Dominicana broadcast live, twelve hours a day (Pacini Hernandez 1995: 47). Under exclusive contract to the station, the best musicians in the country could perform and record only with Petán's permission, and Petán's preference for live music meant that they rarely recorded. By the middle 1950s, La Voz Dominicana employed over ten musical ensembles, consisting of overlapping personnel. These included several dance bands, merengue típico cibaeño groups, a symphony orchestra, and ensembles specializing in Argentinian music, mariachi music, the danzón, and calypso (Incháustegui interview; Lora Medrano 1984: 52, 177, 180).[22]

By broadcasting both típico and big-band merengue, La Voz Dominicana did its part for national consolidation by easing communication across class lines and by popularizing Cibao merengue throughout the country. Accordionist Luis Kalaff told me that Petán "liked these [merengue típico cibaeño] groups a lot, and the radio stations . . . always presented them too. Because in the past, [this music] had only been in Santiago." Radio also linked the Republic with the outside world; Dominicans listened to stations from Cuba, Mexico, Puerto Rico, Colombia, Mexico, and the United States. Recorded music from abroad, especially from Mexico, also gained popularity.

The recording industry in the Republic got off to a creative start at the radio station La Voz del Partido in 1936, when Juan Sálazar Hernández constructed a rudimentary recording system from sundry materials including a steering wheel, sewing machine parts and watch parts. Used primarily to record advertisements, the device once recorded several merengues by an outfit called La Orquesta Benefactor, led by Agustín "Papatín" Ovalles (Incháustegui 1988a: 18). Several years later, conductor Leopold Stokowski, then performing in Santo Domingo, took a liking to the local music and asked to meet its foremost interpreter; he was introduced to Luis Alberti. Stokowski asked the bandleader to make a recording on Stokowski's boat, which was equipped with a recording studio. Alberti's Orquesta Presidente Trujillo thus made its first recording, 30 December 1941, at sea—twenty selections, including at least five merengues. Records were pressed in New York City and released first on Columbia Records, later on RCA Victor, and finally on Alberti's own Alberti Records (Incháustegui interview, 1973c, 1988a: 18–19).

In 1947, Petán bought a Fairchild recording system, founding the Dominican Recording Company and Caracol Records (Incháustegui 1988a: 20). Rafael Trujillo promptly prohibited the importation of foreign records to shield his brother's new business from competition. Possibly because of Petán's penchant for live rather than recorded music, however, Caracol Records never got off the ground, releasing only two 78s (Incháustegui 1988a: 20).[23] In the early 1950s, Frank Hatton imported more modern Ampex recording equipment to record radio commercials and *novelas* (soap operas). While Hatton did not record music, he rented the equipment to others who did so. Luis Alberti and Antonio Morel made several merengue records, which were pressed in the United States and released on various labels (20–21).

Petán's involvement in the music business kept others from entering the field. According to Dominican music historian Miguel Holguin, in this area, the country's "development is atypical, it doesn't reflect what should have been or what was in other places. It was such an iron dictatorship, so ghastly, that if it occurred to me, for example, to make flutes, I'd think that maybe Petán might be thinking about something similar, or he might take an interest in it, and that would make me forget about the flutes. Just thinking that Petán might disapprove" (quoted and translated in Pacini Hernandez 1995: 50).

The Trujillo family's way of doing business ensured them monopolies not only in the music arena but in practically all of the country's major industries. For example, the dictator began his business career in the salt industry. The Dominican salt supply was centered in deposits in the South and dominated by the Michalena family until Trujillo's rise to power. In 1932, the government passed a law forbidding the use of these deposits, maintaining that they were in danger of being exhausted. Trujillo then organized his own company, which took over the salt business and incidentally established the basis of his fortune. He used similar means to gain footholds in the insurance, meat, milk, tobacco, sugar, and other industries (Galíndez n.d.: 187–93). Incredibly, Trujillo and his family employed almost half of the country's labor force directly and another 35 percent through the government by the 1950s (Black 1986: 27). He and his relatives eventually owned as much as 75 percent of the country's economic assets (Kryzanek and Wiarda 1988: 14); by some estimates, Trujillo was one of the two or three richest men in the world when he died (Black 1986: 27).

Although the dictator's fiscal policies were unscrupulous and selfish, the Dominican economy as a whole improved during the regime. Trujillo regained control of the customs receivership from the United States, consolidated internal and external debts, and created a new national currency at par value with the U.S. dollar (Galíndez 1965: 238–40). But while he and his family amassed a fortune, their business decisions often sprang from caprice as much as from profit considerations (Crassweiler 1966: 258).

Because radio and recording were hobbies as much as businesses for Petán, this subjective motivation held particularly true for the music industry, which was managed according to "the owner's whims" (*las chifladuras del dueño*) rather than the profit motive (Pacini Hernandez 1995: 47).

Merengue outside the Dominican Republic

Trujillo's isolationism, combined with a lack of recording opportunities in the Republic, caused Dominican merengue to develop differently abroad than it did at home. This isolationism also led the government to regulate all Dominican contacts with the outside world; rarely were citizens granted permission to travel abroad. Fearing that they would not return, Trujillo rarely allowed Dominican musicians to perform outside of the country, but several performers emigrated anyway. The first of these was bandleader Billo Frómeta, who left for Venezuela in 1936 with his Ciudad Trujillo band (Alberti 1975: 75). Renamed Billo's Caracas Boys, the group was extremely successful and included merengue as a significant part of its repertoire. Singer Alberto Beltrán moved to New York City to work with the well-known group La Sonora Matancera. Although he was primarily a bolero singer rather than a merengue specialist, Beltrán popularized merengues such as "El Negrito del Batey" and "Compadre Pedro Juan" among New York Latinos. Luis Kalaff told me he emigrated first to Puerto Rico and then to New York City, performing accordion-based merengue initially at hotel shows and later at nightclubs for dancing. Also in New York, Negrito Chapuseaux and Rafael Damirón formed a group that played an "Americanized" merengue that featured piano and maracas (Roberts 1979: 145). Meanwhile, Josecito Román and Napoleón Zayas put together authentic merengue big bands in the city. The Dominican musical transplant became popular among New York Hispanics and by the late 1950s had found a permanent niche in the city's Latin music scene.

As part of that scene piano accordionist Angel Viloria established the most successful merengue group outside the Dominican Republic, featuring Ramón E. García on tenor saxophone, Luis Quintero on tambora, and Dioris Valladares on vocals. In spite of its name, Conjunto Típico Cibaeño, the group did not perform típico music. While its instrumentation resembled that of típico merengue, the Conjunto modeled its music on Luis Alberti's cosmopolitan sound. The juxtaposition of small-group instrumentation and a refined sound set Viloria's group apart from most bands in the Dominican Republic, which modeled themselves after either típico tradition or Luis Alberti, but not both.[24]

The small U.S. Dominican community meant that Viloria's audiences were predominantly Puerto Rican; as singer Joseíto Mateo said to me, "It was the Puerto Ricans who originally brought merengue to popularity in New York, who gave their hand to merengue." Mateo recalls that Puerto Rican men often went to dances to meet women, and that dancing merengue helped them out. He remembers that while Dominicans liked to show off with fancy footwork, Puerto Ricans preferred to dance close to their partners:

"For Dominicans . . . merengue is danced with figures; it is for dancing with turns. But Puerto Ricans like slow merengue, so that they can dance very close together." Viloria's merengue hit "La ligadura" (The connection) refers simultaneously to the legato (connected) style of saxophone jaleos and to the physical connection that partners make while dancing merengue (Incháustegui interview).

While the paucity of recording opportunities for merengueros in the Republic limited their international exposure, Viloria's recordings were widely disseminated, and his transplanted music became the best-known manifestation of merengue outside the Dominican Republic. Viloria was a favorite in Cuba, where merengue came to be associated with carnival and Eduardo Davidson created the *pachanga*, a new form that featured a conga-drum rhythm similar to the merengue tambora pattern and dance steps reminiscent of the Cuban *guaracha*.[25] In Haiti, radio broadcasts and touring Dominican bands generated a taste for merengue. Viloria was especially fashionable there in the mid-1950s, as a local recording engineer recalled: "That thing hit like a bomb. The Haitians loved the *merengue* because it had a lively beat for dancing. They were doing it in every nightclub, especially down by Carrefour. The Dominican girls were there and would teach the guys how to dance" (Averill 1989a: 104). Merengue grew so popular in Haiti that it spawned a new Haitian music, konpa (Averill 1989a: 104–5). Moreover, Trujillo's use of merengue as propaganda may have inspired Haitian dictator Duvalier's similar use of konpa. While merengue's international popularity grew, Trujillo's isolationism maintained a split between Dominican music at home and abroad: While Angel Viloria was the top merenguero on the global stage, he was not extraordinarily popular in his native land.

Yet for his own purposes, Trujillo did not hesitate to take advantage of the fame that Dominican music had gained abroad. In 1955, when he decided to organize the Feria de la Paz y la Confraternidad del Mundo Libre (Fair of Peace and Brotherhood in the Free World), remembering his 1939 trip to the impressive New York City World's Fair, he set out to create a positive image for his regime in the eyes of the international community.[26] Among other strategies, he contracted Xavier Cugat's slick New York City Latin band to record an LP of merengues arranged for cosmopolitan tastes. The spoken introduction to the song "¡Ay, que merengue!" from this album exhorts:

¡De todos los continentes, a la Feria en	"From all of the continents, let's go
Santo Domingo!"	to the fair in Santo Domingo!"
"¡Bravo!"	"Bravo!"
"¡Allá los esperamos a todos!"	"We are waiting for you there!"

Trujilloist folklorist Nolasco considered merengue's international diffusion as important as its status as a national symbol within the Dominican Republic: "The example of dynamic nationalism provided by Generalisimo Trujillo and the healthy drive that he has patriotically and arduously devoted to all that is authentically ours have resulted in the appreciation of merengue as our native dance par excellence. Bursting geographical confines, merengue's animation and captivating rhythm are becoming known and have been cordially praised abroad" (1956: 340). Despite Trujillo's isolationist policies, then, merengue's international recognition as a typically Dominican music buttressed its role as a national symbol at home.

Totalitarianism and Popular Culture

As Trujillo's economic policies began to fail in the late 1950s, internal opposition to his regime mounted. Hostility to the regime outside the Republic also grew because of its well-publicized human rights abuses. On 30 May 1961, Trujillo was assassinated while being driven to his estate in San Cristóbal. The assassins, backed by Dominican business and military leaders and with arms provided by the CIA, had planned an immediate transition to a non-Trujilloist military government, but this plan failed. Trujillo's personal secretary, Joaquín Balaguer, who was serving as titular head of state at the time, retained this post and had more than two dozen conspirators arrested and executed. But Balaguer was unable to maintain authority in the face of widespread discontent. All of Trujillo's close family members left the country by November 1961, taking with them a large part of the country's movable wealth; the Trujillo era was over.

Trujillo scholars have debated whether the regime should be considered totalitarian. In many ways, Trujillo was a caudillo like those before him in the Dominican Republic. Some make a distinction between Latin American dictators such as Trujillo, who have no "ideological philosophy," and European twentieth-century totalitarian leaders (Galíndez n.d.: 4). Along these lines, Crassweiler notes a likeness between Trujillo and the despots of the ancient world (1966: 298). However, while Trujillo's rule lacked the immersion in ideology that colored Hitler's and Stalin's regimes, the dictator developed an ideology based on Mediterranean-style fascism overlayed with a facade of U.S.-style democracy. As under European totalitarians, freedom of speech and thought were curtailed, and citizens lived under the constant threat of being denounced to authorities by acquaintances, friends, or family members. Totalitarianism depends on modern transportation systems and the mass media, as Wiarda further suggests; while pre-twentieth-century despots exercised absolute control of politics and the military, control of thought processes and expressive culture depends on modern technology (1968: 16–18, 180–81). Indeed, what most distinguishes Trujillo from past rulers of the Republic such as Santana, Baez, and Heureux is his access to better communication systems. This enabled him to dominate the country more completely, effecting a regime with totalitarian elements.

A nice example of the benefits wrought for totalitarian regimes by the development of mass media lies in the contrast between the ways Trujillo and earlier caudillos appropriated merengue for their own uses. Where past leaders had benefited from the personal praise afforded them by the music, Trujillo systematically used the mass media to make merengue a tool of nationalistic propaganda. As Averill suggests, merengue became the "leitmotif" of Caribbean dictatorship (1989a: 134).[27]

Ñico Lora.
PHOTO COURTESY OF JOSÉ DEL CASTILLO AND MANUEL GARCÍA ARÉVALO, FROM *ANTOLOGÍA DEL MERENGUE*

Tambora player with accordionist and saxophonist.
PHOTO BY PAUL AUSTERLITZ

The güira.
PHOTO BY VICTOR CAMILO

*J*uan Francisco García.

*J*ulio Alberto Hernández.

*L*uis Alberti.

Merengue/jazz master saxophonist
Tavito Vásquez.
PHOTO BY VICTOR CAMILO

Merengues dedicated to and featuring a
photo of the dictator Trujillo.
FROM A REMO RECORDS ALBUM COVER. PHOTO BY
ROBERT C. LANCEFIELD

PART II

The Contemporary Era, 1961-1995

Chapter 5

Merengue in the Transnational Community

The assassination of Trujillo and the flight of his family and close associates in 1961 set off a year of celebration. The capital of the Republic, Ciudad Trujillo, reverted to its former name of Santo Domingo, and people danced in the streets to merengues denouncing the fallen dictator. Antonio Morel, who had recently been performing Trujilloist music, popularized an adaptation of a rural merengue, "Mataron al chivo" (They killed the goat):

Mataron el chivo	They killed the goat
en la carretera	On the highway.
déjenmelo ver,	Let me him,
déjenmelo ver.	Let me see him!
Mataron el chivo	They killed the goat
y no me lo dejaron ver.	But they didn't let me see him.
(del Castillo and García Arévalo 1989: 53)	

Far from dying with the dictator, Trujillo's favorite music instead lived on to deride him. Pro-Trujillo merengues were even prohibited in 1962 (Pacini Hernandez 1989: 146).[1]

[handwritten margin note: Clearly, it was seen as a popular mode of expression in an alternative language]

Euphoria, Intervention, Resistance, and Commodification

The dictator's death triggered radical changes in every facet of Dominican life, from politics to popular culture. Unable to maintain control, Trujilloist head of state Joaquín Balaguer was forced into exile in 1962. Elections held that year gave Juan Bosch's social democratic PRD (Partido Revolucionario Dominicano, or Dominican Revolutionary Party) a landslide victory. Sworn in on 27 February 1963, Bosch pledged a program of civil liberties and land reform. Soon after taking office, Bosch traveled to the United States, where he was received warmly by President John F. Kennedy. However, the Dominican oligarchy considered the new president a leftist, and a coup d'état was staged on 25 September. Bosch was sent to exile in Puerto Rico, and a triumvirate took control of the government.

Transformations in popular culture and intellectual life paralleled the rapidly shifting political scene, as the end of restrictions on foreign travel and trade opened the Republic to international connections. Starved for these contacts, Dominicans enthusiastically embraced artistic and intellectual ideas, practices, and personalities from outside the country.

After the 1959 Cuban revolution and the imposition of the U.S. trade embargo on Cuba, Latin Caribbean popular music became dominated by Cuban-based styles performed by Puerto Ricans on their island and in New York City. The Puerto Rican band Cortijo y su Combo played a key role in developing *salsa* (sauce), as this music was later dubbed, abandoning the big-band style of 1950s Latin Caribbean music in favor of a smaller *conjunto* (combo) format, which used only two to five wind instruments.[2] Cortijo's popularity inspired Dominican musicians to adapt the conjunto format to merengue. Primitivo Santos was reputedly the first merengue bandleader to do so, and most 1960s groups followed suit. As distinct from salsa conjuntos, merengue conjuntos added saxophones to trumpets and trombones; as substitutes for the accordion, saxophones were essential to the music. Merengue conjuntos (or orquestas, as they were later known) consisted of alto and tenor saxophones, trumpets, trombone, piano, electric bass, tambora, congas, and güira.[3]

The biggest hit of 1962 was a fast and unabashedly driving merengue, "La agarradera," composed by Luis Pérez and performed by his conjunto.[4] Pérez explained to me that his inspiration was the Trujilloist merengue "San

Cristóbal," which was marked by a spicy saxophone jaleo. Pérez wanted to compose a merengue with similar appeal, but without the Trujilloist text: "When Trujillo was killed, all of those [Trujilloist] merengues disappeared automatically, and I wanted to compose a merengue with a similar use of the saxophones. So "La agarradera" comes out, with a similar saxophone part, and it becomes a hit. I know that it was because of this." Omitting the introductory paseo and merengue sections, "La agarradera" was structured around a catchy and driving saxophone jaleo performed at breakneck speed. Pérez told me that the exuberant quality of the piece was intended to capture the rural accordion aesthetic. A poignant amalgam of new elements and characteristics rooted in rural and barrio aesthetics marked the arrangement: It combined a novel fast tempo and aggressive quality with traditional tambora rhythms and saxophone jaleos (similar to those in musical example 10) that evoked típico music. Pérez's youthful and dynamic lead singer, Johnny Ventura, helped ensure the merengue's success. Joseíto Mateo believes that Ventura's charisma and this euphoric new sound expressed the jubilant mood of a people celebrating the end of a tyrannical dictatorship: "When Trujillo was killed in '61, Johnny Ventura entered the scene. Johnny Ventura, who was younger than I, came out with a happier merengue . . . because people didn't have to fear the political situation anymore. . . . You see, when people are enslaved, music is held back, sad songs come out. But when Trujillo fell, we became a free people, and so Johnny Ventura came out" (interview).

Ventura himself agrees that this uninhibited sound expressed the political freedom of the times; he told me that song lyrics and dance also reflected a new openness: "When Trujillo died, a political euphoria swept the Dominican Republic. And as youths of twenty-one years, we naturally participated in this. I began to record my music which didn't have the restrictions [of Trujillo-era merengue] in the texts, performance style, or dance style. And this helped make me famous." Merengue texts were emancipated sexually as well as politically; the suggestive double meanings traditional in merengue cibaeño resurfaced. Although double-entendre songs had not entirely disappeared during the Trujillo era, they had often been suppressed to make the music suitable for the ballrooms of the elite. "La agarradera" (The handle) refers to the way men and women handle each other, pressing their bodies close together, while dancing merengue. Its fourth line tells of a woman who died of the "shot" (ejaculation) that her squeezing provoked!

LA AGARRADERA
(The handle)

Oye, este merengue es de la
    agarradera [repite].
Lo baila las niñas y también
    las viejas [repite].
	Listen, this merengue is about the
	    handle [repeat].
	Little girls dance it, and so do
	    older women [repeat].

La agarradera no la bailo yo [repite];
La bailó una vieja y del tiro se
    murió [repite].
	I don't dance the handle [repeat];
	An old lady danced it, and she died of the
	    shot [repeat].

Ya, mi compadre y la vecina de
    al lao [repite]
La agarradera segurito que han
    bailao [repite].
	Now, my buddy and his [female]
	    neighbor [repeat]
	Have certainly danced the
	    handle [repeat].

Oigan mujeres cuando vayan a
    fiestar [repite],
La agarradera es lo que deben
    bailar [repite].
	Listen, women, when you go to a
	    party [repeat],
	The handle is what you should
	    dance [repeat].

While the staid 1950s merengue had suited Trujillo's high-class salons, it was out of place in the barrios; Luis Pérez's innovations and Johnny Ventura's dynamism manifested the pulse of the Dominican masses. Moving from elite contexts to the street, mass-mediated merengue changed from a ballroom to a truly popular music; I thus call it *pop merengue.*

In the early 1960s, the United States represented freedom and modernity; after all, the United States was known as a democracy, and President Kennedy had supported Juan Bosch's innovative social and economic program. The fast tempos and spectacle of rock 'n' roll seemed to embody North American modernity and liberty, just as Trujillo-era merengue stood for suppression. According to Ventura, "Without a doubt, this music and performance style was more in tune with what North American society was becoming in those years, and what the societies of all the countries dependent on the United States were gradually becoming. . . . You can be sure that traditional merengue was completely identified with the tyranny and had been usurped by the enormous popularity that rock 'n' roll had awakened in Dominican youth" (1978: 24).

Because merengue could hardly compete with rock and salsa, when Ventura started his own band in 1964 he incorporated elements of the contending musics. The group's name, Johnny Ventura y su Combo-Show, reflected the international, modern flavor its music embodied. *Combo,* of course, alluded to Cortijo's eminently popular combo and the conjunto format that Ventura's band shared with salsa, while the Americanism *Show* referred to the choreographic display that Ventura's singers put on at performances. Merengue enthusiast Sixto Reynoso told me about this visual spectacle, an essential ingredient in Ventura's appeal: "When you went to the dances given by Félix [del Rosario] or Rafael Solano [other bandleaders], you went to dance and to hear the music. When you went to Johnny Ventura's dance, you went to see the *musicians* [actually, the singers] dancing. This was called the Combo-Show" (p.c.). Ventura's clothing and stage presence resembled Elvis Presley's; even the merenguero's wry smile was similar to that of the North American rocker. Ventura explains that he borrowed the idea for the Combo-Show from rock 'n' roll: "Although I was an adolescent at this time, and did my acrobatics to the beat of rock and [the] twist, I carried the spirit of, and a calling for, merengue within me. . . . It occurred to me to create a bit of a mixture of classic merengue and this rock and twist" (1978: 24–25). It proved a winning combination: Johnny Ventura y su Combo-Show became the top merengue band of the 1960s, and other merengue bands copied his innovative use of dance on the bandstand.

During the dictatorship, there had been only three major dance bands in the country. When the Trujillo family's retreat from the music industry allowed new talent to come to the fore, bands proliferated. Other than Johnny Ventura's group, the most important of the new conjuntos were led by Félix del Rosario and Rafael Solano. A saxophonist and arranger, del Rosario had long been interested in giving merengue a different sound; he had arranged the innovative jazz-influenced version of "Skokiaan" discussed in Chapter Four. When he organized Los Magos del Ritmo (The Rhythm Magicians) in 1964, del Rosario wanted a "new sound, a new timbre," he told me, so he omitted the alto saxophone, trumpets, and trombone from the group, using only tenor and baritone saxophones and a rhythm section. During this period, Latin band leaders in New York City were conducting similar experiments with instrumentation; for example, Joe Cuba replaced the entire horn section with vibraphones. While Ventura's band had mass appeal, members of the middle class loved del Rosario's group, which received critical acclaim. Pianist Rafael Solano, a veteran of La Voz Dominicana, entered the musical market with his own merengue band in 1970.[5] While Solano catered to popular taste by adopting a conjunto format, his sound retained the sophistication of 1950s merengue.

Merengue and the Aborted Revolution of 1965

While an optimistic mood reigned, the political situation remained unstable; the armed forces ousted the government on 24 April 1965. Pro-Bosch, pro-Constitution military men competed for power with a rightist wing of the military, while thousands of unarmed demonstrators took to the streets of Santo Domingo in support of the Constitutionalists. When that faction took over downtown Santo Domingo, anti-Bosch officers—the Loyalists—clashed with them, and civil war broke out. The pro-Bosch faction was on the verge of victory when President Lyndon Johnson of the United States ordered an invasion of the Dominican Republic; 23,000 U.S. troops entered the country from 28 to 30 April (Black 1986: 38). While ostensibly undertaken to protect the lives of U.S. citizens residing in the Dominican Republic, the intervention, most analysts agree, was motivated by Johnson's mistaken belief that the Contitutionalist faction was dominated by Communists. Fighting continued until combatants agreed to a cease-fire on 31 August. U.S. authorities set up a provisional government, and campaigning for presidential elections began. Bosch ran for president, but terrorist attacks frustrated his efforts. Trujilloist Joaquín Balaguer, back from exile, campaigned effectively and won the election of 1 July 1966. As Jan Knippers Black writes, it seems "remarkable that the election results were accepted as legitimate, since the election "took place while the country was under military occupation by U.S. Marines, an occupation that had come about precisely to prevent . . . the reinstatement of Bosch" (1986: 40–41).[6]

Johnny Ventura explains that merengue was enlisted in the Revolution of 1965, as Constitutionalists called the civil war: "We sang to the soldiers who were fighting, because a feeling of inertia and discouragement came about at a certain point among the Constitutionalist troops. Somehow or another, we had to encourage and support them, to promote patriotism. And they sustained themselves" (interview). It may seem paradoxical that Ventura, whose musical style was so influenced by North American rock, enlisted that music to oppose U.S. hegemony. But Ventura spells out the peculiar effectiveness of this contradiction: "If I had the power in those days, I might have done other things to save merengue from extinction, but I didn't have that power. Being the home-boy that I am, I had to limit myself, heeding the advice of a saying which I later learned: 'If you can't beat 'em, join 'em'" (1978: 24–25).

The United States that had represented freedom in 1964 violated Dominican sovereignty in the following year; an inconsistency that must have generated mixed feelings among many Dominicans. Incorporating musical materials from the neocolonial power in a time-tested national symbol was a culturally empowering move that helped offset Dominicans quashed hopes for political self-determination. A form of popular culture partaking of both dominance and subordination, Ventura's music served as a subtle form of resistance to U.S. hegemony that was analogous to the strategies of using merengue as "semiological guerrilla warfare" employed during the U.S. occupation of 1916–24 (Eco 1986).

Marketing Merengue

While Dominican bands were appropriating U.S. styles, the country's music industry began to adopt marketing strategies; Johnny Ventura's business manager, William Liriano, ran the Combo-Show (or Johnny Ventura y Asociados, as it was officially called) as a capitalist venture. He believed that "to sell popular culture, one should use the same marketing tools that one uses to sell fritters, canned juice, or automobiles" (Liriano 1986: 35), an approach that helped set Johnny Ventura apart from his peers. Dance bands had traditionally played for upper-middle-class or elite audiences, working steady jobs in one establishment and at private parties. Liriano wanted to capture a larger market: Dominican barrio dwellers and campesinos. Because most of Ventura's competition came from foreign music, mainly heard over the radio, Liriano stressed live performance, booking the group at dances all over the country. He also made innovative use of advertising and other methods of promotion, and geared the band's style and performance to the tastes and the customs of his target audience.

"Knowing the profile of the consumer whom you wish to capture as a segment of the market, you are in a position to design your product, but you design it so that it will respond to the desires or the needs, the requirements or the expectations, of this client," Liriano believed (1986: 35). And he designed his product to respond to the tastes of the Dominican masses. Liriano reached out to rural Dominicans by arranging the band's touring schedule to coincide with *fiestas patronales*, or local patron saints' festivals. He also studied regional dance customs; when he learned that people preferred to dance on Sundays in certain areas and on Saturdays in others, he adjusted the group's performance schedule accordingly (37). Others in the music business adopted Liriano's innovative practices.

Television had long been a medium of merengue diffusion, and the Dominican television industry grew fast in the newly liberated commercial environment.[7] Live midday variety shows featuring merengue performance, games, and other forms of entertainment became popular in the 1970s. Each show was generally assigned two or three merengue groups for each day of the week; viewers could thus tune in on specific days to catch favorite groups. These programs coincided with *la hora de comida*, the hour when most Dominicans eat the main meal of the day.[8] Johnny Ventura often performed on television and eventually hosted his own TV game show, backed up by the Combo-Show. Television personality Yaqui Nuñez del Risco suggests that TV only enhanced the visual appeal of merengue as performed by Johnny Ventura and other merengueros like him: "On television, the sound element alone is not sufficient. A visual image must also be present, and a band's impression of motion is appealing when there is a headlining group [of singer/dancers] who put on a show while merengue is being sung" (1986: 7). In the 1950s, bands performing at live dances or on the radio delivered aural excitement while seated. Television in the post-Trujillo era, however, demanded the visual spectacle of musicians on their feet and singers who danced.

The Merengue Boom

Under President Joaquín Balaguer, the Dominican Republic became a transnational community (Georges 1990; also see Grasmuck and Pessar 1991). Balaguer demonstrated incredible staying power, heading the Dominican government for all but eight years between 1966 and 1996. (The opposition PRD party was in power from 1978 to 1986).[9] Sometimes called "Trujilloism without Trujillo" because of Balaguer's association with the dictator and his continued use of state-supported violence, the early years of Balaguer's rule saw progovernment death squads assassinate over a thousand Dominicans in efforts to subdue opponents (Black 1986: 42, 48).[10] But the passive resignation of the Trujillo era was over; radicalized by the aborted Revolution of 1965, the opposition insisted on making its voice heard. Other Dominicans, however, welcomed the stability that the new regime provided, and by the 1980s, Balaguer's violence had lessened. Also, despite the president's past connections to Trujillo, there were fundamental differences between the two leaders. Balaguer's policies attracted foreign aid and investment, fostered the growth of the middle classes, and benefited Dominican business interests, even if the country's overall standard of living declined. While Trujillo instituted a one-party system, Balaguer allowed opposition parties to exist, maintaining power by persecuting his opponents and rigging elections. Most significantly, where Trujillo was intensely personalistic and isolationist, the new leader maintained a relatively low profile and opened the country to foreign, especially U.S., influences. While Trujillo had used political power to advance his own business interests, Balaguer encouraged investment by transnational corporations. His courting of global capital resulted in foreign domination of all major private sectors of the Dominican economy; the U.S.-based Gulf and Western Corporation invested so heavily in the Dominican Republic in the 1970s and 1980s that some called the country a "company state" (Black 1986: 8).

As foreign influences moved into the country, a growing number of Dominicans were moving out. The lifting of a ban that Trujillo had placed on internal migration, combined with steady population growth and the failure of Balaguer's land reform program, led to massive rural-to-urban flight, which overcrowded cities and encouraged out-migration. In his early years, Balaguer often gave political opponents the choice of migration or "disappearance," which precipitated an exodus of middle-class Dominicans to the United States (see Vilas 1979). A declining standard of living and changes in U.S. immigration law also fomented out-migration. The burgeoning Dominican diaspora was part of the general trend of increased intercourse between Dominicans and the outside world and it affected the lives of expatriates and island dwellers alike.

External as opposed to domestic/active/passive donal distinction
(From artificial/artificio to internal/active/subordinate)

With one foot in modernity and the other in tradition, merengue played an important role in arbitrating these new Dominican realities. The national music was a link with the Dominican Republic for those in the diaspora, and its creative incorporation of outside elements served to domesticate transnational popular culture at home.

Just as merengueros had borrowed from rock 'n' roll in the 1960s, many young Dominicans turned to disco in the 1970s and early 1980s. As Brito Ureña writes, many of the participants at a 1983 merengue festival listened to North American music rather than to merengue: "The 'tum tum' of American (United States) music was heard from most of the [radios of] the cars that were parked in this area and it did not seem that the listeners were in the Dominican Republic at the Merengue Festival, but rather in 'Feverlandia' (Saturday Night Fever, John Travolta)" (1987: 72). At first, many bandleaders, including Johnny Ventura, added disco songs to their repertoires in their effort to remain popular. "We incorporated almost all of the Bee Gees' songs into the repertoire of my band, and the public applauded a lot when we sang those songs in English," Ventura told me. But he "felt that we were doing something ridiculous. Because I was accustomed to creating, always creating songs, and modifying merengue. So I discovered that the basis of disco was in the beat of the bass drum; that's where the attraction was to the young people. So I began to use the bass drum in merengue, and the young people went back to dancing merengue." Ventura's use of a bass drum (called the *drum* or *bombo* and played with a pedal by the güirero) to execute a discolike beat during certain sections of arrangements was widely imitated and became standard practice in pop merengue.

Johnny Ventura
Wilfrido Vargas

Johnny Ventura, the top merenguero during the 1960s, gave way in the 1970s and 1980s to bandleader and trumpeter Wilfrido Vargas.[11] Wilfrido Vargas y sus Beduinos started out as a quartet (trumpet, piano, bass, drum set) that played bossa nova, rock, and some salsa and merengue. In the early 1970s, Vargas adopted a conjunto format and changed to an all-merengue repertory. He directed the band, sang occasionally, and played trumpet and assorted other instruments such as synthesizer and harmonica.[12] Vargas's music continued the trends set by Luis Pérez and Johnny Ventura, who had sped the music up and borrowed from salsa and rock; Vargas used even faster tempos and appropriated more outside elements. Like his predecessors', Vargas's innovations did not cloud típico aesthetics. His megahit "Abusadora" used an even faster tempo than had "La agarradera," and like Ventura's hit fore-grounded flashy saxophone jaleos evocative of accordion-based merengue.[13] In the most striking part of the "Abusadora" arrangement, a saxophone jaleo produces a seamless, perpetually moving sound because the two saxophon-ists breathe in different places.[14] This novel, exciting, accordionlike effect, combined with the arrangement's breakneck tempo and sheer danceability, made "Abusadora" a huge success in the Dominican Republic, the diaspora, and among Latinos throughout the Americas.

Vargas's music was often marked by shifting ideas; sudden changes of key and innovative percussion rhythms hitherto unknown to merengue provided contrast with traditional progressions and drumming. Vargas's group was also notable for featuring several lead singers, each with a dynamic, personal style. Propelled to transnational popularity, Vargas produced a stream of hits. He frequently recorded merengue versions of Haitian konpa, Colombian *cumbia*, and other genres, and also used elements of these musics in original compositions; his pioneering and influential use of synthesizers in merengue was likely influenced by Haitian music. Based on the Haitian konpa hit "Men sirop" by Tabu Combo, Vargas's 1985 release "El jardinero" combines Cibao-style tambora, güira, and saxophone rhythms with konpa, synthesizer sounds, rap music, and jazz-informed horn voicings.[15]

Many bands practiced what was called *fusilamiento* (shooting, assassina-tion), basing merengue arrangements on foreign hits. While Wilfrido Vargas often drew upon Colombian and Haitian material, most fusilamiento was based on Latin American or Spanish romantic *baladas*. Salsa versions of bal-adas were also recorded. New York City Latin-music promoter George Ne-nadich told me that fusilamiento was employed as a marketing strategy aimed at cashing in on the enormous popularity of baladas on the international Latin music market to create new audiences for merengue and salsa: "Bal-lads appeal to a lot more people [than salsa and merengue], and it's a novelty to hear a salsa [or merengue] that's a ballad. It's cute." Balada-merengue ap-pealed to non-Dominicans because its texts did not treat specifically Do-minican themes; baladas generally spoke of romantic love rather than com-menting on local events in the manner of típico merengue. Borrowing from and adapting elements of non-Dominican musics thus continued to promote merengue's transnational success.

The Maco Rhythm and Subido Exuberance

Wilfrido Vargas's rhythmic innovations functioned primarily to provide contrast to the typical Cibao-style tambora and güira patterns, which continued to serve as the rhythmic basis of his music. However, a different beat, called *el maco* (the toad) and illustrated in musical example 11, came to be used as the basis of many merengues beginning in the late 1970s. The origin of this rhythm is the subject of much controversy, but Negrito Truman's 1961 hit, "La cúcara," is the earliest manifestation that arranger Luis Pérez could recall. Later incorporated into merengue, this rhythm marked a novel musical type in the 1960s. Pérez believes that the drumming on "La cúcara" was influenced by Cortijo's arrangements of the Puerto Rican *plena*, and that its cowbell part is borrowed from Haitian konpa.[16]

Musical Example 11
The Maco Rhythm

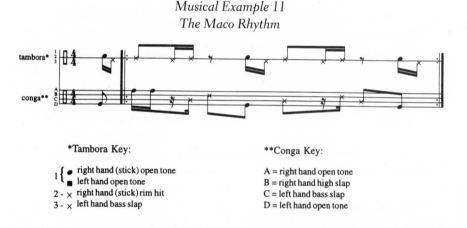

*Tambora Key:

1 { • right hand (stick) open tone
    ■ left hand open tone
2 - × right hand (stick) rim hit
3 - × left hand bass slap

**Conga Key:

A = right hand open tone
B = right hand high slap
C = left hand bass slap
D = left hand open tone

A band called Cheché Abreu y sus Colosos began using this beat, which they called *el mangué,* in the late 1960s. Abreu told me that he and his percussionists created it as a fusion of the Cuban son and merengue. This band gained fame in 1977 with a mangué-infused hit, "El berigüe," and in the following year it released a tune called "El mangué." Abreu told me that he used this novel rhythm as a marketing strategy: "Here in Santo Domingo, there were so many groups that had made big hits on the radio, like Johnny Ventura, Félix del Rosario. . . . So I felt that the only way I could get over on the radio would be to create my own style of music." Bandleader Aníbal

Bravo also claims to be the inventor of this rhythm, which he calls *el chucuchá*; he had a big hit by that title around 1978. As he told me, Bravo's reasons for deviating from the usual merengue beat were similar to Abreu's: "When I started my band, . . . I figured that, since I don't have money or a name, I need to invent something different, that isn't the usual thing that everybody else is doing. And so I invented . . . this new rhythm."

In the 1980s, Pochi y su Coco Band, Jossie Esteban y la Patrulla 15, and other groups, especially Los Hermanos Rosario, gained great popularity by basing their styles on this rhythm, by then considered a type of merengue rather than an independent genre and known as the maco rhythm.[17] By the 1990s, the maco was more prevalent than the typical Cibao-style percussion pattern. While the latter has a lilting four-beat cadence, the maco emphasizes a two-beat pulse evocative of disco music; recording engineer July Ruiz attributes the maco's popularity to its similarity to North American dance rhythms (interview). Indeed, partygoers often abandon the ballroom dance position and dance disco-style to maco arrangements.

While Latin jazz musicians sometimes dismissed pop merengue as a commercial music devoid of musical substance, the music suited the dancing public, which required the *contagioso y caliente* (catchy and hot) quality of its driving percussion rhythms and spicy horn arrangements. Dominicans enjoy dancing and partying, value *alegría* (happiness, euphoria), and joke that "there are more holidays than work days here." Their "goodnaturedness and spontaneity" have been commented on by observers, who also assert that for Dominicans "the dance is the social act *par excellence* in both the country and the city" (Ferrán 1985: 9). Merengue fan Miguelina Rodríguez Vidal told me that this spirit is captured by songwriter Luis Días in the Fernandito Villalona hit "El carnaval," extremely popular in Dominican carnival celebrations during the 1980s: "In Santo Domingo people live with a lot of happiness. People dance in the street, they sing at night, they sing in the daytime. And Luis Días's music speaks of this: 'Dance in the street!'"

Dominicans consider the hot aesthetic of pop merengue *subido* (rising or animated); as early as in the 1950s, Joseíto Mateo cried, "¡Súbelo!" (Raise it! Pump it up! Get hot!), to the band at the beginnings of instrumental portions of merengue arrangements. Martha Davis likens the ability of pop merengue to lift spirits to the function of a musical type called the *salve secular*, which is performed at rural religious rituals in the Republic: "The temporary transcendental state attained by means of repetition and aspects of the social environment in which *salves seculares* are performed is called *subido*. . . . This preference for the *subido* is well known to Dominicans in commercial *merengue*: the elimination of the *paseo*, the increased importance of the *jaleo*, and a greatly increased *tempo*" (1981: 37, 73). Although the transcendental state reached in salve contexts is not identical to the exhilaration experienced at merengue discotheques, an undeniable likeness exists between the musically induced euphoria that imbues Afro-Caribbean religious and recreational events.[18]

Gage Averill writes that Caribbean musical "exuberance" exhibits "a synchrony of collectivity within a temporal frame that could be called 'virtual time'" (1989a: 20). Suzanne Langer used the latter term in her discussion of temporality and music, which contrasts the virtual time of music with the "sequence of happenings" (1953: 104–19). In a similar vein, Ruth Stone applies Alfred Schutz's (1964: 170) notion of "inner" musical time to Kpelle music in West Africa; while the Kpelle are conscious of sequential time, they deemphasize it, using musical events to "elaborate the present": "Kpelle time is like a bubble in that while it is invariably expandable, at some point it must cease to expand. At the point the bubble bursts, in a similar way the participants move to another present in time through a leap or a shock" (1982: 72).[19] African and African American musics often achieve such effects. As John Chernoff explains, in Dagomba drumming in Ghana, "a change at just the appropriate moment will pace people's exposure to the deeper relationships of the rhythms, involving an audience for different lengths of time with the various rhythms which have been judged to fit most properly" (1979: 113).

James Brown brings his band to "the bridge" (the second sections of his arrangements) at the exact moment that the audience is receptive to the change.[20] Merengue elicits similar responses. Merenguero Wilfrido Vargas told me that he gets his best musical ideas, including the "Abusadora" saxophone jaleo, on the bandstand, and that he tries them out on the spot. I had the opportunity to experience this type of spontaneous arranging when I performed with Victor Waill, a singer and arranger who had worked extensively with Vargas. In the middle of a tune, Waill would tell the piano and bass players to switch keys, or cue rhythmic shifts in the percussion section. He built the momentum gradually, waiting until the crowd was primed for a change, and then introduced the new rhythm or harmony, provoking an emotional and kinesthetic response that changed the feeling in the whole room—*¡Se subió!* (It rose! It soared!)—or in Stone's terms, the bubble burst and the crowd entered another affective state.

Subido exuberance is catching; Dominicans often attribute merengue's popularity to the fact that it is *una música contagiosa* (a contagious music). Novelist Ishmael Reed also intimates an analogy of African American music to infectious disease by referring to 1920s jazz as "jes' grew," implying that the music was a virus that "just grew," to the satisfaction of many, and to the chagrin of racist whites (1972).

The Transnational Merengue Industry

As exhilarating as merengue can be, the music probably could not have carved a place in the transnational market without the recording industry's help. The powerful New York City–based Fania Record Company moved into the Dominican Republic in the 1970s, promoting salsa performers such as Celia Cruz and Willie Colón and buying radio stations (Falette 1988: 11–12). As Fania's exclusive distributor in the Republic, the Dominican impresario Bienvenido Rodríguez became the most successful individual in Dominican music; by 1988, he would own a radio station, a record factory, and a record distributorship, as well as the country's top record company, Karen Records (12). Rodríguez began to promote and record Wilfrido Vargas in 1975, breaking down market barriers to sell up to twenty-thousand records. His subsequent production of the band Los Hijos del Rey (Sons of the King), which featured singer Fernandito Villalona, was even more successful; their LP "El mayimbe" sold sixty-thousand copies (2, 3). In the mid-1980s, Rodríguez began to promote bandleader Juan Luis Guerra, who achieved unprecedented success in the transnational market (see Chapter Six).

The growing Dominican middle class formed the consumer base of the burgeoning merengue industry. Dominicans in New York City and Puerto Rico, who were better off economically than those on the island, were also major consumers, as were non-Dominican merengue fans. Karen Records and its principal competitor, Kubaney, became the central movers of one of the Dominican Republic's top export items.

The advancement of Dominican recording technology helped give merengue a competitive spot next to disco and salsa in the market. All recording was done on two-track equipment in the Republic during the 1960s, but by the early 1980s, sophisticated twenty-four-track recording was the norm (Ruíz interview). Because modern recording equipment allows each instrument or section of a band to record separately, every part can be recorded as many times as necessary to achieve the desired effect; the several tracks are then mixed by a recording engineer. Dominican percussionist Isidro Bobadilla told me that the calculated nature of this process belies deep-seated notions about popular music's spontaneity: "Popular music is not spontaneous, no; [recordings] are planned out. I have had several disagreements with people who claim that there is a lot of spontaneity in popular music. But where is it? . . . In the studio, you can say, 'Change this,' 'Get rid of that,' 'No, I don't like it, let's do it again,' until you come out with a product that is very intricate, very thought-out." Recording engineer July Ruiz points out that members of his profession perform a creative role in the music; he attributes his sensitivity to the nuances of merengue recording to his own prior experience as a professional saxophonist. Ruiz told me that until the 1990s, merengue was recorded exclusively in the Dominican Republic because there were few Dominican engineers in the diaspora, and non-Dominican technicians lacked sensitivity to merengue: "We [Dominican recording engineers] heard merengue in the cradle." A friend added that "they even heard it in their mothers' wombs."

Patriotism and Payola

Because the price of cassettes, LPs, CDs, and sound systems was prohibitive for many Dominicans, recorded music was perhaps most often heard on the radio—in homes, buses, and *colmados*, neighborhood grocery stores that serve as informal social centers. Radio plays a role in creating musical preferences throughout the world; Peter Tagg believes that it "probably does more to influence public taste than anything else" (in Wallis and Malm 1984: 242). Theodor Adorno expressed an extreme form of this opinion, holding that a song "will be drummed into the listeners' ears until they cannot help . . . [but] love it" (1976: 34). In the 1960s, Dominican radio aired mostly North American music, salsa, and baladas; merengue was programmed mostly on weekends (Rodríguez 1986: 15–16). Merengue radio play increased dramatically in the 1970s and 1980s; by 1986, Dominican music accounted for 70 percent of what was aired (17).[21] A parallel trend in the preference for native popular culture occurred in television; surveys indicate that while U.S. shows had dominated Latin American television programming in the 1970s, by the late 1980s most working-class Dominicans preferred local shows to U.S. imports. The turn toward local television programming, according to some observers, indicated "resistance to cultural imperialism, notably U.S. imports" (Straubhaar and Viscansillas 1991: 53). Similarly, Dominican radio announcer Willie Rodríguez relates the increase in merengue radio play to nationalistic feelings (1986: 16).

Dominican radio programming was determined by deejays, who aired songs based on personal taste, advertisers' preferences, and payola—under-the-table cash incentives—that record companies provided in return for playing specific records. A man who works in Dominican broadcasting told me that "in the Dominican Republic, it is the deejay that decides. He plays the music that appeals to him, that he likes. And, how should I put it, when an artist, or the representative of an artist from a record company, wants to promote a record, well, he shows a radio announcer which record it is that he wants to move. And, I'd say that he gives him something under the table, as we say. This is called *payola*." Practiced in many countries, payola often consists of gifts or services instead of cash bribes (see Segrave 1994; Wallis and Malm 1984: 242–46). It developed in the Dominican Republic during the 1960s, when compensation most generally took the form of gifts other than money. The shift to cash inducements began around 1970 (Solano 1992: 201–2). Dominican music businessman Ramón Falette writes that at first, about U.S. $5–25 was given per month for each record; by 1988, rates had risen to U.S. $15–$230 per month (Falette 1988: 58–62). By the mid-1990s, according to a musician, bribes in the diaspora could run in the thousands of U.S. dollars paid to *deter* deejays from playing particular records.

Dominicans often objected to this practice for its unfairness to musicians who do not have the support of major record companies. One bandleader extremely popular in the 1980s told me he got no airplay in the 1990s because he could not award payola. He said that payola costs can exceed record production costs and calls payola "the assassin of our musicians." The practice may indeed create an alliance between record companies and radio stations in which the former impose musical preferences "not always based on quality" (Pérez 1991: 20). Evoking Adorno's view that the mass media manipulate popular preference, Falette credits Dominican payola with "controlling the taste of the whole society" but points out that no alternatives or solutions have yet been proposed (1988: 62).

One reason may lie in payola's connection to the general economic corruption of the country, a problem exacerbated by low salaries and high prices. High inflation rates and wage freezes (often mandated by The International Monetary Fund) have made it difficult for most Dominicans to make ends meet. Corruption is tempting for workers such as police officers, who as of 1990–91 received as little as U.S. $50 monthly, as well as for professionals, who sometimes received as little as U.S. $300 monthly. In the Dominican Republic, I was shocked to be accosted by police officers, who left me alone after I gave them a few pesos. But a friend told me that he did not mind when this happened, since only a small amount of money is involved, and the police needed these funds to support their families. While nothing can pardon bribery, the corrupt underground economy clearly fills the vacuum created when salaries fail to keep up with inflation. Unlike Dominican workers and professionals, transnational Dominican record companies earn U.S. dollars that a lopsided exchange rate renders extremely remunerative in the Republic. Unlike other sectors of the economy, record companies' profits, like payola rates, have risen with inflation. While the increased radio play that merengue enjoyed in the 1980s and 1990s was no doubt associated with patriotic feelings, growing payola rates likely also played a role; deejays did not receive payment for non-Dominican music (Falette 1988: 66–67).[22]

Keeping Up Appearances: Merengueros, Advertising, and National Identity

While many connected to the recording industry profited from the growth of the merengue business, musicians often moved up the social scale but not necessarily up the economic ladder. "Until this time," Johnny Ventura told me, "being a musician was a romantic, bohemian thing. . . . We made a musician into a . . . profession." Indeed, barrio youths who join successful merengue bands may achieve the appearance, if not the reality, of elevated class status. But, as Teófilo Barreira warns, while merengue performance may be a "principal avenue of social mobility," this mobility often results in feelings of "alienation" (1986: 42–46). Natanael "la Güira" Cabrera, one of the most talented and sought-after güira players in the Dominican Republic, told me that "I used to be a kid that people ordered around, and things like that. I used to sell bottles on the street." After he began to appear on television, people treated him differently: "I changed social status a bit. . . . People see me differently. . . . They see me as an artist now." But social status is not synonymous with economic status. Producers and some bandleaders profited greatly from merengue, but most performers fared less well; in 1991, percussionists usually received about U.S. $30 per performance, while trumpeters, saxophonists, bassists, and pianists could make U.S. $45 or more. Musicians usually played one to four times a week (J. Cabrera Torres interview; Jérez 1991). As one merenguero told me, "Musicians are poorly paid; they exploit you here, because most of the money goes to the bandleader. I'll give you an example: If a band plays a dance for $20,000 [about U.S. $2,000 in 1991], the leader . . . pays the musicians. He keeps all the rest of the money. One bandleader . . . bought a car after having a band for six months." Musicians who insist on more money run the risk of being replaced.[23]

Natanael la Güira told me that his new social position placed him in a difficult predicament. Like performers of other popular musics, merengue musicians are known for their characteristic style of dress (see Barthes 1991; Hebdige 1979: 100 ff.). Natanael la Güira was expected to wear the clothes befitting his new status as a top merenguero, but he couldn't afford them: "People are always around artists, they are always looking at them, to see how you are. People check out my *fílings* ["feelings," style], clothing. . . . [I] have to wear expensive clothes, even [clothes bought] in a boutique, where they sell imported clothes, which are expensive." Singer Joel Cabrera Torres agrees; being a musician, he told me, is "a question of keeping up appearances." Indeed, an aura of flashy escapism hung over the entire merengue culture.

Merengue proved equally valuable for entrepreneurs outside the music industry. Dominican advertising executives foregrounded the national music in commercials for tobacco and rum, which, like merengue, are homegrown products. The Barceló rum company led the way in developing commercials with folkloric themes. Building on many types of Dominican music, Barceló ads made prodigious use of merengue, the best-known native genre. José Rivera, the campaign's creator, told me that the commercials used songs from all over the country: "We based the campaign on tradition and folklore. . . .

The commercials are based on work songs, love songs, songs of happiness. . . . And they are almost all songs of rural origin, peasant songs . . . from the South, the North, the East." While studio arrangers altered the music, Barceló strove for authenticity and hired the eminent folklorists Fradique Lizardo and Dagoberto Tejeda to oversee the project. Rivera compared his campaign to advertising that entreated U.S. citizens to "buy American"; he claimed that it promoted national identity while selling rum: "Selling this also transmits culture, *our* culture, our own culture, our identity as a nation. And at the same time, it serves as a vehicle for the promotion of our product. . . . It is the same in the United States: it's always, 'Made in USA,' appealing to nationalism. This is the same idea." He said he had sought a wholesome image; the commercials depicted healthy, traditional activities such as serenades and farm work. Instead of showing people drinking rum, the commercials focused on activities that occur *before* people have a drink: "It is after what the commercial depicts that the rum consumption takes place," he explained.

Other rum companies ran similar campaigns. While identifying their brand of rum with Dominicanness, for instance, the Brugal company's ads suggested that music is inextricable from national identity. A television shot shows a decanter of vodka, while an announcer explains that "this bottle contains the essence of the Russian people." The top of the bottle comes off, and Russian-sounding music plays. The scene shifts to a bottle of Brugal rum. The announcer continues: "In the same way, Brugal rum represents the essence of the Dominican people." Merengue plays when the Brugal bottle top comes off. The Bermudez rum company's television commercials paired prominent Dominican musicians of the past with the best contemporary performers. One ad coupled composer Julio Alberto Hernández, a pioneer of merengue as Euro-Dominican concert music, with singer Maridalia Hernández of the group 4:40, one of the best artists of the 1990s. Another paired a highly regarded bolero singer of the 1950s with pop merengue idol Sergio Vargas; together, they sang:

Este es mi pais,	This is my country,
Esta es mi gente.	This is my people.
Bermudez es mi ron,	Bermudez is my rum,
Y merengue es mi ritmo.	And merengue is my rhythm.

The National Genre as an Aesthetic Border Zone

Beginning in the 1970s, considerable debate developed between those who considered pop merengue a "deformation" of traditional merengue and those who regarded it as a logical development of earlier forms of the music. Fradique Lizardo contends that it underwent such drastic changes in the late twentieth century it ceased to be merengue. The Fernandito Villalona hit "El carnaval," he claims, "is not a merengue, not a mangulina, not a *carabiné*, nor anything else that corresponds to our musical genres" (in "Fradique dice" 1986). Papa Molina, who led the top merengue band of the 1950s, concurs, suggesting that the drastic changes the music suffered warrant giving it a new name. Because rhythmic structure is often a determinant of musical genre, Molina asserts, "when the rhythmic structure changes, the music changes, and the genre's name should change." He adds that North American popular music has taken different names at different points in its development (p.c.). Other musicians and fans, however, point out that contemporary merengue shares much with earlier merengue and that musical types can evolve without losing their integrity as genres.

Bandleaders Aníbal Bravo and Cheché Abreu's attempts to coin new names for the music fell in with Lizardo's and Molina's position. About the term *el mangué* for his music, Abreu told me that "since we played it differently than merengue, I named it *el mangué*, in order to respect the tradition of the original Dominican merengue, . . . in order not to show a lack of respect for merengue." The neologisms may have failed to stick in part because music industry promoters continued to sell the music as merengue, a "name brand" whose market value outweighed any commercial benefits that the new names could have provided. The industry's strategy developed in dialogue with merengue fans. While Haitian, Cuban, and Nigerian audiences took "delight in neologistic terms for performance styles" (Waterman 1990a: 17; also see Averill 1989a: 122; Robbins 1989), Dominican audiences were clearly *not* delighted by the coinage of new names for their music. According to Jeffrey Kallberg, composers of European classical music make strategic choices regarding genre in dialogue with their audiences; his remarks apply equally to Caribbean bandleaders and their fans: "The meaning of a term . . . is connected to the willingness of a particular community to use that word and not another" (1988: 243). In spite of the rhythmic and harmonic changes in the music, and in spite of some bandleaders' promotion of new terms, fans continued to call Dominican popular music *merengue*.

If we look at music as a "social phenomenon," Kallberg suggests, a musical type's symbolic significance is clearly related to its definition as a genre (1988: 243). The late twentieth century was marked by far-reaching changes in Dominican society: exuberant liberation from dictatorship, foreign intervention, and unprecedented intercourse with the outside world. According to Christopher Waterman, "popular music is a public arena for the symbolic negotiation of continuity and change" (1990: 16). Stylistic changes kept Dominican music in step with new social realities, while the retention of traditional musical elements and adherence to the label *merengue* forged links with the past. At the same time, the use of outside elements turned the national music's aesthetic space into what Américo Paredes calls a "borderzone," a "sensitized area where two cultures come face to face" (1978: 68; also see Rosaldo 1988: 86). Using popular music as a customs office, merengue musicians and fans charged creative tariffs that domesticated incoming culture. Stubborn adherence to a time-tested national symbol thus gave Dominicans jurisdiction over the aesthetic borderland during a period marked by dizzying transnationalization.

Chapter 6

Innovation and Social Issues in Pop Merengue

■n the midst of the conservative aesthetic encouraged by the investment-conscious merengue industry, the music continued to change in exciting ways; brilliant innovations challenged the time-tested formulas. And while most of its song texts expressed conventional values, merengue also served as a site for negotiating hard questions about race, social class, gender relations, and sexuality.

Arguments flared over the value of fusilamiento. Many Dominicans criticized the fusion of foreign music with merengue as a commercial gimmick devoid of artistic merit. The term itself is pejorative: *Fusilamiento* means firing a gun and thus implies that merengue assassinates non-Dominican music. On the other hand, fusilamiento also may intimate that non-Dominican songs are "fired up" by merengue's hot sound (Manuel 1995: 112). Moreover, critics praised the use of foreign compositions in merengue when the arrangements and singing were of high caliber. Merengue cibaeño typically employs simple harmonies; as one musician told me, non-Dominican elements "enrich the harmonic palette" of the music. The king of merengue, Joseíto Mateo, pointed out to me that fusilamiento was not invented in the 1970s, and that besides holding on to Dominican audiences that might otherwise be lost to foreign musics, it improved the music: "They have used music from other countries [in merengue]—cumbias, baladas. But there is nothing new about this; I was doing it thirty years ago. . . . And since it [other music] has a different musical structure, more beautiful arrangements could be made."

Singer Alex Bueno's acclaimed mid-1980s Orquesta Liberación owed much to Manuel Tejada and Ramón Orlando's innovative merengue versions of Latin American romantic songs. Combining sophisticated balada-style arrangements and elements of funk and jazz with Cibao-style tambora, güira, and saxophone rhythms, these arrangers brought a polished sound to the music. In 1986, another young arranger, Juan Luis Guerra, told me that "young musicians are interested in merengue. . . . There is a tendency to refine merengue with different types of arrangements, violins and things like that, which do not diminish the drive that merengue has by nature." Ramón Orlando later founded his own critically acclaimed group, whose style combined spicy maco rhythms with sophisticated arrangements.

A composer, arranger, and singer, Guerra emerged as the most innovative presence in merengue in the 1980s and 1990s. He was born in the capital and, after stints at the Autonomous University of Santo Domingo and the Dominican Conservatory, studied jazz at the Berklee College of Music in Boston. Guerra had a special liking for the North American vocal quartet Manhattan Transfer, known for its jazz-influenced arrangements, and formed his own vocal quartet in the Dominican Republic in 1984.[1] The group's name, 4:40, reflected Guerra's schooled aesthetic: Its music was to be sung perfectly in tune, measured against the standard pitch of Western music, the note A at 440 cycles per second (Tejeda 1993: 114). Performing Guerra's vocal arrangements of merengue and other genres to prerecorded tapes of his orquesta arrangements, the group appealed primarily to the middle and upper classes, as well as to students, artists, and intellectuals from all sectors of society. Its sophistication evoked Trujillo-era salon merengue; like Luis Alberti and the other big-band merengueros, Guerra refined the music with cosmopolitan influences. The group's first LP, "Soplando" (Blowing), released in 1985, consisted largely of jazz-influenced merengues and featured inspired saxophone improvisation ("blowing") by Dominican jazz master Tavito Vásquez.[2] It also included a brilliant jazz-tinged arrangement of "Jardinera," the Joseíto Mateo ranchera-merengue hit of the 1950s.

Popular among jazz enthusiasts, the album's cultivated quality and moderate tempos did not entice the dancing public. Under the influence of impresario Bienvenido Rodríguez and Karen Records, 4:40's music evolved in a direction that appealed to a wider audience without abandoning its innovations.[3] Guerra soon enjoyed great success on the Dominican and transnational markets, surpassing previous standards set by Fernandito Villalona: His 1990 release "Bachata rosa" sold more than 3.5 million copies globally, his 1991 North American tour set attendance records, and he won a U.S. Grammy award in 1992 (Pacini Hernandez 1992a: 359).[4]

While 4:40 had performed to the accompaniment of prerecorded instrumental tracks in its early years, Guerra formed a full merengue band in 1989 (Tejeda 1993: 205). Although the group's work was perhaps more intellectual than most merengue, it was still party music; people danced in the aisles at their concerts, and 4:40 records were highly solicited at discotheques and private parties. Guerra's songwriting evinced a sentimentality influenced by soft-rock composers such as Paul McCartney and Carole King, while his arrangements displayed an innovative take on the blend of Afro-Caribbean rhythms and cosmopolitan sophistication that had often characterized merengue. The group's music combined a remarkable variety of influences, including Cibao-style and maco rhythms, slick balada and jazz-influenced harmonies and orchestration, and sundry elements borrowed from *soukous* (Central African popular music), flamenco, bebop, and funk. "Our main influence" Guerra told me, "is, more than anything else, jazz. . . . Next to this, or along with it, is funk, [especially in the] trumpet rhythms, [which are] combined with the saxophone patterns. We have an incredible mix: merengue saxophones and funk trumpets. A funk sound like Tower of Power or Earth, Wind, and Fire's . . . with an extremely Dominican rhythm." His songs are notable for their sophisticated texts. While merengue cibaeño had always employed wit and irony, its poetic voice was that of the common man and woman, its perspective that of the campesino. The literary sophistication of 4:40's lyrics strikes an entirely new note in merengue. Because it is intended to make people think and dance at the same time, Guerra once called his music *"el merengue dual"* (dual merengue) (Cazorla 1991). As we will see, Guerra's music addressed social issues at the core of Dominican life in the late twentieth-century.

Old and New Attitudes about Race

In the decades following Trujillo's death, merengue fueled arguments over the hot issue of race, particularly debates about whether the country's identity was primarily African or Hispanic. Like Trujillo, Joaquín Balaguer propagated an anti-Haitian, racist sense of Dominican identity, identifying as inferior the many residents of the Dominican Republic of Haitian origin or descent. During the 1980s and 1990s, he used xenophobia and racist rhetoric to galvanize electoral support in much the same way European and North American politicians did (Fennema and Loewenthal 1987). In *La isla al revés: Haití y el destino dominicano* (The island upside down: Haiti and Dominican destiny) (1983), Balaguer argues that the Dominican Republic is threatened not by U.S. imperialism, but by *Haitian* imperialism "directed against the independence of Santo Domingo and against the Hispanic-American population" that began during the nineteenth-century Haitian occupations of Spanish Santo Domingo. Balaguer writes that while the military peril has faded, "biological" factors, such as the "fecundity characteristic of the Negro," pose threats to Dominican destiny. Both Haitian overpopulation and "barbaric customs that make incestuous unions possible" are purportedly dangerous to Dominicans, "corrupting the ethnic physiognomy" (as quoted and explicated in Fennema and Loewenthal 1987: 33–40).[5] It is difficult to ascertain the extent to which Dominican citizens subscribe to these views. Balaguer's book sold over 10,000 copies; I have heard Dominicans of all social classes refer to the growing Haitian presence in their country as an "invasion"; and I have witnessed mistreatment of Haitians in the Dominican Republic. On the other hand, I have observed friendly relations between Dominicans and Haitians, and according to anthropologist Carlos Andújar, who has researched relations between Haitians and Dominican sugar workers, when members of the two groups share lifeways, good relations are the rule (p.c.).

The mood of democratization and influx of external influences that followed Trujillo's fall kindled new currents of Dominican humanistic and social scientific thought in the 1960s and 1970s; the ensuing reconsideration of conventional notions about national and racial identity was associated with the anti-Balaguer resistance. Folklorist Fradique Lizardo advocated renouncing Hispanophilism and celebrating the African influences on Dominican culture. Reminding his compatriots that merengue's status as a national symbol had been mandated by Trujillo, Lizardo once declared that "to say merengue is the national dance of the Dominican Republic is false." He also suggested that palos drumming be adopted as a national music, noting that this genre is performed in virtually all regions of the country (in Ysálguez 1975a: 51).

Afro-Dominican musics found advocates also among members of the *nueva canción* (new song) movement, which originated in Chile in the 1960s and spread throughout Latin America, using local musics in the struggle against rightist authoritarian regimes, economic inequity, and U.S. imperialism. A coterie of young artists and intellectuals sometimes called "the alternative generation" created a Dominican brand of nueva canción. Prominent in this movement was the group Convite, which featured sociologist Dagoberto Tejeda Ortiz and guitarist-composer Luis Días. Like the Dominican-Haitian communal work teams after which the group was named, Convite was a collaborative effort dedicated to serving the community. In addition to being a musical ensemble, Convite investigated, educated, and politicized; the group's members conducted fieldwork and held workshops to promote their musico-political agenda (Sálazar Díaz 1978; Tejeda Ortiz 1978). Like Lizardo, members of Convite were especially interested in Afro-Dominican musics, which they considered expressions of genuine peoples' culture. While advocating the preservation of this rural authenticity, Convite also used Afro-Dominican forms as fodder for their own compositions. Groups such as Los Guerreros del Fuego and Asa-Difé, led by José Duluc and Tony Vicioso, continued to work in this idiom during the 1980s and 1990s.

Convite's spokesperson, Dagoberto Tejeda Ortiz, believes that while mainstream popular music such as merengue is rooted in people's culture, it is denatured by close association with the capitalist music industry: "The musical and folkloric expressions of the people have been both disfigured and undervalued, and have been substituted with commercial, alienated songs" (in Sálazar Díaz 1978: 23). But Convite did not shun merengue, believing that, disassociated from reactionary influences, the preeminent Dominican popular music could promote a progressive vision. In line with this notion, when a nueva canción festival, Siete Días con el Pueblo (Seven Days with the People), said to be the largest such festival ever held in any country, was organized to challenge Balaguer's regime in 1974, it featured performances by sympathetic merengueros Johnny Ventura and Cuco Valoy in addition to top local and foreign nueva canción artists (Pacini Hernandez 1995: 120–21).

In their celebration of the Republic's African roots, Dominicans who were involved in or sympathetic to the nueva canción movement challenged their compatriots' traditional Eurocentric prejudices. The question of merengue's origin was central to a debate that developed between conservative Dominicans who insisted on the Republic's Hispanic identity and the constituency that promoted the country's African heritage. The traditionally minded faction claimed that merengue had little or no African influence, while progressive thinkers celebrated its African-derived aesthetic.

Juan Luis Guerra, who was associated with the nueva canción movement as a youth, spoke forcefully of the music's African roots without negating its syncretic nature: "Unequivocally, you can't take merengue out of Africa. No matter how much you may want to, you can't take it out of Africa. Forget it—the rhythms are African, period. Of course there are these influences, which are melodic: the melodies are European, the harmony, just like in jazz" (interview). Afro-Dominican ritual drumming held particular interest for Guerra; while he did not use it in his arrangements, he referred to it in lyrics. His song "Guavaberry" speaks of the regional customs of *cocolos,* the Dominicans of Anglophone Caribbean descent who live in and around the city of San Pedro de Macorís in the East. With their dark skin and non-Hispanic roots, cocolos had remained on the margins of Dominicanness ever since their arrival in the country in the nineteenth century. Guerra's song pays homage to the cocolo guavaberry beverage and drumming tradition, celebrating the truly Caribbean, versus solely Hispanic, nature of Dominicanness. The song's bilingual text acknowledges the cocolos' Anglophone background:

GUAVABERRY

I like to live in the streets of San Pedro de Macorís [repeat].
I like to sing my song in the middle of Malecón [repeat].
Drinking my guavaberry, watching the sun go down,
Woman, that's all I need, in San Pedro de Macorís.

Quiero vivir junto a tí en San Pedro de Macorís [repite].
Quiero bailar mi canción en el medio del Malecón [repite].
Bebiendo guavaberry al ritmo de un tambor,
O, bailando feliz, en San Pedro de Macorís.

I want to dance in the streets of San Pedro de Macorís [repeat].
I want to hear the sound of cocolo beating the drums [repeat].
Drinking my guavaberry, watching the sun go down,
Woman, that's all I need in San Pedro de Macorís.
¡Cocolo de San Pedro!

Guerra may have intended the English in part to attract North American audiences; he told me that he hoped his English-language music would appeal
to this listenership. Ironically, English is the language of both a marginalized
Afro-Dominican group and of the hegemonic United States.

Guerra expressed his enlightened view of the relationship between Dominican and African cultures in both the music and the video produced to
promote his hit "A pedir su mano" (To ask for her hand). This piece combines
a melody taken from a Central African soukous song, vocal arrangements
marked by South African inflection, and merengue rhythms. The video jux-
taposes African and Afro-Dominican images: A black Dominican man looking at pseudo-African masks in a museum; scenes of gagá, an African-influenced processional music performed in sugar-producing areas of the
Dominican Republic during Holy Week; and footage of cocolo drumming
and dance. The video implies that while African arts can be admired in mu-
seums, they are better appreciated as living Dominican culture. Guerra's
high-profile celebrations of the Republic's African roots paved the way for the
use of Afro-Dominican ritual drumming by others: Kinito Mendez's Rocka-
banda and Sergio Vargas's Orquesta used palos drumming in several mainstream merengue hits of the early 1990s. Even so, musical challenges to prevailing Dominican attitudes have not had a substantive impact on Dominican
attitudes about race, which on the whole remain Eurocentric.

Bachata and Social Class

Despite merengue's phenomenal success, another native music began making inroads on Dominican taste in the 1970s. *Bachata* is distinguished by its
guitar-based instrumentation, association with barrio and rural culture, and
texts that use street language to comment ironically on the bitter realities

faced by impoverished Dominicans. Several musical types, including merengue, are performed within the rubric of bachata. The most common of these is the Cuban son or *bolero-son*, which is Dominicanized through the use of characteristic chord progressions and dance steps. Bachata employs a tight, nasal vocal quality, one or two guitars, marimba or electric bass, *maracas* or güira, *bongó* (for Cuban genres), and tambora (for merengue).[6] Bachata's association with rural and barrio culture precluded its endorsement by the dominant society; while it was arguably the single most popular music among the Dominican majority, bachata was long considered a "marginal" music (Pacini Hernandez, 1995). Until mainstream musicians began performing this music in the 1990s, even bachatas that outsold merengue hits received no airplay on major radio stations, appeared on no hit-parade lists, and were usually unavailable in middle-class record stores. The notion that bachata was marginal thus reflected not its audience size, but its lack of acceptance by the dominant society.[7]

As merengue gained popularity during the 1970s and 1980s, bachata musicians included it in their repertoires. For example, guitarist and singer Eladio Romero Santos told me that he began his career performing non-Dominican musics — "boleros, because at that time, merengue was not big; it was all boleros and a lot of foreign music. Rancheras and *corridos.*" During the merengue boom of the 1970s, Romero decided to record the Luis Alberti song "La muñeca" (The doll). He told me that while the record was not promoted on the radio, it sold better than did Rafael Solano's orquesta version of the song later released. Romero then decided to specialize in merengue.

Singer Blas Durán gained fame with the novel, twangy, electric-guitar sound of his bachata-merengue. His 1987 song "Consejo a las mujeres" (Advice to women) outsold many pop merengue hits.[8] Durán refers to bachata's successful challenge to merengue's monopoly in the tune's spoken introduction: *"Fuera del ancho, que llegó el estrecho!"* (Out with the wide, the narrow one has arrived). As interpreted by Pacini Hernandez,

> This seemingly nonsensical wisecrack . . . cloaked a David-to-Goliath message to the mainstream music system that they'd better make room for bachata. As he [Durán] explained: "Wide means fat people, and narrow a skinny one. In other words, you get out, because I've arrived, and I'm better than you are" (interview). Durán's boast was

right on the mark: . . . by successfully incorporating the long-popular merengue into bachata, Durán directly challenged the orquestas on their previously exclusive turf. (1995: 200)

Born in the disenfranchised barrios and *campos* (countryside), the humble bachata was indeed music of the "thin" people—while merengue belonged to the establishment fat cats.

Pop merengue's flashy and escapist aura appealed to the aspirations of many Dominicans, but it did not speak to the day-to-day realities faced by the impoverished majority that lived in campos and barrios. By contrast, bachata's homespun style and skillful use of street language kept it in tune with rural and barrio tastes. Bachata often used bawdy double entendre. In this excerpt from Duran's "Consejo a las mujeres," "bones" refers to erections, and "ear" refers to the female genitals:

Una mujer se casó con un hombre que	A woman married a one-eyed man,
era tuerto,	
Yél le daba de comer huesos, huesos,	And he gave her bones, bones,
muchos huesos.	lots of bones to eat.
Una mujer se montó en una bicicleta,	A woman got on a bicycle,
Yde lejo se le vió que se le menió	And from far away, you could see her
una oreja.	move an ear.

As bachata gained ground on merengue, bandleaders such as Musiquito, Wilfrido Vargas, and Juan Luis Guerra began to record orquesta versions of bachatas. Guerra showed special interest in the genre, producing several son-bachata hits whose texts couched bachata's sexual references in his own characteristically literary style. I once stopped to join a man who was watching, from the street, a videotape of an orquesta merengue-bachata being shown in a bar. He was frustrated with the middle-class Dominicans who had once disparaged bachata and now embraced it: "Well, well, bachata is in the salons now. In times past, high-class people criticized bachata, but now they're dancing to it themselves." Blas Durán himself pointed to this double standard in a newspaper interview, noting that while music critics censured his music as lewd, they praised Guerra's bachatas, many of which also "qualif[ied] as vulgar" (Guzmán 1990). Indeed, Dominicans do often evaluate musical styles according to class associations.[9] When middle-class musicians adapt campesino and barrio genres, the results are called *elevaciónes* (exaltations); Luis Alberti's and Juan Luis Guerra's contributions to the history of merengue are considered artistic milestones. But when rural and barrio musicians adapt salon styles, the results are derided as *deformaciónes* (deformities); bachata is often subject to such criticism, and even pop merengue has been criticized for its association with barrio life and because its performance rarely exhibits the level of professionalism of the 1950s big bands. While acknowledging the artistic merit of 4:40's bachatas, Pacini Hernandez is disappointed at Guerra's failure to actively educate international audiences about bachata's roots, especially in light of his nueva canción background (1995: 208; also see 1992a: 363). On the other hand, the success of Guerra's bachata had a legitimizing effect on the genre as a whole, opening the door for street-level bachata to enter mainstream society. By the mid-1990s, guitar-based bachata was available in middle-class record stores and was played at bourgeois discos, even if most singers had abandoned bawdy lyrics. The front cover of the 1 August 1995 issue of *Bemoles*, a Dominican music magazine, went so far as to proclaim that "Merengue Falls" while "Bachata Singers Gain Ground."

Merengue, the Body, and Gender Relations

The merengue dance step has remained fundamentally the same since the early twentieth century; couples continue to execute the characteristic footwork, moving in one direction on the floor as they perform turns and other figures similar to those used in salsa, swaying their hips from side to side.[10] North American influences and the maco rhythm encouraged couples to abandon the ballroom position to dance disco-style, without touching each other. Merengue fans have also sometimes imitated the steps that singers performed on stage. Additionally, couples have the option of dancing while pressing their groins close together (*pegado*, stuck). The dance thus offers social sanction for intimate physical contact between men and women; as Joseíto Mateo said to me, merengue is a "music of taking advantage; it gives [men] a chance to embrace a woman without doing anything immoral." Combine close contact with undulating hip motion, and this dance mode can be sexually arousing.

This sensuous dance conspires with bawdy lyrics and spicy drumming to lend merengue contexts an air of libidinous mirth, heightened by the revealing clothes that women customarily wear to fiestas. While there is an uninhibited playfulness about all this, Dominican sexuality is phallicentric and misogynistic. The hot maco rhythms and lustful lyrics of Pochy y su Coco Band's megahit "La faldita" (The miniskirt) express this brand of carnal appetite; the appeal to "*¡Subelo un chin!*" (Raise it a bit! Pump it up!) simultaneously calls for a hotter music and a higher hemline. Note the lecherous reference to a woman's "voluminous thigh," which reflects the Dominican preference for a buxom body type.

LA FALDITA
(The miniskirt)

Me gusta esta faldita	I like the miniskirt
Que tú siempre te pones,	That you always wear,
Ay oye mamacita,	Listen, mama,
No uses pantalones.	Don't wear slacks.
Cuando vas caminando	When you walk around
Con esa chulería,	Wearing that awesome thing,
Se va subiendo todo,	Everything gets pumped up!
¡Que tiene mamá mía!	My mama has a lot!
¡Ay que chula, te queda la faldita!	Oh, it looks hot on you, that miniskirt!
¡Ay que chula, te queda mamacita!	Oh, it looks hot on you, little mama!
Cuando tú te la pones,	When you wear it,
Los tigueres en la esquina	The wolves on the corner
Te van chequeando todo,	Really check you out,
Y atras de tí caminan.	And follow behind you.
Ay, no te la quites,	Oh, don't take it off,
Dejate en la faldita,	Stay in the miniskirt,
Para chequearte en tela	So I can check out the cloth.
¡Esa pierna tan gordaza!	That thigh is *voluminous*!
¡Ay que chula, te queda la faldita!	Oh, it looks hot on you, that miniskirt!
¡Ay que chula, te queda mamacita!	Oh, it looks hot on you, little mama!

Esa faldita, que tu te pones,	The miniskirt that you wear,
A mi me encanta, no pongas	I love it; don't wear slacks.
pantalones.	
¡Subelo un chin!	Pump it up!
¡Subelo un chin!	Pump it up!
¡Subelo un chin!	Pump it up!
¡Ay que chula, te queda la faldita!	The miniskirt that you wear,
¡Ay que chula, te queda mamacita!	I love it; don't wear slacks.

Because of this air of male-dominated sexuality, many Dominicans believe that unaccompanied women should not go to discotheques and that performing merengue music is no fitting occupation for women. Miguelina Rodríguez Vidal told me that "in Santo Domingo people generally think that [playing] merengue is only for men," that any woman that plays it must be "a crazy girl, a bad girl." Beginning in the 1970s, however, factors such as the changing roles of women in the Dominican diaspora influenced women to enter occupations that had previously been considered for men only (see Pessar 1987). All-female merengue bands began to emerge in the middle 1980s. Pianist Belkis Concepción led the first of these in 1984. Singer Jocelyn Quezada told me in 1990 that many people had thought that women incapable of playing percussion and brass instruments; when this supposition was disproved, female merengue bands gained acceptance:

> People were kind of shocked, like, to see women . . . playing the tambora, the congas. You know, if you wear a dress, and you have to open your legs and hold the tambora, that's kind of awkward. And also the brass instruments . . . that's like macho territory. They never thought a woman could do that. They could play a violin, flute. They got up there, and they played those instruments, and people were shocked, and they were mostly curious to see if it works. The audience was not too thrilled; they thought, "Nah, well, a female group is not going to sound kosher." But when they go out there, they see the band, and they like it. . . . The audience really accepts the female groups now.

Although the rise of these groups represented a break with traditional gender roles, female merengue musicians were not necessarily politically active as feminists. Most of the all-woman merengue bands were formed by success-ful male bandleaders as businesses, and Dominicans often referred to them as the "property" of the male businessmen. For example, the most popular of these groups, Las Chicas del Can, was formed by Wilfrido Vargas and often accompanied Vargas's group on tour.

Merengue fan Rodríguez Vidal told me that female bands' popularity owed something to their sex appeal: "The female merenguera has a double attraction—the attraction of being a woman, and the contagious music. She can take advantage of her art in two ways—the show of being an artist, [and] her sex appeal, [which] attracts men." While sexuality was not central to the images projected by the first all-woman bands, the most popular wore se-ductive outfits and danced provocatively on stage. Their success inspired some male bands to use alluring women as backup singers or dancers. Tra-ditional-minded Dominicans criticized this practice as pornographic, while feminists called it sexist; indeed, the voyeurism on which it relies evokes Laura Mulvey's notion of the "male gaze" as central to patriarchal society (1975). However, Dominican anthropologist Carlos Andújar views erotic *Haiti* dance on the merengue bandstand as the same kind of celebration of fertil-ity that characterizes much African-influenced expression (p.c.).[11]

Formed soon after Belkis Concepción's group, the band Millie, Jocelyn, y los Vecinos (Millie, Jocelyn, and the Neighbor) included male musicians, yet many Dominicans considered it a female group because its leaders were women. One of the band's founders and lead singers, Millie Quezada, told me that although the rise of women's liberation helped the group gain acceptance, she did not consciously set out to challenge existing gender roles. Her sister and fellow group member, singer Jocelyn Quezada, disagrees: "We were making a statement, because Dominican men are very male chauvinist; I mean, women stay home and cook. So, when we stood up in front of a band, . . . women in the audience would identify with us. And the songs that we used to sing, we were at-tacking men: If you don't take care of your woman, you're going to lose her. So we had a lot of woman fans, we still do" (interview). Female merengueras often recorded songs with such feminist messages. Nueva canción artist Sonia Sivestre recorded a merengue that stated, "I don't want to be your laundress, your cook, your slave . . . I want to be your companion" (*No quiero ser tu lavandera, tu cocin-era, tu esclava . . . quiero ser tu compañera*), while another female band went far-ther, declaring, "I don't like marriage" (*No me gusta el matrimonio*).

Typically, the music's ironic, witty tone allowed serious subjects to be treated in a lighthearted way. "Me dejaste sola," composed by Luis Días and performed by Belkis Concepción, tells of a woman who did everything expected of Dominican wives, performing a seemingly endless list of chores. Despite all this, her man only smoked, drank, consorted with other women— and finally left her:[12]

ME DEJASTE SOLA
(You left me)

Colé el café a levantarme,	I made the coffee as soon as I got up,
Te hize tu té y tu chocolate.	I made your tea and your hot chocolate.
Te lavé ropa, remendé trapo,	I washed your clothes and mended a rag,
Pa' que fumara, yo compré	I bought you cigarettes, so that you
el tabaco.	could smoke.
Te emborrachaste, pagé la cuenta,	You got drunk, I paid the bill,
Y tú, de jumo, no diste cuenta.	In your stupor, you didn't even notice.
Tenía querías por todas partes.	You had girlfriends all over the place.
No te hice nada y me deshonraste.	I didn't do anything to you, and
	you degraded me.
Me dejaste sola.	You left me.
Te cargué el agua, lavé tus piernas,	I fetched the water and washed your feet,
Cuidé la casa y limpié la cisterna.	I took care of the house and cleaned
	the water tank.
Tenías querídas por todas partes.	You had girlfriends all over the place.
No te hize nada y tu me	I didn't do anything to you, and you
deshonraste.	degraded me.

Some feminists might argue that such songs have limited value, since they are often composed by men and do not resolutely challenge patriarchal attitudes. But singer Jocelyn Quezada told me that, in her opinion, by representing a female perspective they serve an important purpose: "[Women] identify with what we do. They come up to us and they say that 'You know, when I'm . . . [mad] at my husband, I just take one of your albums, and I pick a song, and I, just . . .—you know, 'cause they don't *dare* say that to their men. They're not supposed to . . . open their mouth." In a staunchly patriarchal culture, any open expression of the female perspective is a significant act of self-empowerment.[13]

It is important to remember that the assertion of women's viewpoints, Guerra's challenges to racist attitudes, and Ventura and Valoy's alliance with the nueva canción movement were exceptional cases. While bachata provided a voice for the disenfranchised Dominican majority, and nueva canción fomented resistance to an authoritarian regime, most pop merengue was allied with mainstream Dominican society and promoted conventional attitudes. As the social action group Convite argued, it was essentially escapist fare created by the capitalist music industry. Nevertheless, Convite member Luis Días, who has composed several merengue hits, also told me that merengue's malleable, multifaceted quality makes it the "the most complete" of all Dominican musics (p.c.); over and over it has provided an avenue for bold artistic innovations. Merengue's paradoxical alliance with both hegemony and resistance is typical of popular culture in general; as Richard Middleton writes, popular music puts its "finger on that space, that terrain, of contradiction—between 'imposed' and 'authentic,' . . . to organize it in particular ways" (1990: 7).

Johnny Ventura.
PHOTO COURTESY OF KUBANEY RECORDS

Felix del Rosario.
FROM A GAMA MUSICAL RECORDS ALBUM COVER.
PHOTO BY ROBERT C. LANCEFIELD

Wilfrido Vargas y sus Beduinos. PHOTO BY VICTOR CAMILO

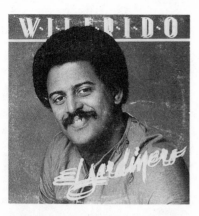

(top left) **W**ilfrido Vargas.
FROM A KAREN RECORDS ALBUM COVER.
PHOTO BY ROBERT C. LANCEFIELD

(top right) **L**os Hermanos Rosario.
PHOTO COURTESY OF KAREN RECORDS

(left) **J**uan Luis Guerra.
PHOTO COURTESY OF KAREN RECORDS

(below) **J**uan Luis Guerra and 4:40 in concert.
PHOTO BY VICTOR CAMILO

(l. to r. in photo below) **S**ongwriter Luis Días, saxophonist Tavito Vásquez, photographer Victor Camilo, and bandleaders Tony Vicioso and José Duluc.

PHOTO BY VICTOR CAMILO

Maridalia Hernández.

PHOTO COURTESY OF
KAREN RECORDS

Dancing to orquesta merengue in New York City, 1990.

PHOTO BY PAUL AUSTERLITZ

Chapter 7

Merengue on the Global Stage

Migration patterns have changed in recent years, as the Dominican out-migration proves. Those who have left the Republic since the 1960s are not cut off from their native land, and they are not displaced persons in their adopted countries—in short, they are transnationals. As the U.S. government heralded the Dominican Republic as a "showcase of the Alliance for Progress," and despite a growing middle class, most Dominicans' standard of living declined steadily in the late twentieth century. Electricity and water were scarce, and a series of economic recessions, each worse than the last, plagued the country. The deteriorating economy combined with Balaguer's repressive political policies and changes in U.S. immigration law to precipitate a massive out-migration of Dominicans to New York City, Puerto Rico, Venezuela, and elsewhere beginning around 1965. By 1990, an estimated 900,000 Dominicans—12 percent of the country's population—lived in New York City alone (Moya Pons 1995: 436).

While early studies of Dominican migration to the United States had posited that most entrants were from rural and lower-class backgrounds (González 1970; Hendricks 1974), later studies revealed that many were members of the middle class, forced to take jobs lower on the social scale than they would have held at home (Grasmuck and Pessar 1991: 13–14; Ugalde Bean, and Cárdenas 1979: 242). U.S. dollars Dominicans in the diaspora were able to send to their families in the Republic by the middle 1980s accounted for 10 percent of the Dominican GDP (gross domestic product), almost equal the amount earned by the county's chief export industry, sugar (Georges 1990: 236). During the recession in 1990, a Dominican leftist reckoned that the Dominican economy was "kept alive thanks to the remittances sent by Dominicans living abroad" (Féliz 1990: 13). Transnational capitalism and the information revolution have made the world smaller than it has ever been before. Such remittances, along with high rates of return migration and telephone links, forge a network between migrants' home and host societies that coalesces into what Roger Rouse describes as a "single community spread across a variety of sites," or a "transnational migrant circuit" (1989: 15).

While the view of immigrant musics as "transplants" from home societies is useful for looking at genres cut off from their countries of origin (Qureshi 1972: 38; Reyes-Schramm 1989: 25), it does not apply to transnational musics such as merengue. A comprehensive ethnomusicology of migrant musics must take into account the extent of contact between home and host societies, perhaps using a tripartite model that contrasts (1) *transplants*, in which the migrant community is isolated from the home society (usually for political reasons), such as Vietnamese music in the United States (see Reyes-Schramm 1989); (2) *transnational circuits*, in which there are high return rates and high-volume mass media communication between home and host societies, such as Caribbean musics in the United States (see Averill 1989a; Hebdige 1987; Roberts 1979); and (3) *continua*, in which home and host societies are geographically contiguous with poorly defined borders, such as Mexican music in the United States and Haitian music in the Dominican Republic (see Loza 1993; Peña 1985). In today's world, transnational circuits and continua are clearly more common than transplants. Even in earlier periods, wholesale transplantation of music was not necessarily the rule; for example, European immigrants to the United States often influenced popular music in their home countries.[1] Border identities were celebrated as early as 1916, when *Atlantic Monthly* writer Randolph Bourne called for Anglo-Americans to "make something out of this trans-national spirit [that characterizes immigrant cultures] instead of outlawing it" (Glick Schiller, Basch, and Blanc-Szanton, 1992: 212).

Nevertheless, the information revolution has brought a qualitatively new type of transnationalism in recent years. As we have seen, in the Republic merengue served as an aesthetic border zone, mediating the outside influences that inundated the country during the late twentieth century. The music also became central to life in the Dominican diaspora and found fans among non-Dominicans.

Merengue Unfolds in the Diaspora

Primitivo Santos was the first merengue bandleader to settle in the United States after Trujillo's fall. While he had been one of the first to adopt conjunto instrumentation, Santos for years retained the staid complexion of 1950s merengue. (Shortly before his return to the Dominican Republic in 1985, after more than twenty years in New York City, Santos began to incorporate the later merengue innovations; perhaps his impending move sharpened the bandleader's awareness that his earlier style was passé in the music's country of origin.) Although Joseíto Mateo never lived in the United States, he had worked there steadily since 1963, when he sang with típico accordionist Luis Kalaff in New York's Club Caborojeño. In 1967, Mateo, Alberto Beltrán, and Primitivo Santos brought merengue to New York's colossal Madison Square Garden for the first time. For Mateo, that concert was a rite of passage symbolizing the arrival of merengue on the global stage (interview). Also promoting merengue among Latinos in the United States was New York–born Dominican Johnny Pacheco, who had led Latin bands in the city since the early 1960s. Although he specialized in Cuban music (as most New York Latin musicians did in the 1960s and early 1970s), Pacheco included the merengue "Los diablitos" on his 1973 LP "Tres de café y dos de azucar." Other *salseros* soon began to record merengues, and by 1976, the music's popularity among New York Latinos was surpassed only by salsa's (Rondón 1980: 291).

As New York's Dominican community grew, bands specializing in merengue sprang up in the city; by the early 1980s, several such groups were active in the metropolitan area. The first of these to establish a following in the Dominican Republic was Millie, Jocelyn, y los Vecinos, founded by sisters Millie and Jocelyn Quezada (lead singers) and their brother Rafael (lead trumpeter, musical director, and arranger). The family band began by playing informally at neighborhood parties in New York and in 1973 made its first record and turned professional. Millie Quezada told me that in its early days, the group provided "Dominican Yorks," as Dominican New Yorkers were known, with a link to their home country:

> The nostalgic effect—that's the reason that los Vecinos were formed. We really were very nostalgic. We didn't have any of the language or anything. And so, we kind of were trying to keep our roots, and out of that, the group was born. It was really out of a need, not only us, but the people in our neighborhood, to kind of stay in tune with what was happening with our music and with our cultural background in general. . . . That's why we called the group los Vecinos.

Her words bear out one Dominican writer's belief that merengue is the New York Dominican community's single most important "physical-cultural" link with the Republic (Canelo 1982: 33). In 1982, Millie y Jocelyn became popular outside of New York City, generating hits in the United States, the Dominican Republic, Colombia, and Panama. Rivaling, although not surpassing, Los Vecinos' position as the top New York–based merengueros were La Gran Manzana (The Big Apple) and the New York Band, both of whose names refer to their hometown, possibly as a marketing strategy. La Gran Manzana was notable for its innovative use of synthesizers and for its Haitian influence, while the New York Band specialized in merengue flavored with baladas and *soca* (Trinidadian popular music), and featured four distinctive lead singers.

In Puerto Rico as well, the large Dominican community spawned excellent merengue bands. The first of these to gain transnational exposure was Conjunto Quisqueya, displaced from the top spot when singer Jossie Esteban and his group La Patrulla 15 moved to Puerto Rico in 1976. Esteban's charisma and witty texts, which often used streetwise double entendres, made his music phenomenally popular both in the diaspora and in the Dominican Republic. The group's success also rested on its unique musical style, created by arranger and pianist Alberto "Ringo" Martínez, whose arrangements relied heavily on the maco rhythm and made inventive use of electronically produced clap sounds evocative of disco.[2] Although musically excellent, the bands based in New York and Puerto Rico did not differ qualitatively from Dominican groups; merengue was stylistically transnational.

Merengue's popularity occurred in spite of, rather than through the efforts of, the established Latin music industry. This industry failed to actively promote merengue, partly, music promotor George Nenadich told me, because executives felt that the Dominican Republic was not a lucrative market, but also because the Puerto Ricans, Cuban Americans, and Italian Americans who dominated the industry had no nationalistic interest in doing so. Some Dominicans felt that promoters in New York and Puerto Rico actively worked *against* merengue; according to Dominican deejay Willie Rodríguez, the powerful New York Latin-music company Fania "boycotted" it, not only in New York City and Puerto Rico, but even in the Dominican Republic itself (1986: 17). One New York–based Latin-music promoter told me that "we don't manage any merengue artists; tropical [Spanish Caribbean] music is still divided in this sense." Perhaps referring to misunderstandings between non-Dominican promoters and Dominican musicians, he added that "we used to book merengue, but due to mishaps, we closed it down." To many Dominicans, merengue's global success vindicated the situation; Rodríguez called merengueros "guerrillas of the music, who go to Puerto Rico and place a bomb in the places that they play" (21).[3]

Merengue among Non-Dominicans

Playing with a New Jersey–based Central American band in 1983, I was surprised to discover that the Central American dancing public preferred merengue to Honduran or Salvadorian music. A few years later, the *Village Voice* reported that salsa, "besieged by merengue, . . . is going through hard times" (Fernández 1986: 18); merengue was the most requested Latin Caribbean music in the United States by the mid-1980s. Salsa promoter Nenadich explained to me that Dominican music gained favor during a period when salsa's popularity had ebbed: "What happened was that around 1978, salsa was going through a total downfall. Sales came to a stop, and it became boring and repetitious. And merengue came in with such flair and such excitement. And the artists were completely different, and it revived the generation. Plus, it was something new for the new generation of Latinos that were listening to tropical [or Latin Caribbean] music. It was sort of like a light that came into the darkness." He also said that merengue's popularity in New York served as a conduit for its diffusion all over Latin America and beyond: "Everything happens through New York—music, fashion, food; . . . merengue became popular in the outside world through New York."

While merengue linked Dominican immigrants with their home country, non-Dominicans found it appealing partly because it is easy to dance. After taking a whirl on the dance floor, New York's former mayor Ed Koch called it "the one dance that you can do from the moment you're born" (Cocks 1986). As always, the music's sensuality also contributed to its appeal; *Time* magazine declared that "partners can press hips close enough to grind grain" (ibid.). While merengue negotiated island Dominicans' identity in the face of increased contacts with the outside world, the foreign stylistic elements it incorporated helped make the music palatable to non-Dominicans. Disco influences appealed to New York's Puerto Rican youth, for example, and balada elements contributed to merengue's popularity in South America.

The music's success inspired non-Dominicans to form merengue bands in the mainland United States and Puerto Rico. I performed with several such groups in New York City, Connecticut, and Detroit from 1982 to 1995. In the early 1980s, most Puerto Rican bands in Connecticut specialized in salsa and occasionally played merengue "oldies." By the mid-1980s, however, many of these groups were reproducing the latest merengue innovations, and by the end of the decade most specialized in merengue, with salsa relegated to a minor role in their repertoires.

A common language and similar culture made patterns of Dominican adaptation in Puerto Rico qualitatively different than in the mainland United States.[4] Long popular in the neighboring island, merengue was firmly entrenched there by the 1970s and 1980s. Although salsa remained the preeminent Puerto Rican popular music, merengue soon became the most requested form for dancing. Some Puerto Rican salsa musicians initially resented the inroads of Dominican musicians, who usurped valuable performance opportunities. As time went on, however, Puerto Ricans embraced merengue so thoroughly that many came to consider it their own. In 1995, one Puerto Rican singer told me that "merengue has now become a part of Puerto Rican culture" (Arroyo interview).

Many excellent all–Puerto Rican merengue bands were formed. In 1992, the Dominican pianist and arranger Ringo Martínez produced a group called Caña Brava, whose image was cunningly crafted. First, four light-skinned Puerto Rican men, dressed more like balada or rock singers than merengueros, fronted the band as singers and dancers. Second, naming the group after Cibao accordionist Toño Abreu's composition and featuring this merengue in its repertoire were deliberate marketing strategies, the group's spokesperson, singer Arturo Arroyo, told me: "We wanted to enter the Dominican market. Being Puerto Ricans, we didn't know if the Dominican Republic would accept us. And so, we decided, . . . as a strategy, to use a típico name from the Dominican Republic, and [to play] a classic merengue, also típico to the Dominican Republic, to facilitate our entry." Ultimately, Puerto Rican merengue passed the toughest test: The authentically hot sound of Caña Brava and other bands met with success, not only in Puerto Rico and the United States, but in the Dominican Republic itself.

Transnational Identities

Merengue became a prime marker of ethnic identity for Dominicans in the diaspora. A German politician, irritated by immigrant communities' independent style in another context, once complained that "we called for workers, and we got people" (Grasmuck and Pessar 1991: 208); while migrants may be part of the transnational economy, they negotiate circumstances according to their own agendas. As Nina Glick Schiller, Linda Basch, and Cristina Blanc-Szanton point out, "By maintaining many different . . . identities, transmigrants express their resistance to the global political and economic situations that engulf them" (1992: 11). I once asked a Dominican teenager in New York what kind of music she liked. "American" music, she replied. I pressed, asking whether she cared for Latin music—salsa and merengue. She answered that salsa was not much to her liking but that "of course I like merengue. I'm Dominican." My impression was that although merengue was not her preferred style, she considered it a patriotic duty to speak well of the national music.

Few issues of national and cultural identity have gone untouched by the diaspora experience. Subjected to virulent racism, some Dominicans in the United States embraced the philosophy that "black is beautiful" in the 1960s and 1970s (del Castillo and Murphy 1987–88: 62). Return migration to the Dominican Republic influenced the progressive mood of the 1970s, when many Dominicans reevaluated the island's traditional Eurocentrism. Band-leader Tony Vicioso, however, who performs Afro-Dominican music in New York City and conducts educational workshops in public schools, feels that the diaspora experience has been a double-edged sword. While living in the United States inspired some Dominicans to overcome the conventional Eu-rocentrism, North American materialism only abetted other migrants' notion that Afro-Dominican traditions are part of a backward life-style best left be-hind (p.c.).

Noting what she considers an identity crisis among New York Puerto Ri-cans, bandleader Millie Quezada predicts that Dominicans will face a simi-lar crisis: "Third- and fourth-generation Puerto Ricans have lost, are losing, their language, are losing their heritage. They're going through some kind of turmoil about who they really are, they are Americans or they are Puerto Ri-cans. That's going to happen with the Dominicans." She hopes that promot-ing merengue will preserve Dominican identity in the diaspora: "We're try-ing to do something to keep what we have, because to lose your identity is kind of . . . rough. Living in the United States is—you don't belong here, and you're not there, so you're kind of in limbo."

The influence of diaspora Dominicans eventually grew so strong that it affected Dominican identity on the island, an outcome poignantly reflected in a photograph sent by a rural Dominican woman to her husband in New York, who had supported his family through remittance dollars for many years. To express the well-being of the family and its debt to the father, the woman dressed her sons in borrowed suits and traveled to the nearest city to have the photo taken in a studio, where the family posed in front of a back-drop of the Brooklyn Bridge (Grasmuck and Pessar 1991: 17).

In addition to affirming Dominican identity for those in the diaspora, merengue's stylistic pastiche came to embody a transnational identity for all Dominicans. But identifying with more than one place can be disori-enting. President Balaguer called those in the diaspora *los dominicanos ausentes* (absent Dominicans), an absence not confined to the physical realm, as Millie Quezada told me; it is also feeling psychologically lost between two cultures: "Balaguer has called us absent Dominicans; we're kind of in nowhereland. I feel that we, as Dominicans living outside, are *more* Dominicans because we kind of miss the homeland." She confirmed the idea that merengue plays a decisive role in forging identities on the cusp of the transnational circuit: "We make a point of keeping the music and of telling people who were are. We can survive here. Not just survive, but make something of ourselves and, at the same time, be proud of who we were, where we came from. It's a big deal for us."

In addition to the economic dependency, a "psychic dependency" between Dominicans abroad and on the island caused a mania for emigration (Grasmuck and Pessar 1991: 17); as Dominicans sometimes say, island dwellers are *"loco para irse"* (sic), or "obsessed with the idea of emigrating" (Bray 1987: 164).

Describing the process of applying for a visa to the United States, Juan Luis Guerra's merengue "Visa para un sueño" expresses this state of mind.[5]

VISA PARA UN SUEÑO
(Visa for a dream)

Eran las cinco en la mañana.	It was five o'clock in the morning.
Un seminarista, un obrero,	A seminarian, a laborer,
Con mil papeles de solvencia,	With a thousand documents proving economic solvency,
Que no les dan pa' ser sinceros.	Which do not allow them to be honest.
Eran las siete en la manaña.	It was seven o'clock in the morning.
Uno por uno en el matadero,	Lined up at the slaughterhouse,
Pues cada uno tiene su precio,	Everyone has his price,
Buscando visa para un sueño.	Seeking a visa for a dream.
El sol quemándoles las entrañas,	The sun burning their entrails,
Un formulario de consuelo,	With only application forms to console them,
Con una foto dos por cuatro,	And a two-by-four-inch photo,
Que se derrite en el silencio.	Which melts away in silence.
Eran las nueve en la mañana,	It was nine o'clock in the morning,
Santo Domingo, ocho de enero.	Santo Domingo, the eighth of January.
Con la paciencia que se acaba,	With patience almost at an end,
Pues no hay visa para un sueño.	There are no visas for a dream.

Buscando visa de cemento y cal,	Seeking a visa of cement and limestone,
¿Y en el asfalto, quién me va	Whom will I meet in the concrete
a encontrar?	jungle?
Buscando visa, la razón de ser,	Seeking a visa; a reason to be,
Buscando visa para no volver.	Seeking a visa; never to return.
¡La necesidad, que rabia me dá!	Necessity; I am infuriated!
¿Golpe de poder, que más	A forceful blow; what else can
puedo hacer?	I do?
Para naufragar, carne de la mar,	I'll be shipwrecked, food for the sea,
La razón de ser; para no volver.	Never to return; a reason to be.

The first three lines of the song speak of Dominicans from all social backgrounds arriving at the U.S. consulate at five o'clock in the morning to apply for visas. Many Dominicans seek tourist visas to visit relatives in the diaspora and then overstay the visas to work in the United States. Applicants must convince the U.S. immigration service that they are not only economically solvent but so firmly established in the Republic that it would be disadvantageous to overstay the visa and work in the United States. Because even Dominican professionals often earn no more than U.S. $300 monthly (as of 1991), few Dominicans are able to convince immigration officials of this. Aspiring migrants thus sometimes use falsified documents, which, as the fourth line of Guerra's song seems to imply, preclude an honest interview. At seven o'clock, applicants continue to wait for what likely will be a butchering of their hopes. Line three of stanza two refers to an applicant's musings about bribing the customs officials and also hints at the price in dignity that petitioners pay in the degrading application process.

Near the end of the song the applicant reflects on the coveted destination as a concrete jungle; while most Dominican migrants hope to return to the Republic someday, the applicant most likely will not. "Reason to be" in may refer to the idea that pining for migration has become a raison d'être. The song ends with a reference to the practice of Dominicans emigrating without visas to Puerto Rico in small boats (*yolas*). Because the yolas are not always seaworthy, and emigrants must travel at night to avoid detection by U.S. immigration officials, many have lost their lives in shipwrecks. The sound of a helicopter is woven into the musical mix, evoking the constant presence of the U.S. immigration department on Puerto Rican shores.

The difficulties of transnational identity were mitigated, in part, by merengue's phenomenal success on the global stage. As Millie Quezada explained to me: "I think that [Dominicans] are very proud to know that merengue has escalated into what it is today because, first of all, it makes the country known, because people want to know where is our music coming from, so it's a way of advertising the country. And also, I tend to think that they kind of feel a sense of pride to think that their music has been able to be assimilated by other countries. You know, that's not something that happens often."

In their frequent reports on foreign tours of merengue groups, Dominican newspapers concentrate on performances in Europe, with typical island Europhilism. One 1991 newspaper headline read "4:40 Songs Break Records in Europe" (Cazorla 1991); another article, entitled "Merengue: The International Promoter of Our Country," reported on the German release of a Coco Band LP (Arias 1991). The German version of the record came with liner notes describing merengue instrumentation, with a map of Latin America and the Caribbean that highlighted the Dominican Republic, and with the phone number of a Berlin dance school that offered merengue dance lessons.

Millie Quezada hopes that incorporating North American elements into merengue will make the music, and Latino culture in general, relevant to all Hispanics residing in the United States. "By incorporating these influences, "we are trying to . . . capture the generations of Hispanics that are kind of being lost to rock and to other kinds of music," she told me. "We want them to kind of keep looking for their roots. We're hoping that continues, and so we're trying to rescue them. To keep the youth." Merengue does, in fact, represent pan-Latino identity to some non-Dominicans in the United States. In my experience, however this is more often true outside of New York than within that city. In New York, ethnic boundaries between Latino groups are often sharply drawn, and merengue generally marks Dominican, rather than pan-Latino, identity. In my early days playing Latin music in New York, a Puerto Rican friend once said, "Look across the street there, see that building? That's a Dominican building; almost everyone that lives in there is Dominican." Like most English-speaking New Yorkers, I was unable to distinguish between the various Latino groups; I asked, "How do you know?" He answered, "Well, it's hard to say, exactly; they are just *different*. For one thing, they're always playing those merengue records."

Puerto Ricans outside New York City, however, often feel that merengue belongs to them. When I included merengue in my junior high school music classes in Connecticut, Puerto Rican parents thanked me for teaching "their music." When I visited Puerto Rico in 1995, I was stunned when one woman said that "merengue is not a Dominican thing" (García interview). But the innovative Dominican arranger Ringo Martínez helped me to understand that this music has indeed been absorbed by Puerto Ricans: "Being so close to us, it is logical that . . . [they] would naturally assimilate merengue. . . . These people have added something to the continuing history of merengue." The incorporation of merengue into Puerto Rican culture comes on the heels of a long tradition of Puerto Rican domestication of Cuban musics (see Manuel 1994). Dominican music has also found a place in mainstream Anglo-American culture: A 1995 midwestern television advertisement for the Ameritech telephone company mentions it in passing, and Juan Luis Guerra was asked to present awards in several *non*-Latin categories at the 1992 Grammy award ceremonies (Pacini Hernandez 1992a: 359). Like the tango, cha-cha-chá, and bossa nova, merengue thus became a sonic expression of what Renato Rosaldo calls the "implosion of the Third World into the First" (1988: 85).

Chapter 8

Enduring Localism

$\mathbf{P}$erhaps the most striking aspect of Dominican music culture is the degree to which urban, mass-mediated, transnational musics coexist with rural, orally transmitted musics created by local populations. Even commodified merengue continues to operate on local, as well as national and transnational, levels. As Mark Slobin writes, while the transnationalization of popular culture occasions legitimate fears of cultural "gray out" (Lomax 1968: 4), local arts continue to thrive (Slobin 1992: 1). The whole story of contemporary culture can only be told by considering trends of both loss and invention, according to James Clifford: "To reject a single progressive or entropic metanarrative is not to deny the existence of pervasive global processes unevenly at work. . . . Indeed, modern ethnographic histories are perhaps condemned to oscillate between two metanarratives: one of homogenization, the other of emergence, one of loss, the other of invention. In most specific conjectures both narratives are relevant" (1988: 17).[1]

The Dominican Merengue Complex

Large numbers of Dominicans live in the countryside today; the 1991 population was estimated at 45 percent rural (Georges 1990: 7). Here the "extraordinary religiosity" that Frank Moya Pons observed in nineteenth-century

Dominican culture (1988: 215) still manifests itself in frequent Afro-Catholic rituals in which local music plays a central role. As Martha Davis writes, these festivals are well attended: "There seems, in any region, to be a network of fiesta enthusiasts who attend as many musico-religious events . . . as possible within a radius of up to some eight to ten kilometers from their homes" (1976: 44). I once met a campesino who planned to attend five such all-day or all-night events in the space of a week and a half. In addition to rural rituals held for specific magico-religious purposes, towns celebrate annual regional secular/sacred patron saint's day festivals (fiestas patronales). These feature performance of local recreational and sacred music and dance styles as well as appearances by internationally known pop stars. I once experienced a vivid example of the coexistence of transnational and local music at a rural Afro-Dominican ceremony held in honor of a saint. To my left, a chapel emitted local sacred drumming, while to my right, a group of young people socialized around a car whose radio blasted the latest pop merengue hits.

Some Dominican rural musics are performed only in specific localities; for example, the sarandunga is known only in the town and outlying areas of Baní. Other genres, widely diffused, display extraordinary stylistic variation according to region; for example, while Dominicans in most areas of the Republic perform palos, this genre's melodies, rhythms, and dance steps vary greatly from region to region (see Davis 1976). Similarly, several stylistically distinct rural merengue variants, together constituting a *Dominican merengue complex*, are played in rural regions of the Republic.[2] The most often performed of these, other than merengue cibaeño, is merengue palo echao (or pri-prí) of the South and East.[3] While few regional merengues are played today, a vital pri-prí culture persists. This music calls for one singer, the single-headed balsié drum, the güira, and the one-row accordion (instead of the more common two-row model). Its 12/8 rhythm is markedly different from the 4/4 of merengue cibaeño (see musical example 12). While pri-prí's choreography differs from that of merengue cibaeño, both variants are independent couple dances performed in the ballroom position.[4] Many residents of Villa Mella, a town adjacent to the capital of the Republic, are avid pri-prí dancers, and functions called *pri-prís* are held especially for its performance. Also, the New York City–based band Asa-Difé, which specializes in original compositions built on rural Afro-Dominican musics, performs jazz-tinged pri-prí arrangements on traditional percussion instruments, guitar, key-boards, and saxophone.

Musical Example 12
Merengue Palo Echao (Pri-Prí)

*Balsié Key:

1 = left hand open tone
2 = right hand slide with left foot pressure on drum head
3 = right hand finger slide
4 = right hand open tone

Pri-prí often serves as a secular component of religious rituals and figures prominently in the annual festival of a Villa Mella mutual aid society, La Cofradía de los Congos del Espíritu Santo (The Holy Spirit Congo Brother-hood).[5] I once attended a *banco*, or funeral commemoration, performed by a Villa Mella mutual aid society that included pri-prí performance. A musician informed me that this music was featured at the banco because the deceased woman had been an enthusiastic dancer of pri-prí: "She would dance pri-prí for one or two weeks at a time." At the banco, the spirit of the deceased woman entered the body of a living woman, who proceeded to dance pri-prí for sev-eral hours. Spirits usually enter only family members at such events, but mu-sicians informed me that this woman was "like a sister" to the deceased.[6]

Other regional merengue variants include the following: merengue de atabales, performed in the East on two hand drums called atabales (or palos), and
several güiras in 12/8 meter (see musical example 13);[7] merengue redondo,
performed on the Samaná peninsula on accordion, tambora, and güira in 4/4
meter (see musical example 14);[8] and merengue ocoeño, performed in the
south-central town of Ocoa in 4/4 meter on accordion, marimba, balsié, güira,
and a tube-shaped shaker called the *maraca ocoeño* (Ocoa-style maraca).[9] As

Musical Example 13
Merengue de Atabales

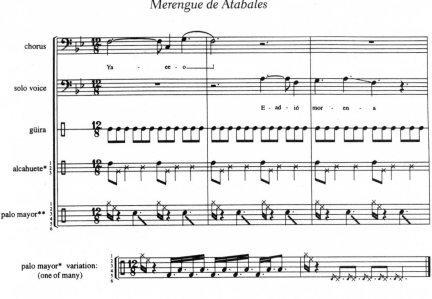

*Alcahuete Key:

1 = right hand open tone
2 = right hand slap
3 = left hand muff

** Palo Mayor Key:

1 = right hand muff
2 = left hand bass muff
3 = descending glissando produced by an open
   stroke with the right hand and a left
   hand first finger slide
4 = right hand open tone
5 = left hand open tone
6 = bass muff with grace note, produced
   with both hands

noted, the fact that all the merengue variants combine independent-couple dance choreography with local, Afro-Dominican elements suggests that they developed from the contredanse-derived nineteenth-century ballroom forms.[10] Other than pri-prí, these musics are rarely performed today; merengue de atabales and merengue redondo are sometimes played at patron saints' festivals, while merengue ocoeño has fallen into obscurity.

Musical Example 14
Merengue Redondo

*Tambora Key for merengue redondo:

The drum is held between the legs, with one head facing up.
A stick is held in the right hand.

1 = right hand (stick) open tone
2 = right hand (stick) light rim shot
3 = right hand light rim shot with a simultaneous left hand
    middle finger tap on the drum head
4 = left hand middle finger tap on the drum head

In addition to overshadowing the other regional variants, merengue cibaeño has influenced the development of a rural form called variously *palos amerengueao* (merenguized palos), *palos cibaeños*, *girapega*, or *gerapega* (Davis 1976: 215). Performed in the central Monte Plata area and as far south as La Victoria, this form combines merengue cibaeño choreography with palos drumming; musicians told me that it has been solicited as a recreational dance at religious festivities because its choreography is similar to pop merengue.[11] As Davis points out, the appellation *palos cibaeños* obviously refers to Cibao influence on the form, while the designation *girapega* derives from the verb *girar* (to twirl or gyrate), suggesting an "'embraced whirl' with a sensuous implication"; palos amerengueao resembles merengue cibaeño in its sensual overtones and dance turns (ibid).

Like the other regional merengues, accordion-based merengue cibaeño is often performed at fiestas patronales and for recreational dancing at religious rituals. Unlike the other variants, however, merengue cibaeño is played in all areas of the country. Martha Davis attended a "Vodú" celebration near the capital in which a Cibao accordionist played merengue during a break from sacred activities (1987: 319,391). The line between sacred and secular music at such events is not always clear; as Manuel Miniño writes, merengue cibaeño has made inroads into even the liturgical portions of magico-religious ceremonies in recent years: "Merengues [cibaeños] with liturgical texts, performed on güira, accordion, saxophone, and tambora, are now being included in ceremonies in various parts of the country. This illustrates Vodú's power of assimilation and adaptation" (quoted in Davis 1987: 318). It also illustrates merengue's ability to adapt.

Although some observers have suggested that performing for tourists often changes local music cultures (Lewin and Kaeppler 1988: xiv, 187), such does not seem to have been the case for merengue. The pop merengue boom of the 1970s and 1980s inspired típico musicians to perform for tourists in such spaces as the Malecón, the beach-front boulevard in the capital where tourists and Dominicans stroll and sit in the evenings. Accordion, tambora, güira, and marimba groups approach people there, playing and asking for money. Musicians have also played at the airport. Other than providing much-needed employment, however, the only effect that I have observed is the benign one of revitalization: Tourism provides a responsive context for contemporary accordion-based merengue, whose performers are highly skilled and expressive. Of course, playing merengue for tourists is related to the genre's status as a national symbol. One Dominican woman told me that she believes that the alegría that merengue musicians generate at the airport offers the ideal greeting to tourists arriving in the Republic: "When any foreigner arrives, . . . the first impression will be one of merriment. There are other things that we do not show tourists. But . . . if a person hears music upon arriving in a country, he or she will immediately feel content, and say that there is a lot of happiness in this country. As soon as he or she arrives, we present him or her with Dominican music, so that every visitor will know what merengue is" (Rodríguez Vidal interview). Her suggestion that some Dominican things are *not* shared with tourists reflects the strategic nature of the choice of merengue cibaeño as a national symbol.

A Transnational Local Music

Although members of all social classes heard accordion-based merengue on the radio during the Trujillo era, típico music was never performed in elite Dominican ballrooms at that time. In New York, however, accordionist Luis Kalaff played in large, luxurious nightclubs beginning in the early 1960s. While Kalaff's music remained true to típico style, he used an expanded group consisting of accordion, tambora, güira, alto saxophone, bass, and conga drums in these larger venues.[12] His widely disseminated recordings may have influenced groups in the Dominican Republic to adopt this expanded instrumentation during the 1970s.

On the island, Tatico Henríquez was the most influential and highly regarded accordionist from the time that he took over for Pedro Reynoso in El Trio Reynoso until he died in 1976.[13] Using accordion, tambora, güira, and marimba format during most of his career, his less nasal singing style was markedly different from that of Pedro Reynoso. During the merengue boom of the 1970s, típico groups began performing in the finer nightclubs, and Henríquez substituted the marimba with electric bass and added conga drums and saxophone to his group to facilitate performance in the larger venues. Other groups followed suit, and the expanded instrumentation of accordion, tambora, güira, alto saxophone, and electric bass became standard for típico music in Cibao's principal city, Santiago de los Caballeros (Román and Luis interviews). The music these expanded accordion-based groups played incorporated influences from pop merengue, and the resulting blend of tradition and innovation was sometimes called *merengue típico moderno* (modern típico merengue).[14]

Lucrative performance opportunities and enthusiastic fans fostered the development of this music in Santiago, where the most innovative and influential of the new wave of accordionist/bandleaders were Francisco Ulloa and Bartólo "El Ciego de Nagua" (The Blindman from Nagua) Alvarado. Ulloa introduced unison rhythmic breaks (*cortes,* or cuts), increased tempos, and a fiery exuberance borrowed from Johnny Ventura and Wilfrido Vargas. El Ciego de Nagua, whom many consider the dean of típico bandleaders, developed a hot yet refined style marked by intricately interwoven accordion and saxophone jaleos. Other notable típico moderno groups were formed by Agapito "El Moderno" Pascual, who used electronic percussion, and Rafaelito Román, who initiated brilliant collaborations with Dominican jazz master saxophonist Tavito Vásquez. (Vásquez also performed with el Ciego de Nagua.) Several female accordionists became active in merengue típico moderno, most notably Manuela Josefa Cabrera, "Fefita la Grande" (Fefita the Great), loved for her musical excellence and dynamic stage presence.

Típico moderno not only incorporated innovations and outside influences but preserved traditional stylistic characteristics, such as sectional form, that had been dropped by the large orquestas. It even came to exert its own influence on pop merengue. Of course, borrowing between típico and salon musics was nothing new; it had been central to merengue and the other contredanse transformations since the nineteenth century.

Structured around orally transmitted arrangements, típico moderno makes prodigious use of collective improvisation. As accordionist Fefita la Grande explained to me: "Musicians hardly ever . . . play a merengue the same way live as he or she recorded it. There are always variations, because . . . you find another *mambito* [*mambo,* jaleo figure], and you stick it in, and the public likes it." When musicians introduce a new rhythmic pattern, their bandmates invent complementary figures. Accordionists usually take the lead, but any player may initiate rhythmic changes; if a tamborero plays a pattern that captures the spirit of the moment, the other musicians may invent parts to highlight the shift. Specific principles of musical organization govern the rhythmic relationships; for example, saxophone and accordion jaleos often link up in the manner illustrated in musical example 10. (Similar patterning of rhythmic shifts characterizes West African music, in which lead drummers often cue dialogues with supporting drummers.)

Merengue típico moderno displays greater rhythmic complexity than does pop merengue. Dancers respond to its perpetually changing pulse; as one fan told me, orquestas generally use "the same rhythm, mostly, more than típico groups, which play a lot of variations, and you can move better." Típico percussionists developed new rhythms called the *guinchao, volao*, and *a juste*,[15] and became known for their flashy, highly improvisational style; as 4:40's percussionist Isidro Bobadilla told me, they "never keep time sedately." As in pop merengue, arrangements often consist solely of repeating jaleos. Saxophonists play patterns in tandem or juxtaposition with accordionists and also take wildly exuberant improvised solos marked by jagged lines, wide leaps, and timbre manipulation; this high-spirited music has been aptly described as an "avant-garde improvisational fest in Caribbean disguise" (McLane 1991: 28).[16]

Típico moderno lyrics display great continuity with earlier merengue cibaeño; compositions by Ñico Lora and Toño Abreu are still often played. Not a large city, Santiago extends a small-town hospitality even at luxurious nightclubs, where típico performers often greet audience members over the public address system. As with musical elements such as jaleo figures, song texts often arise spontaneously. Adolfo Díaz told me that improvised merengues are frequently dedicated to audience members: "For example, I could make up a merengue [dedicated to you] when you arrive at a fiesta. And invent phrases, compose two or three verses right on the spot, and it would work out fine."

Accordion-based merengue was long considered the province of Cibao campesinos, but Dominicans from all social classes and all geographic regions began to take interest in it during the merengue boom. By the late 1980s, accordion-based groups often alternated with large orquestas in top night spots throughout the Dominican Republic as well as in the diaspora. Santiago de los Caballeros naturally led the way in the típico rage; even during the recession of 1991, when inflation hit 100 percent and residents of the capital rarely went dancing, accordion-based groups filled Santiago dance halls even on weeknights. My own observations corroborate bandleader Eladio Romero Santos's opinion of the public's musical preference:

If you are in a nightclub where two groups are playing, one típico group and one orquesta, you will notice that more people will get up to dance when the típico group plays than when the orquesta plays. And when they get up to dance . . . you will see their emotion, their wonder, their delight. And those who do not get up to dance will move in their seats. And when the orquesta, when it begins to play, some of the people will get up to dance. But you will see that they won't have the same vigor that they had when they got up to dance to típico music. (Interview)

While típico musicians adopted aspects of pop merengue, arrangers in the capital became interested in accordion-based music. In the late 1980s, Sergio Vargas's band used típico melodies and accordion sounds on the synthesizer and Henry Hierro's Orquesta had a hit with El Ciego de Nagua's "El diente de oro." Juan Luis Guerra's 1994 album *Fogaraté* included collaborations with Francisco Ulloa's típico group, and just as his forays into bachata had done for guitar-based music, this venture into accordion-based merengue lent the style a new legitimacy.

The development of a típico moderno industry was pivotal to the music's growth. Merengue típico cibaeño was first disseminated through the mass media in the 1950s, when it was a staple of La Voz Dominicana programming. In the post-Trujillo years, few radio stations in the capital played it, while Cibao stations continued to air live accordion-based merengue. Recordings by El Trio Reynoso, Luis Kalaff, Tatico Henríquez, and Guandulito had been available since the 1950s, but the most important record company for accordion-based merengue was founded in the early 1970s by impresario José Luis in Santiago. In addition to producing recordings, Luis promoted the musicians, often thinking up catchy nicknames (Luis interview). In spite of its wide diffusion, merengue típico moderno stayed in touch with its native region; its foremost interpreters were all Cibao natives, and the bulk of its audience remained cibaeños.[17] Impresario José Luis told me these ties exist not only because the music is local to the Cibao, but also because it is *promoted* mainly in this region: "It sells more in the Cibao. It always sells more here, because the groups are located here. It sells in the capital too, but we do more promotion here, and so it sells more here. If it was promoted in the capital, it would sell just as well there, and it would sell even more, because there are more people there." By the 1990s, merengue típico moderno was a transnational music; Santiago accordionists performed regularly throughout the Dominican Republic and the diaspora, several típico moderno groups were based New York City, and the music had been performed in Europe.

The most adventurous of the típico bandleaders, accordionist Agapito "El Moderno" Pascual uses electronic percussion and plans to incorporate synthesizers into his arrangements. Típico merengue's growing visibility inspired rocker David Byrne to ask Pascual to record with him a merengue/rock fusion piece, "Call of the Wild," which is included on Byrne's 1989 album, *Rei Momo*. Although Pascual considered this "an honor," he told me he also felt that Byrne and cocomposer salsero Johnny Pacheco had inadequately oriented him for the project; they had simply asked him to make up an accordion-based introduction and then recorded the rest of the tune. Pascual said, "It wasn't that hard for me, but . . . I had to really make an effort, because it isn't easy to come out, to do something that you're not really leaning towards doing; to put yourself in the middle of a piece that you do not know."

While Byrne's compositional technique does not amount to a wholesale appropriation of Pascual's music, it does raise ethical questions central to all world music fusion. The approach resembled Paul Simon's with the Los Angeles Chicano group Los Lobos. While "All around the World, or The Myth of My Fingerprints" is credited to Simon, much of its musical substance was created by Los Lobos. Band member Louis Pérez said that when the group "got into the studio, there were no songs. . . . We expected him [Simon] to have a song ready for us to interpret when we met him in Los Angeles, but he said, 'You guys just play,' and we said, 'Play what?' We just worked up a bunch of stuff that he eventually got a song out of " (Feld 1988: 35).

The unequal power relationships between northern and southern hemisphere musicians color any homage that such projects pay to so-called "world musics," as Steven Feld suggests. When the Nigerian bandleader Fela Kuti incorporates James Brown's innovations, the economic stakes are small, and the result is a revitalizing circuit. But when Simon or Byrne uses Los Lobos's or Pascual's ideas, the economic "gap between the lion's share and the originator's share [is] enlarged, and the discourse of race and ripoffs [is] immediate and heated" (1988: 37).

Cibao Music and Dominican Identity

Simultaneous operation on transnational, national, and local levels characterizes pop merengue as performed by orquestas as well as merengue típico moderno; despite its entrenchment as a national symbol and its global diffusion, orquesta merengue did not become completely disassociated from its region of origin. Noting that the Cibao is the birthplace of the national music, orquesta leader Cheché Abreu explained to me that "a person from the Cibao is a person [who], even if he is from the upper class, the highest class, understands merengue [cibaeño] just as much as a campesino from the most remote countryside, because it is his music. . . . it's like the Cuban: A Cuban from the city as well as from the country understands the *son montuno*, because it is his music."

The *"hierarchy of regions,* in which the Cibao had always been dominant," that Hoetink noted in the nineteenth-century Republic is still evident today (1982: 50). Cibaeños sometimes even jokingly express a stronger regional than national identity; a Santiago native once told me that "I am prouder to be cibaeño than I am to be Dominican." While regional dialects are rarely sources of pride for noncibaeños, I have heard Cibao natives joke that "I speak two languages: Spanish and cibaeño." As in past periods of Dominican history, the Cibao's greater distance from African-influenced culture than other regions of the Republic accounts, in part, for its primacy.[18]

Dominicans generally consider Afro-Dominican drumming *música folklórica* (folkloric music), a designation that brings images of campesinos and academic study to mind. By contrast, they view syncretic, accordion-based forms such as merengue cibaeño as *típico,* which Langenscheidt's dictionary glosses as "picturesque, quaint, cute, of interest to (or popular with) tourists."

El Ciego de Nagua's merengue tipico moderno group in Santiago de los Caballeros, Dominican Republic, 1991.

PHOTO BY PAUL AUSTERLITZ

Francisco Ulloa.

PHOTO COURTESY OF KAREN RECORDS

Dancing to accordionist Adolfo Díaz's merengue tipico moderno group in New York City, 1990.

PHOTO BY PAUL AUSTERLITZ

Merengue musicians playing accordion, marimba, tambora, and güira for tourists in Santo Domingo, Dominican Republic, 1985.

PHOTO BY PAUL AUSTERLITZ

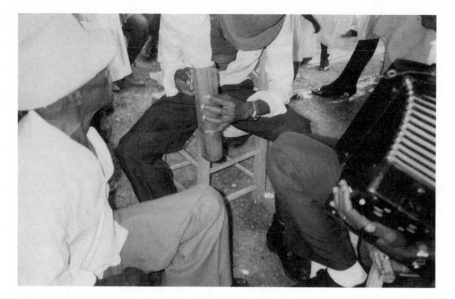

Merengue palo echao, or pri-prí musicians, playing balsié, güira, and one row accordion at a banco, or funeral commemoration ceremony, in Villa Mella, Dominican Republic (the South), 1991. PHOTO BY PAUL AUSTERLITZ

Tambora player performing merengue redondo in Samaná, Dominican Republic, 1991.
PHOTO BY PAUL AUSTERLITZ

Dancing to gerapega, or palos amerengueao, in La Victoria, Dominican Republic (the South), 1995.
PHOTO BY PAUL AUSTERLITZ

Chapter 9

Conclusion

Although merengue is central to Dominican life and identity, some argue that it is not a representative symbol of the Dominican Republic, home to a wealth of African-derived drumming styles whose cultural importance and sheer beauty are denied by the country's dominant Hispanophilic ideology. In efforts to heal "socialized ambivalence" regarding national and racial identity (Herskovits 1937: 295–96), groups such as Convite and Asa-Difé perform Afro-Dominican musics in urban areas; Fradique Lizardo suggests that palos drumming be adopted as the national music (Ysalguez 1975a: 51); and Martha Davis proposes that "Dominican music of greater African influence [than merengue] . . . be recognized by all as genuinely Dominican and gradually become another national symbol. In this way, musical symbols of national identity would more accurately reflect the nature of Dominican culture" (1976: 23). Considering the music in local, national, and transnational perspectives, this book argues that Dominicans have used merengue cibaeño as a national symbol precisely *because* its syncretic quality appeals to the prevailing African-derived aesthetic without offending the prevailing Hispanophilism.

Colonialism lies behind the ambivalence that prevails in the Dominican

Republic. After Spain's retreat as an imperial power, when North American neocolonialism made itself felt, Dominicans were antagonistic toward the impediments that the United States placed on their sovereignty but at the same time attracted to Yankee wealth and modernity. Musicians repeatedly responded to this quandary by incorporating U.S. and other outside elements into an avowedly *Dominican* merengue as their lives became increasingly transnational. The music thus derived viability as a national symbol because it mediated the contradictions of Dominican life, a capacity inherent to much popular culture. "Cultural populists" argue that the expression of societal contradictions is the unique province of oppositional constituencies, but popular arts are not tied to specific groups of people (McGuigan 1992); instead, disparate constituencies use them to promote diverse agendas.[1]

Merengue's history includes periods resembling Adornoesque fantasies of mass culture in the service of the state as well as periods in which the music was clearly oppositional. McGuigan's "critical populism" calls for observers to unravel patterns of hegemony and resistance in popular expression (1992: 5). While merengue was enlisted in opposition to neocolonial hegemony in the transnational arena, it was usually allied with the status quo within the Dominican Republic. Unlike most local musics, merengue was performed in elite ballrooms as early as the nineteenth century. Despite its association with local culture and its rejection by some urbane Dominicans, the music's relative palatability, as compared to Afro-Dominican drumming, made it attractive to elite and bourgeois cultural nationalists during the early twentieth century. And given Trujillo's Hispanocentric worldview, merengue was an effective form of propaganda for his repressive regime. As Convite suggested, late twentieth-century merengue was essentially an escapist product created by the capitalist music industry. This is especially clear when one compares the music to nueva canción, which was self-consciously oppositional, and to bachata, which was a grass-roots alternative to the fare offered by the dominant music industry.

Of course, there were exceptions to merengue's alliance with the status quo. Johnny Ventura's use of merengue to galvanize Constitutionalist troops during the aborted Revolution of 1965 represented an oppositional stance, and Juan Luis Guerra's celebrations of Afro-Dominican culture challenged conventional ideas about race. Nevertheless, most late-twentieth-century merengue was linked to conventional, mainstream society.

But the picture is different in the transnational arena. As Arnold Perris points out, musical nationalism becomes an especially effective oppositional strategy when a subjugated nation's art gains fame on the global stage: "For the tiny nation, so unequal to her conqueror, every cultural achievement which brought her international attention . . . was a subtle act of resistance" (1985: 38). Merengue's status as a national symbol was intimately tied with opposition to neocolonial hegemony. Resistance could be overt or oblique. The Cibao elite's interest in merengue was linked to the propaganda campaign waged against the 1916–24 U.S. occupation of the Dominican Republic. Like Ñico Lora's song "La protesta," this campaign articulated an openly anti-American position. Meanwhile, the pambiche origin theory's ironic comment on the U.S. marines' choreographic ineptness served as a subtle form of "semiological guerrilla warfare" (Eco 1986: 135–44; Fiske 1989: 19, 23–49). In the diaspora, marginalized Dominicans felt vindicated by merengue's transnational success; as Dominican deejay Willie Rodríguez said, merengueros in Puerto Rico were "guerrillas of the music" (1986: 21).

Subsuming outside elements within the national music subtly challenged the inundation of transnational popular culture that accompanied transnational capitalism, although the ensuing stylistic changes were so drastic that some Dominicans argued that merengue should be renamed. Pointing out that North American popular music has repeatedly changed names over the years, Papa Molina argued that "when the rhythmic structure changes, . . . the genre's name should change" (p.c.), and bandleaders' coinage of neologisms for their trademark styles was consistent with this perspective. In addition to undergoing stylistic changes, however, the music retained many traditional elements, and in any case, audiences and industry moguls kept calling it *merengue*. While musical types can be classified according to stylistic characteristics, symbolism also plays a part in genre definition. Jeffrey Kallberg argues that music-makers and their audiences enter negotiated "contracts" in which genres carry specific meanings (1988: 242, 243); similarly, Charles Keil writes that "the very naming of musics is a declaration of solidarity" (1985: 126). By appropriating outside elements into the national music, merengueros forged an expressive borderland ruled by the Dominican aesthetic.

Ninety years after W.E.B. Du Bois articulated the notion of a black "double consciousness" ([1903] 1989: 3), Paul Gilroy argued that this condition remained central to black Atlantic life, and that its "inner ambivalences" are "neither simply a disability nor a constant privilege" (1993: 161).[2] Influenced by Gates's discussion of the "double-voiced" richness of North American black folklore and literature (1988), Gary Tomlinson argues that jazz composer Miles Davis's artistry is marked by the contradictions of his marginal status as an African American on one hand and his mainstream upper-middle-class background on the other: "From this cultural ambivalence, refracted through the unique lens of Davis's psyche, arose a powerfully synthetic Signifyin(g) voice. From ambivalence—or, better, from multivalence—arose musical dialogue" (1992: 86–87).

Poised at expressive borderlands, merengueros, like jazz musicians, partake of a creative tension that imparts to their fluid expression a poignancy with special meaning for the multicultured Americas.

Notes

Preface

1. Although the term *participant observation* originally referred to field methods in sociology and anthropology in which the researcher took part in the daily lives of members of the community under study (see Kluckhohn 1940; Vidich 1955), in ethnomusicology, the term most often refers to the method advocated by Mantle Hood (1960), in which scholars become performers of the music they research.
2. Many non-Hispanic musicians are deeply involved in Latin music, the most prominent of whom include Barry Rogers, Marty Sheller, Cal Tjader, and Larry Harlow.
3. Dominican treatments include numerous magazine articles (see the series by Ysalguez), a book on merengue lyrics (Brito Ureña 1987), and a brief but informative bilingual social history of the music (del Castillo and García Arévalo 1989); also see Pacini Hernandez (1989a, 1991, 1995).
4. Similar schemes have been used by others. For example, Thomas Turino grounds his study of Peruvian music in consideration of history and politics at "local, national, and international levels" (1993: 118), and Krister Malm has written about local, national, and international musics (1992).
5. The multi-locale approach was previously used in ethnomusicology by Gage Averill (1989a).
6. Much recent ethnomusicology of popular music combines ethnography — in varying degrees — with history (cf. Averill 1989a; Guilbaut 1993; Loza 1993; Pacini Hernandez 1995; Waterman 1990).

Chapter 1

1. This and all translations throughout the book are by the author, unless noted. The Torres anecdote is repeated in Coopersmith (1945: 86–87, 1949: 19–20); Hernández (1927: 6); and Roberts (1972: 106–7).

2. Although a similar song text also appears in a nineteenth-century writing by a Spanish military officer, he calls the song a *mangulina* rather than a merengue (López Morillo 1983: 81).

3. Melville Herskovits notes that only a "small proportion of the slaves" came from Madagascar (1958: 47).

4. Rafael Damirón suggests that merengue evolved from the mangulina but provides no supportive evidence (1947: 22).

5. Curt Sachs (1938) provides photos of a Malagasy drums similar to the Dominican tambora. Fouchard notes that, despite the similarity of his own and Lizardo's theories, the Dominican scholar does not cite his Haitian source (1988: 81). Moreover, Lizardo makes no mention at all of Haitian mereng. As we have seen, conspicuous inattention to Haitian music is typical of much Dominican scholarship. While Lizardo's theory is revolutionary in acknowledging the African influence on merengue, his omission suggests that Dominican repudiation of Haiti runs deeper than rejection of Africa.

6. Population estimates have ranged from 72.9 percent mixed, 16.1 percent white, 10.9 percent black, and 1 percent Asian (Lizardo 1979: 25) to the Dominican government's reckoning of 60.4 percent mixed, 28.1 percent white, and 11.5 percent black (Wiarda 1969: 74).

7. In 1881, Pedro F. Bonó complained about the hardship of long-distance travel in the Republic, caused by roads that were "by a proper definition, not roads: those in the neighborhood are paths; those in the savannas are cattle-trails; those denominated royal are nameless passages where absolutely no one has ever lifted a finger. . . . Every old Dominican who finds himself obligated to make a journey, . . . spends the evening before as agitated as if it were the one preceding a battle" (Hoetink 1982: 47).

8. Because race is a socially constructed category, such assessments can be misleading to North Americans; in the United States a person with less than one-quarter African blood is often considered "black," while in the Dominican Republic the same person may be considered "white" (Wiarda 1969: 74). Most Dominicans from the Cibao would not be considered "white" in the United States.

9. Contrasting it with "state coercive power, " Antonio Gramsci defines hegemony as "the 'spontaneous' consent of the great masses of the population to the general direction imposed on social life imposed by the dominant fundamental group, . . . caused by the prestige that the dominant group enjoys because of its position" (1971: 12). Raymond Williams explains that hegemony amounts to a "commonsense" worldview shared by all social classes, which, while often incorporating oppositional positions, ultimately serves the interests of the status quo (1991: 419).

10. The term *Santo Domingo* also refers to the entire colonial entity of Hispaniola and is loosely used to refer to the Dominican Republic. For the Dominican history that follows, Moya Pons 1995 is my primary source; Moya Pons 1986, Pérez-Cabral 1968, and Bosch 1988 have also informed my perspectives.

11. By choosing to name their country *Haiti,* said to derive from an indigenous word meaning "mountainous land," Haitians express an anticolonial posture. By contrast, the Dominican use of a European name (La República Dominicana, or The Dominican Republic) as their country's official designation and an indigenous name (Quisqueya) as a vernacular one reflects mixed feelings rooted in colonial experience.
12. Through most of the nineteenth century, the *Dictionary of the Royal Spanish Academy of Spain* glossed the word *nación* as "the aggregate of the inhabitants of a province, country, or kingdom," making no reference to sovereignty until its 1884 edition changed the definition to "a State or political body which recognizes a supreme centre of common government," and "the territory constituted by that state" (Hobsbawm 1990: 14).
13. Eric Hobsbawn calls such ethnic feelings "proto-nationalism" (1990: 46).

Chapter 2

1. For example, Dominican ethnomusicologist Julio César Paulino suggests that the Caribbean progeny of the contredanse are *"transformaciones de la contradanza"* (contradance transformations [p.c.]), and John Szwed and Morton Marks (1988) document "Afro-American Transformations of European Set Dances." Throughout the book, I use the abbreviation *p.c.* to indicate a personal communication to me—a conversation, letter, fax, or phone call—from an individual.
2. This later developed into the North American contradance.
3. In addition to being a French adaptation of the English name for the genre, the term *contredanse* seems to have alluded to the "longways" choreography in which men and women lined up opposite (*contre*) one another to perform sequenced figures (as in the Virginia reel) (Sachs [1937] 1963: 421).
4. The Caribbean cinquillo rhythm characterizes the Cuban *son* (it is implied in the *clave* rhythm), *tumba francesa,* and *danzón;* Haitian *Vodou* drumming (especially *petwo* style), *rará,* and *konpa;* and Dominican merengue, palos, congos, and *gagá.* In spite of its name, the Caribbean cinquillo is a syncopated duple rhythm (consisting of two pulses with off-beat accents) rather than a true quintuplet (of five equal durations). In performance, Haitian mereng musicians sometimes stretch the Caribbean cinquillo to create rhythms that lie between the duple cinquillo and a true quintuplet; according to David Yih, Vodou drummers also sometimes do this (p.c.). Such stretching is aptly described as a "5/8 effect" in Gradante (1980).
5. A version of the contredanse called the *contradanza española* developed in the Spanish royal court during the early eighteenth century (Cadilla de Martínez 1950: 69). Cuban scholars, however, believe that the French, rather than the Spanish, contredanse was the primary influence on the Cuban contradanza (Carpentier 1961: 71–78; Galán 1983: 59). The African element of the so-called French, or Saint-Domingue, heritage in Cuba survives today in the black mutual aid society called the Tumba Francesa, whose dances combine French figure-dance choreography performed in seventeenth-century period dress with African-influenced drumming (see Alén Rodríguez 1991).

6. Carpentier believes that this rhythm, called the *cinquillo cubano* by Cubans, came to Cuba from Haiti (1961: 75).

7. Like the Venezuelan *fulía* and *bambuco andino*, this music is in 5/8 meter, which seems anomalous, since duple and 12/8 meters predominate in the Caribbean (Soto 1993: 41–42). Cristóbal Soto affirms that Venezuelan merengue uses a true 5/8 rather than the "5/8 effects" of Haitian mereng (p.c.). Colombian merengue, however, is in 2/4 or 6/8 meter and exists in two forms: a rural type performed by wind and percussion *costeño* groups of the northern coast, which are best known for playing the *cumbia* (Elissa Simon, p.c.), and since the 1940s or 1950s, a more commercial type performed by accordion-based *vallenato* ensembles, possibly influenced by Dominican merengue (List 1980; Quiroz Otero 1983: 213–21).

The nineteenth-century Caribbean merengues may also have influenced the development of *maringa* in Sierra Leone. Blacks from the Americas visited and moved to the West African coast during the nineteenth century, bringing creolized expressive forms that have influenced the development of maringa, a syncretic ballroom dance music associated with the elite of North American descent and considered a Sierra Leone "national dance" (Collins 1985: 41, 1987: 177). Maringa eventually lost favor to high-life music. In the mid-twentieth century, Sierra Leonian musicians were exposed to Caribbean music and often performed "Latin numbers and Meringues" (*sic*) (King in Collins 1985: 42). Flemming Harrev cautions that a distinction should be made between nineteenth-century maringa, which may or may not have been influenced by Caribbean music, and postwar Sierra Leonian merengue, which was undoubtedly influenced by Caribbean merengue (p.c.). Another type of maringa, with no known Caribbean connections, is performed in Central Africa (Harrev p.c.; Mukuna 1979).

Although group dance musics developed differently in the English than in the Spanish and French colonies, some fascinating correspondences exist between Afro-American adaptation of these forms in the United States and the Caribbean; early jazz pianist James P. Johnson, for instance, has said that "a lot of my music is based on set, cotillion, and other southern country dance sets and rhythms. . . . Real ragtime . . . was based on cotillion dance tunes, stomps, drags, and set dances" (Szwed and Marks 1988: 33).

8. According to Joan Corominas's etymological dictionary, the Spanish word *merengue* was first documented in 1760, the French *méringue* in 1739 (1954: 351). The *New Encyclopedia Britannica*, however, reports that the confection made of whipped egg whites and sugar called *méringue* was invented by a Swiss pastry chef named Gaspanni in 1720. Little evidence supports the suggestion that méringue gets its name from an English buccaneer dance called the "merry-ring" (Dumervé 1968: 307).

9. Also see Robert Graves's (1952) translation of the novel.

10. See Turino 1993: 122.

11. This idea later became official policy in the Dominican Republic; the country's contemporary *cédula*, or national identification card, still uses the terms *indio claro* and *indio oscuro* (light-skinned Indian and dark-skinned Indian) to refer to light- and dark-skinned Dominicans of mixed European and African descent, respectively.

12. The timbal (or *timbales*) is a small version of the timpani, often used in Cuban music.

13. The melodic rhythms of "Juana Quilina" are similar to those typical of the Cuban contradanza (see Fernández 1989: 122). The Dominican statesman Federico Henríquez y Carvajal, who was born in 1848 (Coopersmith 1949: 21), taught "Juana Quilina" to Nolasco as it appears in musical example 2 (Nolasco 1939: 60, 1948: 164, 1956: 341).

14. A similar text is quoted by Emilio Rodríguez-Demorizi (1971: 123).

15. Ubaldo Gómez informs us that string instruments such as the *tres* or tiple were also used, as were the *atabalito* and *balsié* drums (in Rodríguez Demorizi 1971: 153). The use of balsié, however, is questionable, since this instrument is not local to the Cibao (Lizardo 1988: 269). The wind instrument was usually the baritone horn, although one document indicates use of the saxophone as early as 1898 (Rodríguez Demorizi 1971: 178–79). For the tambora, it is often said that the right-hand skin must come from a male goat, and the left-hand skin from a female goat that has not given birth, since a skin stretched during labor lacks the proper timbre. However, contemporary tambora makers generally disregard this practice, requiring rather that the left-hand skin be tuned higher than the right-hand skin (see Alberti 1975: 83; Hernández 1969: 60; Lizardo 1988: 350–59).

16. The harmonica also arrived from Germany and was occasionally used to play merengue (Fondeur n.d.; Hernández interview and in Incháustegui 1988b: 9).

17. Some Dominicans still criticize the accordion for having "impeded the development of" (Pichardo n.d.a) or even for "strangling" (Lizardo in Ysálguez 1976a: 1) merengue.

18. Décimas are philosophical in tone and consist of ten octosyllabic stanzas that loosely follow the rhyme scheme a-b-b-a-c-d-d-c-c-d.

19. The instrument's harmonic limitations were also criticized in Europe, however: A Finnish folklorist wrote that accordions were "folk music's greatest enemy," and that there was only one way to escape this menace—"Burn them" (Häggmann 1976: 87).

20. The well-known merengue "Juangomero," based on this theme, (see Chapter Three), can be heard at selection 4 on the CD.

21. This is probably a locality.

Chapter 3

1. Between 1903 and 1934, the United States also intervened in Honduras, Cuba, Nicaragua, Mexico, Panama, and Haiti (Manuel 1995: 263).

2. Merengue típico cibaeño is also called *merengue liniero*, or merengue of the (northern) border region.

3. Ñico Lora's group can be heard at selection 1 on the CD. L. Amanzor González Canahuate (1988) includes short biographical articles about and songs by Lora and many other Dominican composers.

4. The tambora can also be tied around the waist with a string to facilitate playing while standing up. Oral tradition credits the development of the one-stick tambora technique to Flinche, a tamborero who often performed with Ñico Lora. As Fradique Lizardo notes, however, the true origin of this playing technique is not known (1988: 29).

5. Because it resembles a kitchen grater, the metal version of the güira is sometimes called *güayo*. See Luis Alberti's (1973) and Miquea Guaba's (1995) methods for tambora.

6. With few hard data on early merengue cibaeño dance style to go on, this discussion relies on oral testimony and reconstruction from later performance practice.

7. "Desiderio Arias" was collected by Julio Hernández, who wrote a piano arrangement of the piece.

8. Alvarado calls this song "La invasión del '16"

9. Although merengue cibaeño is most often notated in 2/2, I write it in 4/4, which most clearly reveals the music's four-beat rhythmic cycle. A sectional merengue cibaeño can be heard at selection 1, and a pambiche can be heard at selection 2 of the CD.

10. In Spain, the term *jaleo* refers to the shouts of encouragement and rhythmic hand clapping of spectators at flamenco performances.

11. Mercado writes that it was previously known as the *rumba* (this bears no direct relationship to the Cuban rumba) (1983: 144).

12. According to Pichardo, a female accordionist, Monguita Peralta, brought this song to Puerto Plata from the Haitian border (n.d.a: 1).

13. In a similar Dominicanization of American speech, the one-step-inspired merengue estilo yanqui was sometimes called *Juan Ester* (John Esther) (del Castillo and Arévalo 1988: 27). Phonetic analysis explains the transformation: in Cibao speech, an initial *s* must be preceded by the vowel *e*, an *s* followed by a consonant is inaudible, a final *p* is barely audible, and a final *r* is pronounced *i*; one-step [wan ete] becomes Juan Ester [wan etei].

14. The pambiche is still performed today as a musical form, but merengue estilo yanqui dance has fallen into disuse. I have thus been unable to find any specific information on its choreography.

15. Hernández researched and wrote about típico music (1927, 1969), as did Peña Morel and García (García 1972; Peña Morel's fascinating writings are, lamentably, available only in manuscript).

16. Among these is the melody in musical example 7 (Incháustegui 1973a).

17. Selection 3 on the CD is an arrangement of this piece recorded by Nilo Menéndez's band in New York City in 1925 (Incháustegui p.c.). The recorded version alters the form as it is indicated in Hernández's original piano composition and features the Caribbean cinquillo rhythm in the güiro throughout. Also see the publications of Hernández's compositions (1927, 1964).

18. The first movement of this work is to be played "No muy aprisa, al tiempo del merengue" (Not very fast, at the tempo of merengue).

19. Selection 5 on the CD is a recording of "Compadre Pedro Juan." Because the initial melodic rhythm of this song, which reverses the first two values of the Caribbean cinquillo, is used in much merengue, I call it the *Dominican cinquillo*.

20. Selection 4 on the CD is a 1950s jazz-tinged arrangement of "Juangomero." Although this piece is most often performed to pambiche percussion rhythms, early concert and salon interpretations likely did not use the tambora and güira, rendering its cinquillo rhythms and sectional form in a stately manner similar to the danza.

21. Later names for the band included Orquesta Lira de Yaque, Orquesta Presidente Trujillo, Orquesta Generalísimo Trujillo, and Orquesta Santa Cecilia.

22. The term *domesticating* is borrowed from Slobin 1992: 66.

Chapter 4

1. José del Castillo and Manuel A. García Arévalo credit this merengue to Isidro Flores (1989: 31–33), while Augustín Pichardo (n.d.a) maintains that a merengue bearing this title was composed by Ñico Lora in the same year. *Colú* and *bolo* in the lyrics are cockfighting terms that refer to political parties (del Castillo and García Arévalo 1989: 33).
2. Trujillo's eventual dictatorship relied largely on intelligence and other counterinsurgency arts that he learned from the U.S. marines (Black 1986: 26).
3. Julio Alberto Hernández told me that Trujillo had considered using Orquesta los Hermanos Vásquez rather than Alberti's group, but while their musical excellence was never questioned, the dictator felt that these musicians lacked the decorum and social graces necessary to perform for the oligarchy. Deborah Pacini Hernandez suggests that their darker skin might also have been a factor (p.c.). Later in the regime, when Trujillo's brother Hector Bienvenido ("Negro") and Joaquín Balaguer served as puppet presidents, the band changed its name to Orquesta Generalísimo Trujillo.
4. Selections 4 to 7 on the CD illustrate the Trujillo-era merengue sound. See Austerlitz 1992: 147–49 for a musical analysis of Alberti's recording of "El sancocho prieto."
5. See Manuel 1985 on the syncopated bass patterns.
6. See saxophone virtuoso Crispín Fernández's books of jaleos (n.d.) and merengue melodies (1986).
7. Selection 5 on the CD features an improvised solo by Tavito Vásquez.
8. Selection 6 on the CD is Joseito Mateo's ranchera-merengue hit, "Jardinera."
9. See Austerlitz 1992: 156–58 for analysis and musical notation of this piece.
10. Accordionist Luis Kalaff was one of the first musicians to perform the mangulina in the capital.
11. Selection 7 on the CD is a recording of "San Cristóbal."
12. Ramon Ferreras (n.d.) documents the details of Trujillo's often misogynistic love life. Also see Crassweiler 1966: 79–81.
13. This lamelliphone is a descendant of the Central African *sanza* or Shona *mbira*. Although small, hand-held versions of this instrument have sometimes been used in the Americas, most western hemisphere lamelliphones are large and serve as basses in ensembles. Similar to (and derived from) the Cuban *marímbula*, the Dominican marimba is a plywood box on which four to six metal tongues are mounted. The player sits on the box and plucks its tongues with a piece of leather (see Thompson 1975–76). While Caribbean lamelliphones are rarely tuned to exact pitches, El Trio Reynoso's recordings prove that they can be; in these performances, the marimba outlines tonic and dominant harmonies in half notes during the merengue section and often switches to Afro-Cuban anticipated bass rhythms during the jaleo section.
14. Guandulito's music can be heard at selection 8 on the CD.
15. In 1990 and 1991, I conducted field research on the following regional merengue variants, which were likely performed during the Trujillo era: *merengue de atabales* of the East, *merengue ocoeño* of the south-central town of Ocoa and outlying regions, *merengue redondo* of Samaná, and *merengue palo echao* (also called *pri-prí*) of the South. These musics are described in Chapter Eight and notated at musical examples 12–14. I also recorded Samaná's *baile del chivo* (goat dance), which some researchers consider a

merengue variant. Originally a rural form, the baile del chivo became popular in Samaná high-society clubs during the 1940s. Associated with a double-entendre song, "Chivo Florete," and featuring choreography that mimics goats performing sexual intercourse, it was later rejected by Samaná socialites. (Coopersmith 1949: 59; Tejada Ortiz 1984: 259).

16. This life-or-death test may have led to the anti-Haitian Dominican saying that "he who is black must speak clearly" (*el que es negro tiene que hablar claramente*); that is, to demonstrate that one is not Haitian.

17. Dominicans still refer to the Dessalines massacre as a formative event in the development of their country. Dominican radio journalist K-Chiro feels that many people "confuse" the U.S. and Haitian occupations: It is more common for Dominicans to complain about the Dessalines massacre than about the atrocities committed by U.S. forces during the 1916–24 and 1965 occupations (p.c.).

18. See Davis on Afro-Dominican magic, healing, and religion (1987). Researchers often refer to these practices as Vodou, but practitioners rarely, if ever, use this term.

19. Such denial still occurs. A friend who once chastised me for having a picture of a saint or *misterio* in my room had a similar picture in her own. I mentioned this to Dominican anthropologist Paula Paulino, who told me that "the more a Dominican criticizes such practices, the more likely it is that he or she believes in them" (p.c.).

20. As mentioned in Chapter One, *Quisqueya* is a Native American term for Hispaniola, still often used in the Dominican vernacular.

21. As stated in Chapter Three, enramás (enramadas) are structures in which rural dances are held.

22. The dance bands included Super Orquesta San José, directed by Papa Molina; Orquesta Angelita (named after Trujillo's daughter), directed by Eulogio Cesteleiro and Rafael Solano; and Orquesta Melodica, directed by Pepín Ferrar. Típico groups were led by Pedro Reynoso, Isidro Flores, Dionísio "Guandulito" Mejía, and Luis Kalaff.

23. These included the Luis Kalaff merengue "Apretaíto," sung by Joseíto Mateo.

24. Angel Viloria's music can be heard at selection 9 on the CD.

25. Helio Orovio p.c. The Cuban pachanga is distinct from the pachanga that developed in New York City in the early 1960s. Although the latter took its name from the Cuban dance, the New York City pachanga was based on Cuban-derived *charanga* music, which was related to the cha-cha-chá and performed on violins, flute, and timbales (see Thompson 1961).

26. Gage Averill suggests that Trujillo's interest in the fair might also have been motivated by a sense of competition with Haitian dictator François "Papa Doc" Duvalier's 1949–50 international fair (the Bicentenaire) (p.c.).

27. Averill applies this term to Haitian konpa as well as to Dominican merengue. Because Trujillo's use of merengue predated Duvalier's use of konpa, however, I am tempted to argue that the *ur*-leitmotif was Dominican.

Chapter 5

1. Although this prohibition remains in effect, musicians performing at private parties are still sometimes asked to play Trujilloist merengues. I once played at an elite social

function in which the Trujilloist merengue "San Cristóbal" was requested. While some band members were willing to play it, one musician refused, saying that Trujillo had killed several of his relatives. When the bandleader asked me to suggest another merengue, I called for "Desiderio Arias," forgetting that this song had been banned by Trujillo because of its association with a rival caudillo. The party goers seemed not to notice.

2. Cuban bandleader Arsenio Rodríguez had pioneered the conjunto format in the 1940s. The return to this instrumentation by non-Cubans in a period when contacts with Cuba had diminished may have represented a self-conscious search for authenticity.

3. Primitivo Santos's band was notable for its innovative addition of the baritone saxophone to alto and tenor saxophones.

4. Pérez had composed this piece in 1955 as a promotional piece for a military dance band. Negrito Truman recorded it for release in Puerto Rico 1959, and Joseíto Mateo also recorded it. Luis Pérez told me, however, that its exuberant quality was not appreciated until the 1960s.

5. Solano had previously led hotel and restaurant bands, but 1970 marked the year that he took a group to "the street," that is, entered the open market (Solano 1992: 199).

6. A CIA officer who had briefed President Johnson on Balaguer quotes the U.S. president as saying, "Get this guy in office down there!" (Black 1986: 41).

7. By 1991, there were six color stations and U.S. cable; 80 percent of urban Dominicans had television sets by the early 1990s (Straubhaar and Viscansillas 1991: 55).

8. Many jobs provide a two-hour midday break during which workers can go home to eat. Additionally, the high unemployment rate leaves many Dominicans in the house, and many women traditionally do not work outside of the home.

9. Juan Bosch did not return to the presidency at this time because he had left the PRD to found the PLD (Partido de la Liberación Dominicana, or Dominican Liberation Party) in 1974.

10. According to Meindert Fennema and Troetje Loewenthal (1987: 33), as "Trujillo's intellectual right-hand man," Balaguer was a mastermind of Trujilloism. The full story of his role in the Trujillo regime will likely not be told until the caudillo's death. Today Balaguer's regime respects a measure of freedom of speech, but issues regarding the president are not always discussed openly. A knowledgeable Dominican informed me that a standard source on Trujillo, Robert D. Crassweiler's biography (1966), was written with Balaguer as a chief informant, with the stipulation that Balaguer's role in the Trujillo regime not be treated in the book (p.c.).

11. See Tejeda and Báez Ureña 1994 for information on other late twentieth-century merengue bands.

12. Although not himself an arranger, Vargas employed an increasingly common technique by which bandleaders and songwriters gave musical ideas to arrangers. Arrangements, then, were collaborations between songwriters, bandleaders, and arrangers. This setup is also used in Anglo pop music; John Lennon and Paul McCartney used it with George Martin. Wilfrido Vargas worked extensively with arranger Luis Pérez, who is responsible for many innovations in merengue. Also seminal to the behind-the-

scenes development of merengue in the late twentieth century were the studio players who recorded the music, such as tamboreró Angel Miró "Catarey" Andújar, saxophonist Crispín Fernández, and pianist Sonny Ovalles.

13. "Abusadora" was composed by a Colombian, Calixto Ochoa (Deborah Pacini Hernandez p.c.). See Austerlitz 1992: 237–38 for an analysis of Vargas's version.

14. Consisting of an eighth rest followed by three eighth notes, the saxophone jaleo employs
the typical merengue cibaeño saxophone rhythm illustrated in musical example 10.

15. "Men sirop" means "here's the syrup" (i.e., "here's the sweet and tasty stuff") in Haitian Creole (Gage Averill p.c.). Vargas's "Jardinero" should not be confused with the
Joseíto Mateo hit "Jardinera," discussed in Chapter Four.

16. Musical example 11 omits the cowbell part used in some variants of this rhythm, il-
lustrating the version popularized by Los Hermanos Rosario and others in the late
1980s. Having arranged for virtually all of the important conjuntos, Pérez has a wealth
of information on, and a relatively objective view of, the development of merengue
style. The brilliant Dominican percussionist Julito Figueroa was also an invaluable
source on merengue drumming (p.c.). As Isidro Bobadilla of the group 4:40 told me,
the sources of percussion rhythms are rarely documented: "I don't think that anyone
can claim to be the creator, because we are talking about things that happened alone;
they were transmitted alone. It was born in a barrio." The conga rhythm of the maco
is often used in conjunction with the típico merengue cibaeño tambora patterns illustrated at musical example 10. The resulting rhythm is called *el caballo* (the horse).

17. These groups generally omitted the cowbell part used in earlier variants of the rhythm.

18. The type of salve referred to here itself stands at the cusp of the sacred and secular; as
Davis explains, it is "basically secular within a religious context" (1981: 26).

19. Alan Merriam suggests that African time is "nonlinear" (1982: 457). Jonathan D. Kramer
(1988) draws an analogy between the architectonic structures of Western music (e.g.,
sonata form) and Western linear time as expressed in Christian doctrine (e.g., the Last
Coming) or in the nineteenth-century novel (plot with climax). He describes a continuum of types of musical time, ranging from "goal-directed linear time" (sonata form) to
"vertical time" (similar to Kpelle "moment time"), suggesting that nonlinear time became prevalent in the West as composers became influenced by non-European music.

20. Charles Keil notes a similar aesthetic in jazz (1966: 347).

21. The number of radio stations also grew, with more than two hundred stations, AM and
FM combined, in the Dominican Republic by 1991 (O. Rivera interview).

22. Shady dealings, while widespread in the merengue industry, are difficult to research. Perhaps the least savory aspect of the merengue industry is the pervasive involvement of the
underworld; as one source told me, "It's hard to make it in the merengue business unless
you have a really heavy drug dealer behind you, which most of them [the bands] do."

23. See Waterman 1982 on parallel economic and social relationships between musicians
and bandleaders in Nigeria. Merengue composers have often fared no better than musicians. Songs are frequently recorded without granting songwriters royalties. A composer told me that the rights to one of his pieces had been appropriated by a recording
company based in the United States. Knowing that travel abroad was beyond the songwriter's economic means, the company informed him that he must make a trip to the
United States to regain the rights.

Chapter 6

1. The other founding members of 4:40 were Roger Zayas-Bazán, Maridalia Hernández, and Mariela Mercado.
2. Merengue-jazz was less visible in the late twentieth century than during the Trujillo era. Nevertheless, Tavito Vásquez continued performing and making occasional recordings until his death in 1995. Additional forays into merengue-jazz have been made by Mario Rivera, Dario Estrella, Juan Colón, the group Asa-Difé, and myself.
3. See Tejeda's 1993 book about 4:40.
4. Meindert Fennema and Troetje Loewenthal (1987: 34–35) write that while *La isla al revés* fails to note this, the book is based on Balaguer's 1939 *La realidad dominicana*, written in the wake of the Haitian massacre of 1937.
5. Cuban-based bachata favors I-vi-IV-V progressions instead of the I-V and I-IV-V characteristic of Cuban music. The lead guitar used in bachata, the *requinto*, is smaller than a standard guitar and sounds similar to the tres, an instrument essential to the son. The requinto part is often carried by the more readily available standard guitar played with a capo. Bachata's use of the Dominican metal güira in place of the Cuban calabash güiro lends it a characteristically Dominican air. The dance step performed to son-based bachata is a Dominican creation: performed in the ballroom position, it consists of two steps forward (or to the side) and two steps back to the original position.
6. Wayno music of Peru is another marginalized music with mass appeal (see Turino 1993).
7. Selection 11 on the CD is Durán's "Consejo a las mujeres."
8. Dominican musics have clear-cut links with social classes. Performed by campesinos at local rituals, the highly African-influenced rural forms have no access to the mass media. The syncretic bachata and accordion-based merengue, while also part of campesino life, enjoy limited access to the mass media and are performed in urban as well as rural areas. As a national symbol, accordion-based merengue is held in higher esteem than bachata. Pop merengue represents the modernity, patriotism, and transnational contacts that the country's official ideology promotes. Popular across class lines, Latin American romantic baladas derive from and symbolize the dominant Spanish-derived culture.
9. Lizardo and Agustín Pichardo assert that early twentieth-century merengue cibaeño did not involve hip motion. Manuel de Jesús Galván's description of dancers "demonstrating the agility of [their] hips" in nineteenth-century merengue, however, is eminently applicable to late-twentieth-century merengue dance.
10. Nigerian bandleader Fela Kuti, who features provocative female dancing at his performances, declared bluntly at a 1992 concert in Northampton, Massachusetts, "This is music for fucking . . . for me, as an African, sex is not immoral. Corruption and oppression are immoral."
11. This is at selection 10 on the CD.
12. See Aparicio 1994 on "female narratives" in salsa and merengue.

Chapter 7

1. Finnish American musicians played a seminal role in the development of twentieth-century popular music in Finland.
2. The claps are used during the saxophone, but not the trumpet, parts of Martínez's instrumental interludes, or mambos.
3. Alan M. Klein details a parallel trend in his engrossing narrative about the success of Dominicans in U.S. major league baseball (1991).
4. See Duany 1990, an important book on Dominicans in Puerto Rico.
5. Jorge Duany's astute analysis of this song (1994: 76–77) informed my explication of it.

Chapter 8

1. The fact that Martha Davis, who has documented the vitality of rural Dominican music (1976, 1981, 1987), also writes about the "Disappearance of Traditional Musical Arts in the Dominican Republic" (1975), demonstrates the inevitable oscillation between the "metanarratives" of "homogenization" and "emergence" that James Clifford describes (1988: 17).
2. The information presented here was gleaned during my 1990–91 field trips (see Austerlitz 1992: 323–44).
3. I conducted fieldwork on this genre near the capital in Villa Mella, and José Castillo informs me that it is also performed in the southwestern area around San Cristóbal and as far east as El Seybo (p.c.).
4. Pri-prí can be heard at selection 13 on the CD. Its basic dance motion consists of four steps per measure: the right foot to the right, the left foot to the right, the left foot to the left, and the right foot to the left. The smallest of the palos drum family, the balsié can produce several distinct sounds. In what is called the palo echao (thrown palo) technique, the performer places the balsié sideways on the ground, sits on it, and manipulates the drum's pitch by pressing or releasing the membrane with the heel of the foot while striking it. Adding to the balsié's timbral palette is a technique in which the drummer runs the tip of a finger across the drumhead to produce a moaning sound.
5. This takes place seven weeks after Easter (Vicioso interview).
6. It should be noted that, as secular music, pri-prí is not considered to have caused the spirit's transfer.
7. Merengue de atabales can be heard at selection 14 on the CD. This performance is distinguished by an expressive, improvised text:

Coro: ¡Ya-ee-oo! [o "¡Oo-ee-oo!"]	Chorus: ¡Ya-eh-oo!, [or "¡Oo-eh-oo!" Singers switch between *e* and *o*. As a result, both vowels are sometimes heard simultaneously, creating an unusual effect].
Solo: ¡Ee, adio' morena!	Soloist: Eh-ay, don't go away, dark-skinned one!

Coro: ¡Ya-ee-oo!

Solo: ¡Ee-ay no te vaya'!

Coro: [Continúa repetiendo "¡Ya-ee-oo!" entre las estrofas del solista].	Chorus: [Continues repeating "Ya-eh-oo" antiphonally with the soloist].
Solo: ¡Oigan lo que me vengo callando!	Soloist: Listen to me, I'm falling down!
¡Ay dio', yo estoy loco [por tí]— bota ese hombre!	Oh, God, I'm crazy about you; get rid of that other man!
Mira con tus ojos de culebra.	Look at me with your snake-eyes.
¡Ee-ay more!	Eh-ay, dark-skinned one!
¡[Si no] me quiere' vivo, muerto meno'!	You don't love me now that I'm alive; you'll love me even less when I'm dead!
¡Ee-jo-ee!	Eoh-yo-eh!
¡Uoy mamaíta, que no te vaya'!	Woy, little mama, don't go away!
¡Ee-jo dolore'!	Eh-yo, the pain!
¿Pero buena Rosa Julia, y qué tu tiene'?	But sweet Rosa Julia, what's with you?
¡Ee-oo-ee!	Eh-oo-eh!
¡Pero bueno, morenita cariñosa!	Well, well, you lovely dark-skinned one!
¡Ee-ay Rosa Julia-ee!	
¡No me quiere' vivo, muerto meno'!	You don't love me alive; you'll love me even less when I'm dead!
¡Ee-oo-ee!	Yeh-oo-eh!
No permito que te vaya.	I won't let you go away.

8. Merengue redondo (literally, round merengue), at selection 15 on the CD, uses a tambora technique in which the drum is held vertically between the legs (instead of horizontally in the lap, as in merengue cibaeño) and played with a stick in the right hand and the palm and fingers of the left hand. Davis writes that pri-prí is also sometimes called merengue redondo in the South, but the southern musicians with whom I spoke do not use this term (1994: 129).

9. Widely used in Africa and the Americas, this instrument is sometimes called a "rainstick" because when tilted sideways, it emits a sound similar to raindrops. It is shaken to produce a maracalike effect in merengue ocoeño (see Lizardo 1988: 217–21). Because merengue ocoeño is rarely performed today, I was unable to record and transcribe it.

10. All the non-Cibao merengue variants call for steps similar to those of pri-prí. El baile del chivo (the goat dance) of Samaná may also belong to the Dominican merengue complex; Jacob Coopersmith (1949: 59) considers it a merengue, while Fradique Lizardo does not (p.c). Chivo performance documented by Coopersmith during the Trujillo era

used "several" guitars, tambora, and güira. Performances recorded by myself and Lizardo use accordion, güira, and tambora (see Austerlitz 1992 for musical transcription and analysis). In el baile del chivo dance, the man stands behind the woman and both jump forward in what is said to mimic the sex act as performed by goats. This form is associated with the song "El chivo florete," which has a humorous, double-entendre text:

EL CHIVO FLORETE
(The sword goat)

No hay animal como el chivo	There's no animal like the goat
Para jugar el florete.	When it comes to playing with a sword.
Por lejos que va la chiva,	No matter where the she-goat goes,
El la lleva el cohete.	He gives her the missile.
Solo: ¡Ay chivo florete!	Soloist: Oh, sword goat!
Coro: ¡Mueve el florete!	Chorus: Move the sword!

11. I audiotaped and videotaped this form in La Victoria in 1995; Davis researched it in Monte Plata, Boyá, and Chirono (1976: 215).
12. Kalaff also used guitar, but only for the performance of nonmerengue genres such as boleros.
13. Dionisio "Guandulito" Mejía, whose group can be heard at selection 18 on the CD, also played an important role in the development of this style.
14. In Santiago, this is most often known simply as *la música típica* (typical, or folk, music), while residents of the capital usually call it *perico ripiao*. I call it *merengue típico moderno* because of the latter term's descriptive quality, and because it differentiates the music from other genres that qualify as típico.
15. The guinchao and volao are related to the pambiche, while a juste employs a stick played on the side of the conga (José Israel Blanco de la Cruz p.c.; Román and Pascual interviews).
16. El Ciego de Nagua's group can be heard at selection 12 on the CD. See Austerlitz 1992: 347–57 and 1986: 129–33 for musical analyses of típico moderno recordings by Francisco Ulloa and El Ciego de Nagua.
17. While musicians from many Dominican regions perform the style, noncibaeños agree that one must live in Santiago to learn to play it properly.
18. As noted, other reasons for its status are that it is the country's most densely populated region and that it is the traditional home of the gentry. The Cibao's reputation for European-influenced rural expressive culture is only partially founded in fact; vital Afro-Dominican palos traditions are native to the region, especially in the San Francisco de Macoris area (Vicioso interview).

Chapter 9

1. In ethnomusicology, Charles Keil (e.g., 1985) and others have expressed cultural populism by foregrounding working-class musics, while Christopher Waterman (1990a)

and Gage Averill (1989a and b) have written about popular music's connection to the middle and dominant classes.

2. These quotes refer specifically to Richard Wright's works, which Paul Gilroy believes are "the most powerful expression of [this] . . . duality which have we have traced down the years from slavery" (1993: 186).

Bibliography

Adorno, Theodor. 1976. *Introduction to the Sociology of Music.* New York: Seabury.

Alberti, Luis. 1973. *Método de tambora y güira.* Santo Domingo.

————. 1975. *De música y orquestas bailables dominicanas, 1910–1959.* Santo Domingo: Taller.

Alcántara, Almánizar José. 1987. "Black Images in Dominican Literature." *New West Indian Guide* 61, 3–4: 161–73.

Alén Rodríguez, Olavo. 1991. "The Tumba Francesa." In *Essays on Cuban Music,* ed. Peter Manuel. Lanham, Md.: University Press of America.

Alix, Juan Antonio. [1927] 1961. *Décimas.* Vol. 2. Reprint. Santo Domingo: Librería Dominicana.

Anderson, Benedict. 1983. *Imagined Communities: Reflections on the Origin and Spread of Nationalism.* London: Verso.

————. 1991. *Imagined Communities: Reflections on the Origin and Spread of Nationalism.* Rev. ed. London: Verso.

Andrade, Manuel J. 1930. *Folk-lore from the Dominican Republic.* New York: American Folklore Society.

Aparicio, Frances R. 1994. "Así Son: Salsa Music, Female Narratives, and Gender (de)Construction in Puerto Rico." *Poetics Today* 15, 4: 659–84.

Aretz, Isabel, and Luis Felipe Ramón y Rivera. 1973. "Un cursillo de folklore." *Pequeño Universo* 4, July–December: 11–98.

Arias, José Francisco. 1991. "El merengue: promotor internacional del país." *El Siglo* 3 June: 8c.

Arzeño, Julio. 1927. *Del folklore musical dominicano.* Santo Domingo.

Austerlitz, Paul. 1986. "A History of Dominican Merengue Highlighting the Role of the Saxophone." Master's thesis, Wesleyan University.

———. 1992. "Dominican Merengue in Regional, National, and International Perspectives." Ph.D. diss. Wesleyan University.

———. 1993. "Local and International Trends in Dominican Merengue." *World of Music* 35, 2:270–89.

Averill, Gage. 1989a. *Haitian Dance Band Music: The Political Economy of Exuberance*. Ph.D. diss., University of Washington.

———. 1989b. "Haitian Dance Bands, 1915–70: Class, Race, and Authenticity." *Latin American Music Review* 10, 2: 203–35.

———. 1994. "Anraje to Angaje: Carnival Politics and Music in Haiti." *Ethnomusicology* 38, 2: 217–48.

Balaguer, Joaquín. 1983. *La isla al revés: Haití y el destino dominicano*. Santo Domingo: Fundación Antonio Caro.

Balibar, Etienne. 1991. "The Nation Form: History and Ideology." In *Race, Nation, Class: Ambiguous Identities*, ed. Etienne Balibar and Immanuel Wallerstien. London: Verso.

Barreiro, Teófilo. 1986. "La orquesta popular: vía de movilidad social." *Acroarte: Primer seminario sobre las orquestas populares en nuestro país* 1, 1: 42–53.

Barthes, Roland. 1991. "Written Clothing." In *Rethinking Popular Culture*, ed. Chandra Mukerji and Michael Schudson. Berkeley and Los Angeles: University of California Press.

Basch, Linda, Nina Glick Schiller, and Cristina Szanton Blanc. 1994. *Nations Unbound: Transnational Projects, Postcolonial Predicaments, and Deterritorialized Nation-States*. Basel: Gordon and Breach.

Béhague, Gerard. 1979. *Music in Latin America: An Introduction*. Englewood Cliffs, N.J.: Prentice-Hall.

———. 1980. "Tango." In *New Grove Dictionary of Music and Musicians*, ed. Stanley Sadie. Vol. 18. London: Macmillan.

Black, Jan Knippers. 1986. *The Dominican Republic: Politics and Development in an Unsovereign State*. Boston: Allen and Unwin.

Bogen, Elizabeth. 1987. *Immigration in New York*. New York: Praeger.

Bosch, Juan. [1970] 1988. *Composición social dominicana: Historia e interpretación*. Santo Domingo: Colección Pensamiento y Cultura. Reprint, Santo Domingo: Alpha y Omega.

Bourguignon, Erika. 1951. *Syncretism and Ambivalence: An Ethnohistorical Study*. Ph.D. diss., Northwestern University.

———. 1969. "Haiti el l'ambivilence socialisée: une reconsidération." *Journal de la Societé des Americanistes* 58: 173–205.

Bourne, Randolph. 1916. "Trans-national America." *Atlantic Monthly* 118: 86–97.

Bray, David B. 1987. "Dominican Exodus: Origins, Problems, Solutions." In *Caribbean Exodus*, ed. Barry Levine. New York: Praeger.

Brito Ureña, Luis Manuel. 1983. *El merengue y la realidad existencial del hombre dominicano*. Thesis, Universidad Autonóma de Santo Domingo.

———. 1987. *El merengue y la realidad existencial del hombre dominicano*. Santo Domingo: Universidad Autonóma de Santo Domingo.

Cadilla de Martínez, María. 1950. "La histórica danza puertorriqueña en el siglo XVI y sus evoluciones." *Revista Musical Chilena* 6, 37: 43–77.

Calder, Bruce. 1984. *The Impact of Intervention: The Dominican Republic during the U.S. Occupation of 1916–1924*. Austin: University of Texas Press.

Canelo, Juan de Frank. 1982. *Donde, por que, como viven los dominicanos en el extranjero*. Santo Domingo: Alpha y Omega.

Carpentier, Alejo. 1961. *La música en Cuba*. Havana.

Cazorla, Roberto. 1991. "Canciones de 4:40 baten record en Europa." *El nacional*, 26 February, 20.

Chaney, Elsa, and Constance R. Sutton. 1985. *Caribbean Life in New York City: Sociological Dimensions*. New York: Center for Migration Studies.

Chernoff, John Miller. 1979. *African Rhythm and African Sensibility: Aesthetics and Social Action in African Musical Idioms*. Chicago: University of Chicago Press.

Clifford, James. 1988. *The Predicament of Culture: Twentieth-Century Ethnography, Literature, and Art*. Cambridge: Harvard University Press.

Cocks, Jay. 1986. "You Can't Stop Dancing: A New Merengue Heats up the Club Scene." *Time*, 6 October, 91.

Collins, John. 1985. *Musicmakers of West Africa*. Washington, D.C.: Three Continents.

———. 1987. "Jazz Feedback to Africa." *American Music* 5, 2: 176–93.

Coopersmith, Jacob Maurice. 1945. "Music and Musicians of the Dominican Republic: A Survey." *Musical Quarterly* 31, 1: 71–78; 2: 212–26.

———. 1949. *Music and Musicians of the Dominican Republic: a Survey*. Washington, D.C.: Unión Panamericana.

Coplan, David B. 1985. *In Township Tonight! South Africa's Black City Music and Theater*. London: Longman.

Corominas, Joan. 1954. *Diccionario crítico etimologico de la lengua castellana*. Vol. 3. Madrid: Gredos.

Crassweiler, Robert D. 1966. *Trujillo: Life and Times of a Caribbean Dictator*. New York: Macmillan.

Curtin, Philip D. 1969. *The Atlantic Slave Trade*. Madison: University of Wisconsin Press.

Damirón, Rafael. 1947. *De nuestro Sur remoto*. Ciudad Trujillo: Publicaciónes de la Secretaría de Educación y Bellas Artes.

Davis, Martha Ellen. 1975. "La desaparición de las artes musicales tradicionales en la República Dominicana." In *Danzas y bailes folklóricos dominicanos*, ed. Fradique Lizardo. Santo Domingo: Taller.

———. 1976. *Afro-Dominican Religious Brotherhoods: Structure, Ritual, Music*. Ph.D. diss., University of Illinois.

———. 1981. *Vozes del purgatorio: Estudio de la salve dominicana*. Santo Domingo: Ediciones Museo del Hombre Dominicano.

———. 1987. *La otra ciencia: El vodú dominicano como religión y medicina populares*. Santo Domingo: Editora Universitaria — UASD.

———. 1994. "Music and Black Ethnicity in the Dominican Republic." In *Music and Black Ethnicity in the Caribbean and South America*, ed. Gerard Béhague. New Brunswick, N.J.: Transaction.

. del Castillo, José, and Manuel A. García Arévalo. 1989. *Antología del merengue/Anthology of the Merengue*. Santo Domingo: Corripio.

del Castillo, José and Martin Murphy. 1987–88. "Migration, National Identity, and Cultural Policy in the Dominican Republic." *Journal of Ethnic Studies* 15, 3: 49–69.

Deschamps, Enrique. n.d. *La República Dominicana: Directorio y guía general*. Barcelona: J. Cunill.

Díaz Díaz, Edgardo. 1990. "La música bailable de los carnets: forma y significado de su repertorio en Puerto Rico (1877–1930)." *Revista musical puertorriqueña* 5, 1: 3–21.

Duany, Jorge. 1990. *Los dominicanos en Puerto Rico: Migración en la semiperiferia*. San Juan, Puerto Rico: Huricán.

———. 1994. "Ethnicity, Identity, and Music: an Anthropological Analysis of the Dominican Merengue." In *Music and Black Ethnicity in the Caribbean and South America*, ed. Gerard Béhague. New Brunswick, N.J.: Transaction.

Duarte, Isis. 1980. *Capitalismo y superpoblación en Santo Domingo*. Santo Domingo: Editora Universitaria—UASD.

Du Bois, W.E.B. [1903] 1989. *The Souls of Black Folk*. Reprint. New York: Bantam.

Dumervé, Constantine. 1968. *Histoire de la musique en Haiti*. Port-au-Prince: Imprimerie des Antilles.

Eco, Umberto. 1986. *Travels in Hyper Reality*. San Diego: Harcourt, Brace, Janovich.

Espaillat, Francisco. 1909. *Escritos de Espaillat*. Santo Domingo: Cuna de América.

Falette, Ramón. 1988. "*Analisis comparativo sobre la aplicación del 'marketing' para el desarollo del mercado discográfico en Santo Domingo*." Thesis, Universidad APEC.

Fanon, Frantz. 1967. *Black Skin, White Masks*. New York: Grove.

Feld, Steven. 1988. "Notes on World Beat." *Public Culture Bulletin* 1, 1: 31–37

Feliz, José Miguel. 1990. "Isa Conde destaca aportes de dominicanos que residen en el exterior." *Actualidad/Listin Diario*, 17 December, 13.

Fennema, Meindert, and Troetje Loewenthal. 1987. *La construcción de raza y nación en la República Dominicana*. Santo Domingo: Editora Universitaria—UASD.

Fernández, Crispín. n.d. *Jaleos de merengue/Merengue Patterns*. Santo Domingo: Educativa Dominicana.

———. 1986. *Melodías del merengue/Merengue Melodies*. Santo Domingo: Educativa Dominicana.

Fernández, Enrique. 1986. "Is Salsa Sinking?" *Village Voice* 2 September, 18, 20–21.

Fernández, Nohema. 1989. "La contradanza cubana y Manuel Saumell." *Latin American Music Review* 10, 1: 116–34.

Ferrán, B., Fernando I. 1985. "Figuras de lo dominicano." *Ciencia y sociedad* 10, 1: 5–20.

Ferreras, Ramón Alberto. 1990. *Trujillo y sus mujeres*. Santo Domingo: Editorial del Nordeste.

Fiske, John. 1989. *Understanding Popular Culture*. Boston: Unwin Hyman.

Fondeur, Román Franco. n.d. "Puntos de vista en el torno del merengue." Santiago, Dominican Republic: Centro de la Cultura de Santiago.

Fouchard, Jean. 1973. *La méringue, le danse nacional de Haiti*. Ottawa: Lemeac.

———. 1988. *La méringue, le danse nacional de Haiti*. 2d ed. Pétion-Ville, Haiti: Henri Deschamps.

"Fradique dice 'Baila en la calle' no identifica carnaval dominicana." 1985. *Ultima Hora/La Tarde Alegre*, 4 July, 1.

Galán, Natalio. 1983. *Cuba y sus sones*. Valencia: Pre-textos.

Galíndez, Jesús de. n.d. *The Era of Trujillo: Caribbean Dictator*. Santo Domingo.

Galván, Manuel de Jesús. [1882] 1989. *Enriquillo: leyenda histórica dominicana*. Reprint. New York: Las Américas.

García, Juan Francisco. 1972. *Canciones dominicanas*. Santo Domingo: Editora Universitaria — UASD.

Gates, Henry Louis. 1988. The Signifying Monkey: A Theory of Afro-American Literary Criticism. New York: Oxford University Press.

Georges, Eugenia. 1990. *The Making of a Transnational Community: Migration, Development, and Cultural Change in the Dominican Republic*. New York: Columbia University Press.

Gilroy, Paul. 1993. *The Black Atlantic: Modernity and Double Consciousness*. Cambridge: Harvard University Press.

Glick Schiller, Nina, Linda Basch, and Cristina Blanc-Szanton, eds. 1992. *Towards a Transnational Perspective on Migration*. New York: New York Academy of Sciences.

González, Nancie L. 1970. "Peasant's Progress: Dominicans in New York." *Caribbean Studies* 10, 3: 154–67.

———. 1972. "Desiderio Arias: Caudillo, Bandit, and Culture Hero." *Journal of American Folklore* 85, 335: 42–50.

González Canahuete, L. Amanzor. 1988. *Recopilación de la música popular dominicana*. Santo Domingo: Corripio.

Gradante, William. 1980. "Merengue." In *New Grove Dictionary of Music and Musicians*. Vol. 12, ed. Stanley Sadie. London: Macmillan.

Gramsci, Antonio. 1971. *Selections from the Prison Notebooks*. ed. and tran. Quintin Hoare and Geoffrey Nowell Smith. New York: International.

Grasmuck, Sherri, and Patricia R. Pessar. 1991. *Between Two Islands: Dominican International Migration*. Berkeley and Los Angeles: University of California Press.

Grossberg, Larry, and Stuart Hall. 1986. "On Postmodernism and Articulation: An Interview." *Journal of Communication Inquiry* 10, 2: 45–60.

Guaba, Miquea. 1995. *Aprendamos a tocar tambora*. Santo Domingo: Mi Estudio.

Guilbault, Jocelyne. 1993. *Zook: World Music in the West Indies*. Chicago: University of Chicago Press.

Guzmán, Reyes. 1990. "Blas Durán reafima su popularidad y su calidad." *Espectáculos/Hoy*, 13 August, 1.

Häggman, Ann-Mari. 1976. "Ruostalaisseutujen pelimannit ja soittimeet." In *Paimensoittimista kisallilauluun*, ed. Heikki Laitinen and Simo Westerholm. Kaustinen, Finland: Kansanmusiikki-Instituutti.

Hall, Stuart. 1981. "Notes on Deconstructing the 'Popular.'" In *People's History and Socialist Theory*, ed. R. Samuel. London: Routledge and Kegan Paul.

Handler, Richard, and Jocelyn Linnekin. 1984. "Tradition, Genuine or Spurious." *Journal of the American Folklore Society* 97, 385: 273–90.

Hebdige, Dick. 1979. *Subculture: The Meaning of Style*. London: Routledge.

———. 1987. *Cut 'n' Mix: Culture, Identity, and Caribbean Music*. London: Comedia.

Hendricks, Glenn. 1974. *The Dominican Diaspora: From the Dominican Republic to New York City — Villagers in Transition*. New York: Teacher's College Press.

Hernández, Julio Alberto. 1927. *Album Musical*. Santo Domingo: Tipografía de Carmen.

———. 1964. *Música folklórica y popular de la República Dominicana*. Santo Domingo.

———. 1969. *Música tradicional dominicana*. Santo Domingo: Postigo.

Herskovits, Melville J. 1937. *Life in a Haitian Valley*. New York: Knopf.
———. [1941] 1958. *The Myth of the Negro Past*. New York: Harper and Brothers. Reprint, Boston: Beacon.
Hobsbawm, Eric. 1990. *Nations and Nationalism since 1780: Programme, Myth, Reality*. New York: Cambridge University Press.
Hobsbawm, Eric, and Terence Ranger. 1983. *The Invention of Tradition*. New York: Cambridge University Press.
Hoetink, H. 1973. *Slavery and Race Relations in the Americas: Comparative Notes on Their Nature and Nexus*. New York: Harper and Row.
———. 1982. *The Dominican People, 1850–1900: Notes for a Historical Sociology*. Baltimore: Johns Hopkins University Press.
Hood, Mantle. 1960. "The Challenge of Bi-Musicality." *Ethnomusicology* 4, 1: 55–59.
Incháustegui, Arístides. 1973a. "Juan Francisco García (1892)." *Listín Diario*, 13 January, 19.
———. 1973b. "Julio Alberto Hernández (1900)." *Listín Diario*, 27 January, 19.
———. 1973c. "Luis Alberti (1906)." *Listín Diario*, 27 March, 24.
———. 1974a. "Don Pancho García a los 82 años." *Listín Diario*, 15 July, 19.
———. 1974b. "Juan Bautista Espínola Reyes (1894–1923)." *Listín Diario*, 29 September, 20.
———. 1988a. *El disco en al República Dominicana*. Santo Domingo.
———. 1988b. Program notes to the concert "Canciones de Julio Alberto Hernández en la voz de Arístides Incháustegui."
Jérez, Nathalie. 1991. "¿Cual es el salario de los músicos?" *Escala*, 16 August, 16.
Jorge, Bernarda. 1982a. "Bases ideológicas de la práctica musical de la era de Trujillo." *Eme Eme* 10, 59: 65–99.
———. 1982b. *La música dominicana, siglos XIX–XX*. Santo Domingo: Editora Universitaria—UASD.
Kallberg, Jeffrey. 1988. "The Rhetoric of Genre." *Nineteenth-Century Music* 11, 3: 238–60.
Keil, Charles. 1966. "Motion and Feeling through Music." *Journal of Aesthetics and Art Criticism*. 24, 3: 337–51.
———. 1985. "People's Music Comparatively: Style and Stereotypes, Class and Hegemony." *Dialectical Anthropology* 10, 1–2: 119–30.
Klein, Alan M. 1991. *Sugarball: The American Dream, the Dominican Game*. New Haven, Conn.: Yale University Press.
Kluckhohn, Florence. 1940. "The Participant-Observation Technique in Small Communities." *American Journal of Sociology* 46, 3: 331–43.
Kramer, Jonathan D. 1988. *The Time of Music*. New York: Schirmer.
Kryzanek, Michael J., and Howard Wiarda. 1988. *The Politics of External Influence in the Dominican Republic*. New York: Praeger.
Langer, Suzanne. 1953. *Feeling and Form*. New York: Scribner.
Larghey, Michael. 1994. "Composing a Haitian Cultural Identity: Haitian Elites, African Ancestry, and Musical Discourse." *Black Music Research Journal* 14, 2: 99–117.
Lewin, Olive, and Adrienne Kaeppler, eds. 1988. *Come Mek Me Hol' Yu Han'*. Kingston: Jamaica Memory Bank.
Liriano, William. 1986. "Mercado y dimensión económica de las orquestas populares." *Acroarte: Primer seminario sobre las orquestas populares en nuestro país* 1, 1: 34–40.

List, George. 1980. "Colombia." In *New Grove Dictionary of Music and Musicians,* ed. Stanley Sadie. Vol. 4. London: Macmillan.

Lizardo, Fradique. 1975. *Danzas y bailes folklóricos dominicanos.* Santo Domingo: Taller.

———. 1978a. "Cronología del merengue." *Suplemento/Listín Diario,* 5 August.

———. 1978b. "Historia del merengue." Paper presented at Encuentro con el Merengue, Santo Domingo.

———. 1979. *La cultura africana en Santo Domingo.* Santo Domingo: Taller.

———. 1988. *Instrumentos musicales folklóricos dominicanos,* Vol. 1. Santo Domingo: UNESCO.

Lomax, Alan. 1968. *Folk Song Style and Culture.* Washington, D.C.: American Association for the Advancement of Science.

López Morillo, Adriano. 1983. *La segunda reincorporación de Santo Domingo a España.* Santo Domingo: Sociedad Dominicana de Bibliófilos.

Lora Medrano, Luis Eduardo. 1984. *Petán: La Voz Dominicana, su gente . . . sus cosas . . . y sus cuentos.* Santo Domingo: Tele-3.

Loza, Steven. 1993. *Barrio Rhythm: Mexican-American Music in Los Angeles.* Urbana: University of Illinois Press.

McGuigan, Jim. 1992. *Cultural Populism.* London: Routledge.

McLane, Daisanne. 1991. "Dance-Till-You-Drop Merengue." *New York Times,* 6 January, 28,38.

Malm, Krister. 1992. "Local, National, and International Musics: A Changing Scene of Interaction." In *World Music—Musics of the World: Aspects of Documentation, Mass Media, and Acculturation,* ed. M. P. Baumann. Wilhelmshaven, Germany: Florian Noetzel.

Manuel, Peter. 1985. "The Anticipated Bass in Cuban Popular Music." *Latin American Music Review* 6, 2: 250–61.

———. 1994. "Puerto Rican Music and Cultural Identity: Creative Appropriation of Cuban Sources from the Danza to Salsa." *Ethnomusicology* 38, 2: 249–80.

———. 1995. *Caribbean Currents: Caribbean Music from Rumba to Reggae.* Philadelphia: Temple University Press.

Marcus, George E. 1986. "Contemporary Problems of Ethnography in the Modern World System." In *Writing Culture: The Poetics and Politics of Identity,* ed. James Clifford and George E. Marcus. Berkeley and Los Angeles: University of California Press.

Martínez-Fernández, Luis. 1991. "Caudillos, Annexation, and the Rivalry between Empires in the Dominican Republic, 1844–1874." *Diplomatic History* 17, 4: 571–97.

Mercado, Dálmaso. 1983. "Memorias de un músico rural dominicano." *Eme Eme* 35, 67: 131–61.

Merriam, Alan. 1964. *The Anthropology of Music.* Chicago: Northwestern University Press.

———. 1982. *African Music in Perspective.* New York: Garland.

Middleton, Richard. 1990. *Studying Popular Music.* Philadelphia: Open University Press.

Miniño, Manuel. 1983. *Merengues de Luis Alberti.* Santo Domingo: Santo Domingo.

Moya Pons, Frank. 1986. *El pasado dominicano.* Santo Domingo: Fundación J. A. Caro Alvarez.

———. 1988. "Modernización y cambios en la República Dominicana." In *Ensayos sobre la cultura dominicana,* ed. Bernardo Vega et al. Santo Domingo: Fundación Cultural Dominicana.

————. 1995. *The Dominican Republic: A National History.* New Rochelle, N.Y.: Hispaniola Books.

Mukuna, Kazadi wa. 1979. "The Origin of Zairian Modern Music." *African Urban Studies* 6: 31–40.

Mulvey, Laura. 1975. "Visual Pleasure and Narrative Cinema." *Screen* 16, 3: 6–18.

Nolasco, Flérida de. 1939. *La música en Santo Domingo y otros ensayos.*

————. 1948. *Vibraciones en el tiempo.* Ciudad Trujillo.

————. 1956. *Santo Domingo en el folklore universal.* San Cristóbal: Impresora Dominicana.

Nuñez del Risco, Yaqui. 1986. "La importancia de las orquestas populares en la producción de un espacio de la televisión." *Acroarte: Primer seminario sobre las orquestas populares en nuestro país* 1, 1: 6–12.

Orovio, Helio. 1981. *Diccionario de la música cubana.* Havana: Letras Cubanas.

Ortiz, Fernando. 1952–55. *Los instrumentos de la música afrocubana.* 5 vols. Havana: Publicaciónes de la Dirección de Cultura del Ministerio de Educación.

Pacini Hernandez, Deborah. 1989a. "Music of Marginality: Social Identity and Class in Dominican Bachata." Ph.D. diss., Cornell University.

————. 1989b. "Music of Marginality: Social Identity and Class in Dominican Bachata." *Latin American Music Review* 10, 1: 69–91.

————. 1991. "*La lucha sonora:* Dominican Popular Music in the Post-Trujillo Era." *Latin American Music Review* 12, 2: 106–21.

————. 1992a. "Bachata: From the Margins to the Mainstream." *Popular Music* 11, 3: 359–64.

————. 1992b. "Merengue: Race, Class, Tradition, Identity." In *Americas: An Anthology,* ed. Mark Rosenburg, A. Douglas Kincaid, and Kathleen Logan. New York: Oxford University Press.

————. 1993. "Spanish Caribbean Perspectives on World Beat." *World of Music* 35, 2:48–69.

————. 1995. *Bachata: A Social History of a Dominican Popular Music.* Philadephia: Temple University Press.

Paredes, Américo. 1978. "The Problem of Identity in a Changing Culture: Popular Expressions of Culture Conflict along the Rio Grande Border." In *Views across the Border: The United States and Mexico,* ed. Stanley R. Ross. Albuquerque: University of New Mexico Press.

Paulino, Julio César. 1985. "Búsqueda de intérpretes, músicos, y danzas." *Suplemento/Listín Diario,* 2 November, 9.

————. 1987. "El pambiche." *Suplemento/Listín Diario,* 9 May, 14.

————. 1992. "Apuntes para la historia: un merengue llamado pambiche durante la intervención del 1916." *Listin Diario/La Tarde Alegre,* 7 September, 6.

Peña, Manuel. 1985. *The Texas-Mexican Conjunto: A History of a Working-Class Music.* Austin: University of Texas Press.

Peña Morel, Esteban. 1929. "Notas criticas sobre nuestro folklore musical," sec. 2–4. Photocopy.

Pérez, Sara. 1991. "Radio y discos: juntos pero no reburujados." *El nacional,* 13 January, 20–21.

Pérez-Cabral, Pedro Andrés. 1967. *La comunidad mulata.* Caracas: Gráfica Americana.

Perris, Arnold. 1985. *Music as Propaganda: Art to Persuade, Art to Control.* Westport, Conn.: Greenwood.

Pessar, Patricia. R. 1987. "Dominican Women in House and Industry." In *New Immigrants in New York*, ed. Nancy Foner. New York: Columbia University Press.

Pichardo, Agustín. n.d.a. "Retrospectiva del merengue." Photocopy.

————. n.d.b. Untitled. Photocopy.

Quintero Rivera, A. G. 1986. "Ponce, the Danza, and the National Question: Notes toward a Sociology of Puerto Rican Music." *Cimarrón* 1, 2: 49–65.

Quiroz Otero, Ciro. 1983. *Vallenato: hombre y canto.* Bogota: Icaro.

Qureshi, Regula. 1972. "Ethnomusicological Research among Canadian Communities of Arab and East Indian Origin." *Ethnomusicology* 16, 3: 381–96.

Ramón y Rivera, Luis Felipe. 1976. *La música popular de Venezuela.* Caracas: Armitano.

Reed, Ishmael. 1972. *Mumbo Jumbo.* New York: Avon.

Reyes-Schramm, Adalaida. 1989. "Music and Tradition from Native to Adopted Land through the Refugee Experience." *Yearbook for Traditional Music* 22: 25–35.

Rivera González, Luis. 1960. *Antología musical de la era de Trujillo, 1930–1960.* 4 vols. Ciudad Trujillo: Publicaciónes de la Secretaría de Estado de Educación y Bellas Artes.

Roberts, John Storm. 1972. *Black Music of Two Worlds.* New York: William Morrow and Company.

————. 1979. *The Latin Tinge.* New York: Oxford University Press.

Robbins, James. 1989. "Practical and Abstract Taxonomy in Cuban Music." *Ethnomusicology* 33, 3: 379–89.

Rodríguez, Willie. 1986. "Impactos de las orquestas populares en la programación de las radio-emisoras del país." *Acroarte: Primer seminario sobre las orquestas populares en nuestro país* 1, 1: 15–26.

Rodríguez Demorizi, Emilio. 1971. *Música y baile en Santo Domingo.* Santo Domingo: Colección Pensamiento.

Rondón, César Miguel. 1980. *El libro de la salsa: Crónica de la música del Caribe urbano.* Caracas: Editorial Arte.

Rosado, Marisa, ed. 1977. *Ensayos sobre la danza puertorriqueña.* San Juan, Puerto Rico: Instituto de la Cultura Puertorriqueña.

Rosaldo, Renato. 1988. "Ideology, Place, and People without Culture." *Cultural Anthropology* 3, 1: 77–87.

————. 1993. *Culture and Truth: The Remaking of Social Analysis.* Boston: Beacon.

Rouse, Roger. 1991. "Mexican Migration and the Social Space of Postmodernism." *Diaspora* 1, 1: 8–23.

Royce, Anya Peterson. 1982. *Ethnic Identity: Strategies of Diversity.* Bloomington: University of Indiana Press.

Rueda, Manuel. 1990a. "1—dos teorías sobre el merengue." *Isla abierta/Hoy*, 15 December, 2.

————. 1990b. " 2—dos teorías sobre el merengue" *Isla abierta/Hoy*, 22 December, 2.

Sachs, Curt. 1938. *Les instruments de musique de Madagascar.* Travaux et Mémoires de Institut d'Ethnologie, no. 28. Paris: Université de Paris.

————. [1937] 1963. *World History of the Dance.* Reprint. New York: Norton.

Saint-Cyr, Jean Franck. 1981–82. "La méringue haitienne." Revista INIDEF 5:62–74.

Sálazar Díaz, Juan. 1978. "Convite: de los congos a la bambaulá (*sic*), todo es herencia africana." *Ahora*, 3 July, no. 764, 22–24.

Schutz, Alfred. 1964. *Collected Papers II: Studies in Social Theory*. The Hague: Martinus Nijoff.

Segrave, Kerry. 1994. *Payola in the Music Industry: A History, 1880–1991*. Jefferson, N.C.: McFarland.

Shelemay, Kay Kaufman. 1980. "Historical Ethnomusicology: Reconstructing Falasha Liturgical History." *Ethnomusicology* 24, 2: 233–58.

Slobin, Mark. 1992. "Micromusics of the West: A Comparative Approach." *Ethnomusicology* 36, 1: 1–88.

Smith, Anthony D. S. 1983. *Theories of Nationalism*. 2 ed. New York: Holmes and Meier.

Solano, Rafael. 1992. *Letra y música: Relatos autobiográficos de un músico dominicano*. Santo Domingo: Taller.

Somer, Doris. 1991. *Foundational Fictions: The National Romances of Latin America*. Berkeley and Los Angeles: University of California Press.

Soto, Cristóbal. 1993. "No se ha caído el merengue caraqueño." *Revista de la Fundación Bigot* 27, July–August: 36–45.

Stone, Ruth. 1982. *Let the Inside Be Sweet: The Interpretation of a Music Event among the Kpelle of Liberia*. Bloomington: University of Indiana Press.

Straubhaar, Joseph D., and Gloria M. Viscansillas. 1991. "Class, Genre, and the Regionalization of Television Programming in the Dominican Republic." *Journal of Communication* 41, 1: 53–69.

Sutton, Constance. 1987. *Caribbean Life in New York City*. New York: Center for Migration Studies.

Szwed, John, and Morton Marks. 1988. "The Afro-American Transformation of European Set Dances and Dance Suites." *Dance Research Journal* 20, 1: 29–35.

Tejeda, Darío. 1993. *La historia escondida de Juan Luis Guerra y los 4:40*. Santo Domingo: Ediciones MSC, Amigos del Hogar.

Tejeda, Darío, and Higinio Báez Ureña. 1994. "La música popular contemporanea en la República Dominicana: Nuevas expresiónes, nueva musicalidad (1961–1994)." Thesis, Universidad Católica Santo Domingo.

Tejada Ortiz, Dagoberto, ed. 1984. *Cultura y folklore de Samaná*. Santo Domingo: Alfa y Omega.

Thompson, Donald. 1975–76. "The New World Mbira: The Caribbean Marímbula." *African Music Society Journal* 5, 4: 140–48.

Thompson, Robert Farris. 1961. "Portrait of the Pachanga: The Music, the Players, the Dancers." *Saturday Review*, 28 October, 42–43, 54.

Tomlinson, Gary. 1992. "Cultural Dialogics and Jazz: A White Historian Signifies." In *Disciplining Music: Musicology and Its Canons*, ed. Katherine Bergeron and Philip V. Bohlman. Chicago: University of Chicago Press.

Turino, Thomas. 1993. *Moving Away from Silence: Music of the Peruvian Altiplano and the Experience of Urban Migration*. Chicago: University of Chicago Press.

Ugalde, Antonio, Frank D. Bean, and Gilbert Cárdenas. 1979. "International Migration from the Dominican Republic." *International Migration Review* 13, 2: 235–54.

Vega, Bernardo. 1985. *Nazismo, fascismo, y falanguismo en la República Dominicana.* Santo Domingo: Fundación Cultural Dominicana.

Vega, Carlos. 1966. "Mesomusic: An Essay on the Music of the Masses." *Ethnomusicology* 10, 1: 1–17.

Ventura, Johnny. 1978. "El merengue en el presente." Paper presented at Encuentro con el Merengue, Santo Domingo.

Vilas, Carlos. 1979. "Clases sociales, estado, y acumulación periférica en la República Dominicana 1966–78." *Realidad Contemporanea* 2: 31–58.

Vincent, Sténio. 1910. *La République d'Haiti: tell qu'elle Est.* Brussels: Sociéte Anonyme Belge d'Imprimerie.

Wallis, Roger, and Krister Malm. 1984. *Big Sounds from Small Peoples: The Music Industry in Small Countries.* London: Constable.

Waterman, Christopher. 1982. "'I'm a Leader, not a Boss': Popular Music in Ibadan, Nigeria." *Ethnomusicology* 26, 1: 59–72.

―――. 1990a. *Jùjú: A Social History and Ethnography of an African Popular Music.* Chicago: University of Chicago Press.

―――. 1990b. "'Our Tradition Is a Very Modern Tradition': Popular Music and the Construction of Pan-Yoruba Identity." *Ethnomusicology* 34, 3: 367–79.

Wiarda, Howard. 1968. *Dictatorship and Development: The Methods of Control in Trujillo's Dominican Republic.* Gainesville: University of Florida Press.

―――. 1969. *The Dominican Republic: Nation in Transition.* New York: Praeger.

―――. 1982. *The Dominican Republic: A Caribbean Crucible.* Boulder: Westview.

Wilcken, Lois. 1992. "Power, Ambivalence, and the Remaking of Haitian Vodoun Music in New York." *Latin American Music Review* 13, 1: 2–32

Williams, Raymond. 1991. "Base and Superstructure in Marxist Cultural Theory." In *Rethinking Popular Culture*, ed. Chandra Mukerji and Michael Schudson. Berkeley and Los Angeles: University of California Press.

Wilson, William A. 1973. "Herder, Folklore, and Romantic Nationalism." *Journal of Popular Culture* 6, 4: 819–35.

Yih, Y. M. David. 1989. "Sources and Destinations of the Eighteenth-Century French *Contredanse.*" Photocopy.

Ysálguez, Hugo Antonio. 1975a. "El merengue tiene su origen en Africa." *Ahora*, 8 December, no. 630, 50–51.

―――. 1975b. "Julio Alberto Hernández: 'El merengue es dominicano.'" *Ahora*, 15 December, no. 631, 50–51.

―――. 1975c. "Luis Alberti rechaza influencia negroide en el merengue." *Ahora*, 29 December, no. 633, 50–51.

―――. 1976a. "Etnomusicólogo considera es producto de aculturación, compositor llama anti-patriotico a Fradique Lizardo." *Ahora*, 19 January, no. 636, 50–51.

―――. 1976b. "Papito Rivera niega atabales sea el baile más extendido." *Ahora*, 26 January, no. 638, 52–53.

―――. 1976c. "René Carrasco aporte datos sobre el origen del merengue." *Ahora*, 1 March, no. 642, 52–53.

―――. 1976d. "Tim (*sic*) Pichardo afirma: 'El merengue desapareció de la República Dominicana.'" *Ahora*, 9 February, no. 639, 52–53.

Interviews

Abreu, Cheché (bandleader). 1990. Santo Domingo.

Alvarado, Bartólo (accordionist). 1991. Santiago, Dominican Republic.

Arroyo, Arturo, Adam Canuela, and Kirk Coleman (singers). 1995. San Juan, Puerto Rico.

Bobadilla, Isidro (percussionist). 1991. Santo Domingo.

Bravo, Aníbal (bandleader). 1995. Santo Domingo.

Cabrera, "Fefita la Grande" Manuela Josefa (accordionist). 1991. Santiago, Dominican Republic.

Cabrera Torres, Joel (singer). 1990. Santo Domingo.

Cabrera Torres, Natanael (güirero). 1991. Santo Domingo.

Cuevas, Marty (music publisher). 1994. New York.

Díaz, Adolfo (accordionist). 1990. New York.

Esteban, Jossie (bandeader). 1995. San Juan, Puerto Rico.

Fernández, Crispín (saxophonist). 1990. Santo Domingo.

García, Hilda (ASCAP representative). 1995. San Juan, Puerto Rico.

Guerra, Juan Luis (bandleader). 1985. Santo Domingo.

Hernández, Julio Alberto (composer). 1985. Santo Domingo.

Incháustegui, Arístides (music historian and singer). 1985. Santo Domingo.

Jesús, Andrés de (saxophonist). 1990. New York.

Kalaff, Luis (accordionist). 1990. New York.

Lora, Antonio (accordionist). 1985. Santiago, Dominican Republic.

Luis, José (record company owner). 1991. Santiago, Dominican Republic.

Martínez, Alberto "Ringo" (arranger and pianist). 1995. San Juan, Puerto Rico.

Mateo, Joseíto (singer). 1985. Santo Domingo.

Nenadich, George (music promoter). 1990. New York.

Pascual, Agapito (accordionist). 1991. Santiago, Dominican Republic.

Pérez, Luis (arranger). 1990, 1995. Santo Domingo.

Pichardo, Agustín. 1985. Santiago, Dominican Republic.

Quezada, Jocelyn (singer). 1990. New York.

Quezada, Millie (bandleader). 1990. New York.

Rivera, José (business executive). 1991. Santo Domingo.

Rivera, Otto (radio announcer). 1991. Santo Domingo.

Rodríguez Vidal, Miguelina. 1991. Santo Domingo.

Román, Rafaelito (accordionist). 1990, 1995. Santiago, Dominican Republic.

Romero Santos, Eladio (guitarist). 1991. Santo Domingo.

Rosario, Félix del (saxophonist). 1985. Santo Domingo.

Ruíz, July (recording engineer). 1990. Santo Domingo.

Santos, Primitivo (bandleader). 1985. New York.

Tejada, Manuel (arranger). 1985. Santo Domingo.

Tolentino, Pavín (bandleader). 1985. Santiago, Dominican Republic.

Ulloa, Francisco (accordionist). 1985. Santiago, Dominican Republic.

Vargas, Maxy (composer). 1990. Santo Domingo.

Vargas, Wilfrido (bandleader). 1985. Rural Cibao, Dominican Republic.

Vásquez, Reina, (daughter of saxophonist Avelino Vásquez). 1985. Santiago, Dominican Republic.

Vásquez, Tavito (saxophonist). 1985. Santo Domingo.

Ventura, Johnny (bandleader). 1990. Santo Domingo.

Vicioso, Tony (bandleader). 1994. New York.

Waill, Victor (bandleader). 1985. New York.

Index

Guerra, Juan Luis, 97, 110–11, 131, 134,
150; 4:40 band and, 106–7, 121; salon
merengue and, 113–14; típico moderno
merengue, 144
guinchao rhythm, 143, 166n.15
Gulf and Western Corporation, 91

Haiti: contredanse in, 28–29; Dessalines
massacre and, 9, 65, 160n.17, 163n.5;
Dominican nationalism and, 50–51,
108–11; Dominican Republic and,
9–10, 16–17, 19–20; merengue in, viii-
ix, 2–4, 15–17, 75, 103, 154n.5,
158n.12; music of, in Dominican Re-
public, 124; origins of, 9, 155n.11; Tru-
jillo's anti-Haitian campaign, 63–67
Hall, Stuart, 7
Harlem renaissance, 22
Harlow, Larry, 153n.2
harmonica, 157n.16
Hatton, Frank, 72
hegemonic values, culture and, 7–8,
154n.9
Henríquez, Tatico, 63, 141, 144
Henríquez y Carvajal, Federico, 37,
157n.13
Herder, Johann Gottfried, 11
Hernández, Julio Alberto, 1, 32, 35–36,
42–43, 46–48, 79, 102
Hernández, Maridalia, 102, 122, 163n.1
Herskovitz, Melville, 6–7
Heureaux, Ulises ("Lilís"), 27–28, 30, 77
Hierro, Henry, 144
Hispaniola. *See* Dominican Republic;
Haiti
Hobsbawm, Eric, xiv
Hoetink, H., 6, 146
Holguin, Miguel, 72
"Horacio Salió," 52–53, 159n.1

identity. *See* nationalism and national
identity
Incháustegui, Arístedes, 67–69
independent couple dances, 16

indigenista movement, 20
indios, in Dominican Republic, 20,
156n.11
instruments: for bachata merengue, 113,
163n.7; in conjuntos, 84; and
merengue, 15, 23, 25–26, 31–33,
62–63, 78, 157nn.4–5, 159n.13; and
non-Cibao merengue variants,
136–138, 164n.4; típico moderno
merengue, 141–42. *See also specific instruments and types of instruments*
Islamic music: Caribbean music influenced by, ix

jalemengue, 59
jaleo merengue section, 38–40, 43, 56, 85,
97, 158n.10
"Jardinera," 106, 162n.15
jazz, merengue and, ix, 22, 56, 58–59,
96–97, 106–7, 152, 163n.2
Jazz Band–Alberti, 48–49
Jiménez, Ramón Emilio, 41–42
Johnny Ventura y Asociados, 89–90
Johnny Ventura y su Combo-Show, 87,
89–90
Johnson, Lyndon (President), 88
Jossie Esteban y la Patrulla 15, 95, 126
"Juan Ester" merengue, 158n.13
"Juana Quilina," 23–24, 157n.13
"Juangomero," 45–47, 158n.20
a juste rhythm, 143, 166n.15

Kalaff, Luis, 63, 71, 74, 125, 141, 144,
160nn.22–23, 166n.12
Kallberg, Jeffrey, 103–4, 151
Karen Records, 97, 107
Keil, Charles, 151
Kennedy, John F. (President), 84, 86
King, Carole, 107
Klein, Alan M., 164n.3
Kluckhohn, Florence, xiii
Koch, Ed, 128
konpa (Haitian music), viii–ix, 75, 93–94,
160n.27

racial attitudes and, 108–11; Eurocentrism in Dominican Republic and, 20–21; merengue and, xiv-xv, 46–49, 100–102, 151–52; merengue as art, music for, 42–46; radio broadcasts of merengue and, 99–100; sovereignty and, 155n.12; syncretism in Dominican Republic, xiv–xv; transnationalism and, 129–34; Trujillo's cult of, 60, 63–67; U.S. occupation of Dominican Republic and, 30–31. *See also* regionalism

Native American culture, in Dominican Republic, 20

Nenadich, George, 93, 127–28

New York Band, 126

New York City: Dominican diaspora in, 125–27; merengue in, 74-76, 122, 128, 133–34; Puerto Rican music in, viii, 128–29, 133–34; típico moderno merengue in, 145

Nigerian music, 103, 162n.24, 163n.13

Nolasco, Flérida de, 23, 64, 76

nueva canción movement, 109–11, 119

Nuñez de Cáceres, José, 9

Nuñez del Risco, Yaqui, 90

Ochoa, Calixto, 162n.13

"Oh Coconut!," 23

Orlando, Ramón, 106

Orquesta Angelita (band), 160n.22

Orquesta Bohemia (band), 48

Orquesta Generalísimo Trujillo (band), 159n.3

Orquesta Liberación (band), 106

Orquesta los Hermanos Vásquez (Vasquez Brothers Orchestra) (band), 49–50, 56, 159n.3

Orquesta Melodica (band), 160n.22

Orquesta Presidente Trujillo (band), 54–55, 72

Orquesta San José (band), 55–56, 58

Ortiz, Fernando, 4

Ovalles, Agustín "Papatín," 72

Ovalles, Sonny, 162n.12

pachanga merengue, 75, 160n.25

Pacheco, Johnny, 125, 145

Pacini Hernandez, Deborah, xiii, 34, 112, 114, 159n.3

"Pacone," 66–67

Palladium (New York City): merengue in, viii

palo echao (pri-prí) merengue, 4, 64, 67, 136–38, 148, 164nn.3–4

palos musical genre, 5, 67, 109, 136, 149; palos amerengueao (cibaeños, girapega/gerapega), 139–40, 148

pambiche (Yankee) merengue, 12, 38–42, 47–48, 50, 66, 158nn.11–12, 166n.15

"Pambiche es mejor que dril," 40–41

Panama Canal, 30

Paredes, Américo, 104

participant observation, xii–xiii, 153n.1

Partido de la Liberación Dominicana (PLD), 161n.9

Partido Revolucionario Dominicano (PRD), 84, 91

pasadías, 33–38

Pascual, Agapito ("El Moderno"), 142, 145

paseo merengue section, 16–17, 38, 43, 96

Paulino, Julío César, 40–41

Paulino, Paula, 160n.19

payola, radio broadcasts of merengue and, 99–100, 162n.22

Peace of Ryswick, 8

Peña Morel, Esteban, 2–3, 43

Peralta, Monguita, 158n.12

percussion. *See* drums

Pérez, Luis, 84–86, 92, 94, 145, 161n.4, 162n.16

Pérez, Pedro, 59

perico ripiao, 63, 166n.14

Perris, Arnold, 151

Pichardo, Agustín, 33–35, 163n.11

plena (Puerto Rican music), 94

Pochi y su Coco (band), 95, 115

politics, merengue and, 35–38, 62, 67–70, 77, 85–86, 88–89; nueva canción movement and, 109–10

Pons, Frank Moya, 9

MERENGUE

Dominican Music and Dominican Identity